D0931975

NAACP Youth
and the Fight for
Black Freedom,

DATE DUE

MAR 2 1 2018			

Sunderland Public Library
Twenty School Street
Sunderland, MA 01375
413.665.2642
413.665.1435 (fax)

DISCARD

NAACP Youth and the Fight for Black Freedom, 1936–1965

Thomas L. Bynum

The University of Tennessee Press / Knoxville

Sunderland Public Library
Twenty School Street
Sunderland, MA 01375

Copyright © 2013 by Thomas L. Bynum.
All Rights Reserved. Manufactured in the United States of America.
Cloth: first printing, 2013.
Paper: first printing, 2014.

All photographs are from the Library of Congress, Prints and Photograph Division,
Visual Materials from the NAACP Records.

Library of Congress Cataloging-in-Publication Data

Bynum, Thomas L.
NAACP youth and the fight for black freedom, 1936–1965 / Thomas L. Bynum. —
First Edition.
    pages cm
Includes bibliographical references and index.
ISBN-13: 978-1-62190-153-2

1. National Association for the Advancement of Colored People—History—20th
   century.
2. African American youth—Political activity—History—20th century.
3. African American college students—Political activity—History—20th century.
4. African Americans—Civil rights—History—20th century.
5. Civil rights movements—United States—History—20th century.
6. Youth movements—United States—History—20th century.
I. Title.

E185.5.N276B96 2013
323.1196'073—dc23
2013001462

Dedicated to all of the young people of the NAACP, who fought tirelessly and valiantly to make America a beacon of DEMOCRACY, and to the youth who continue to make this country live up to its ideals!

Contents

Illustrations

Acknowledgments

While completing my doctorate in history at Georgia State University, I enrolled in a seminar on the civil rights movement taught by Dr. Jacqueline A. Rouse. In this class, she mentioned that someone should research the National Association for the Advancement of Colored People (NAACP) youth councils and college chapters' involvement in the Black Freedom Movement. Dr. Rouse noted that John Bracey had raised the idea several years previously at a conference hosted by the Association for the Study of African American Life and History. When Dr. Rouse mentioned it, the class was exploring the role of the Student Nonviolent Coordinating Committee (SNCC) in the sit-in demonstrations and voter registration in the South. SNCC's direct action campaigns fascinated me. Although the young people in SNCC piqued my interest, I knew that several prominent historians had already researched this organization. What could I add to the existing scholarship? And would it drastically change how historians viewed the organization?

Searching for a dissertation topic, I decided to take Dr. Rouse up on this offer. At first, the idea of researching information on the NAACP did not appeal to me because the *only* thing I knew about the NAACP was that it worked through the courts to achieve racial equality. Familiar with this popular narrative, I thought research on the association's youth chapters would reveal a similar story. When I decided to research the youth chapters of the NAACP, the idea intrigued me only because there had been no comprehensive study of their involvement in the Black Freedom Movement. Research on the youth chapters has fundamentally changed the way I see the NAACP and youth participation in the black freedom struggle for racial equality. Little did I know that my research would reveal a different story about the youth councils and college chapters of the NAACP—a story I had not anticipated, but one that well deserved to be told. I am grateful to Dr. Bracey, who raised this idea, and to Dr. Rouse, who followed up on the idea in her seminar class.

Dr. Rouse not only provided me with an excellent research topic, but she also served as the chair of my dissertation committee. I am thankful for my dissertation committee, which consisted of Drs. Rouse, Glenn T. Eskew, Vicki Crawford, and Patricia Sullivan. The committee's thorough and meticulous reading of every page of my dissertation, and their insightful comments, greatly benefited me as I transformed the dissertation into a book. I could not have asked for a better dissertation committee. To this renowned team of scholars, I say thank you for your valuable insight, which helped me to expand the scope and depth of this project into my first book. Dr. Rouse, I would like to thank you personally for mentoring me after the dissertation. Not only did you provide much-needed advice on how to transform the dissertation into a book, but you also provided important advice on how to navigate the professoriate. Thanks for pep talks you gave me when I became discouraged or frustrated, and thanks particularly for answering my numerous questions about the professoriate and book manuscript. Your wisdom has been invaluable!

I would like to thank my family and friends for the support they have provided me over the years as I worked on this book project. Thanks for the many prayers, the encouragement, and the belief you all had in my ability to complete this project. Your kind words sustained me and gave me the courage to see this project to its fruition. To my father, Joseph L. Darden, thank you for teaching me how not to take life too seriously. As a result, I have learned to find humor in life's adversities. To my mother, Verna Bynum Farmer, thanks for your many sacrifices and selflessness in rearing me and my siblings— Reginald, Jennifer, Valerie, Victoria, and Crystal. Your wisdom and courage continue to inspire me. Thanks to Catina Davis for proofreading drafts of the manuscript during the early stages of the book project. Special thanks to my friend, Jeraldine "Jeri" Cunningham, for proofreading drafts of the manuscript during the early and final stages of the book project. Your meticulous eyes found mistakes I overlooked.

I particularly thank Dr. Mario Owens for reading the first draft of my book proposal and for providing insightful editorial comments. Since 2008, you have had tremendous influence on this project. You have always believed in my abilities as a writer and academician. You have been a source of inspiration and encouragement in more ways than I can express. Thanks for listening to my ideas, challenges, and frustrations about this project—and for allowing me to vent without judging me. Ever the voice of reason, you would always tell me the truth (whether I liked it or not) and provide helpful advice. As you put the pages together for your book, know that I will be there to support you and to provide the listening ear that you gave me so many times before. To my best friend, Kenya L. Reid—as well as to your mom, Pearl S. Reid—who has provided unwavering support to me in my personal and professional endeavors, I say thank you. Since we met eighteen years ago at Clark Atlanta University, you have been a source of inspiration for my life. I have always admired your tenacity and courage to fulfill your life goals. The editorial assistance your mom and you provided for the dissertation, and now book, has been immensely beneficial. Only you can finish my sentences, at times, without asking me what the heck I was thinking. I have always said you have a way with words! You are the epitome of black womanhood, and I am glad you are part of my life.

I would also like to thank Drs. Tara White, Rose Thevenin, Devin Fergus, and Louis Woods for the many in-depth intellectual conversations and debates we have had about black history and our own research. Louis, I am particularly struck by the conversations you and I have at work and during the long drive from Nashville to Murfreesboro, when we carpool. In many ways, comrades, these intellectual conversations and debates have forced me to think critically about my own work and how it fits within the larger black protest tradition. Our dialogue has shaped my understanding of history and has helped me craft my arguments and discourse in meaningful ways. As the saying goes "Iron sharpens iron." Again, thanks for the feedback and advice you all have given me over the years, which has tremendously benefited me. Tara and Rose, thanks for listening to my many ideas and for expressing your belief in this work and in the important contribution it would make to the historical profession. You have always forced me to think critically about the role of women in the Black Freedom Movement, and I could count on you to help me to express that fact in a stimulating and cogent manner. Since our participation in the W. E. B. Du Bois Institute at Harvard on "African American Struggles for Civil Rights in the 20th Century," Devin, you have been a great role model and have provided valuable feedback for this project. I would like to particularly thank you for asking the tough questions about this work and for prodding me to think critically about how this work connects to larger struggles waged by black Americans for racial equality in this country. Also, thanks for the valuable advice and tips on how to navigate the publishing world, particularly on how to respond *judiciously* to the readers' reports from reviewers of the manuscript. Special thanks to my colleague Dr. Pippa Holloway, who graciously read sections of the manuscript and offered invaluable feedback during the early stages of this project.

I would also like to thank Barbara Patton, executive director, Office of Institutional Equity and Compliance at Middle Tennessee State University, for the financial support she has provided me for travel to archival sites and conferences to present my research. I would also like to thank the College of Liberal Arts at Middle Tennessee State University for the financial support I received to complete this project. During the spring semester 2012, I was awarded the Tennessee Board of Regents Access and Diversity Grant, which provided funds for travel to the Library of Congress so that I could complete the final stages of research on this project. It also provided support for a six-hour course reduction load, which allowed me to complete the final written revisions for the book project. The financial support I have received from the Middle Tennessee State University has been very beneficial to me in completing this book project. Always special thanks to the staff at the Library of Congress for assisting me with finding documents I needed for this project. Particularly, thanks to Jennifer Brathovde at the Library of Congress, who graciously located information for me over the phone when I called to inquire about information I had failed to write down concerning the source of a document.

Lastly, I would like to say thank you to my students, who have caused me to think critically about my research and the history I teach. The discussions

I have had over the years in classes with students have shown me that, as a scholar, there is a lot more to be learned about history than what is contained within the pages of books. I can only hope that the information contained in these pages will produce more stimulating conversations about the history of the NAACP youth movement and research on the NAACP youth councils and college chapters than these pages can capture. After all, history is constantly being constructed and reconstructed—a truism that will always keep us searching and documenting the vast annals of history.

Introduction

This book tells the story of the NAACP youth councils and college chapters' fight for racial equality in the United States. Because civil rights historians have focused largely on the activism of young people within the Congress of Racial Equality (CORE) and the Student Nonviolent Coordinating Committee (SNCC) during the 1960s, the contributions of NAACP youth to the struggle for racial equality in the United States have received little scholarly attention. Although historians often note that the NAACP worked primarily through the courts, this work highlights the direct action activities of the youth councils and college chapters to break down racial discrimination in the United States. Working within the scope of the association's national agenda, the youth chapters staged antilynching demonstrations, campaigned for equal educational and employment opportunities, challenged discrimination and segregation in public facilities, and called for full civil liberties. Historian Rebecca de Schweinitz asserts that the association "used a wide range of protest strategies, some substantially more confrontational than those traditionally associated with the organization."[1]

NAACP Youth and the Fight for Black Freedom contributes to the scholarship on youth activism, particularly black youth, and the long history of the black freedom movement. Underscoring the civil rights activities of the youth councils and college chapters from the 1930s to the 1960s, it shows how instrumental they were in the fight for racial equality in the United States. This work not only illuminates the long struggle for racial equality, but it also shows that youth activism of the 1960s was connected to a history of youth protest against racial inequalities, starting in the 1930s. Recounting all of the specific activities and events of the association's youth chapters in one book is impossible. Hundreds of NAACP youth chapters were organized across the United States, and their activities to achieve racial equality were voluminous. The hope is that this work will inspire more local and regional studies that will, in turn, further explore the NAACP youth chapters' contributions to the struggle for racial equality.

Although young people are often viewed as too immature and naïve to mount serious political action, this book argues that youths were political actors who played a major role in the fight for racial equality in the United States. NAACP youths saw themselves as "agents" or promoters of social change within the black community and mainstream American society. They challenged the status quo and the racial barriers that relegated them to second-class citizenship. In many ways, the youth chapters propelled the NAACP to diversify its civil rights strategy beyond court action to a wide range of direct action tactics in its fight for racial equality.

Spawned by a youth-organizing tradition that emerged in the 1930s, NAACP youth activists staged organized protest demonstrations against lynching, educational inequalities, and Jim Crow segregated facilities and businesses. Rebecca de Schweinitz maintains that youth activists led "street demonstrations to publicize NAACP legal cases and protest unjust court decisions or questionable criminal charges against blacks."[2] Although historians have given much attention to the protest activities of black youth during the 1960s, black youth activism did not begin with the mass sit-in demonstrations of 1960. As previously mentioned, some of the earliest and primary protest activities of black youth can be traced to the NAACP youth chapters during the 1930s. "Children and youth who participated in the sit-ins and other protest demonstrations of the early 1960s built on a militant youth-organizing tradition that began in the 1930s. During that decade, the NAACP, in response to youth activism and fears about potential youth radicalism, developed (with the help of and pressure from young members) a strong youth program that officially encouraged the use of direct-action techniques,"[3] remarks de Schweinitz. This work argues that the NAACP youth councils and college chapters were early initiators of grassroots organizing and nonviolent direct action tactics, such as boycotts, marches, picketing, and sit-ins. Ultimately, the direct action methods employed by NAACP youth chapters during the 1930s and 1940s continued throughout the 1950s and 1960s, providing a framework for other youth activists. Many of the young people who would later join SNCC in the 1960s had begun their activism within the youth chapters of the NAACP. Moreover, the long tradition of activism within the NAACP youth councils and college chapters established a youth protest tradition among black youth.

In this vein, the story presented here highlights the NAACP youth councils and college chapters' crusade against racial inequalities and their determination to make democracy work in America. More important, it reveals the courage of NAACP youth to fight against enduring racial strictures that barred black Americans from the rights and privileges of first-class citizenship. To the youth of the NAACP, their fight was to be recognized as Americans—to have their humanity affirmed—and to be treated with respect and decency. To tell this remarkable story, this book draws primarily on the papers of the NAACP, particularly Part 19: Youth File, Series A-D, which span the years 1919 to 1965. These microfilmed papers include annual reports, correspondences, memoranda, youth programs, financial reports, local chapter and conference minutes, and newsletters, which detail the activities of the NAACP youth groups at the local and national levels. This work also incorporates information from *The Crisis* (official organ of the NAACP), newspapers, and other relevant secondary sources. Situating the NAACP youth groups' activism within the context of a youth protest tradition that began in the 1930s, this research offers a broader understanding of black youth activism, particularly highlighting the intergenerational and generational efforts of black Americans to achieve racial equality. More specifically, it provides a broad analysis of the activities of NAACP youth chapters, noting their contributions to the struggle for racial equality in the United States.

During the early 1930s, NAACP executive secretary Walter White, appealed to the national board of directors to revamp the youth program. At the organization's twenty-sixth annual national convention, held in St. Louis, Missouri (1935), Juanita Jackson, special assistant to Walter White, challenged the association to begin plans immediately for a national youth movement. As a former youth leader, Jackson was aware of the role that youth and youth organizations played in the fight for social change, particularly in free speech, antiwar, and workers' rights demonstrations. She called on the NAACP to rally its youth around the injustices that plagued their lives. The association did just that. In 1936, the NAACP National Board of Directors appointed Jackson as the first national youth director and commissioned her to restructure the youth program. Consisting of mostly junior branches (with members ranging in age from fourteen to twenty-one years old) and some college chapters, the NAACP youth division was poorly structured, lacking both a national youth agenda and a youth director. Jackson blended these units into a national youth agenda focused primarily on directives from the national office.

Working within the scope of the association's national agenda, the junior and youth councils and the college chapters campaigned for antilynching legislation, equal education and employment opportunities, and civil liberties. The youth chapters also promoted black history and campaigned to rid public schools of textbooks that promoted racist ideas about African Americans. Under the guidance of Juanita Jackson, this new youth division gave young people a voice within the association and harnessed their collective energies to fight against racial inequalities. Many of the campaigns staged by the association's youth division were coordinated with other interracial youth organizations. Groups such as the Young Men's Christian Association (YMCA), Young Women's Christian Association (YWCA), the National Council of Methodist Youth (NCMY), the Southern Negro Youth Congress (SNYC), the American Youth Congress (AYC), American Students Union (ASU), Student for Democratic Action (SDA), the National Student Association (NSA), Young Adult Council (YAC), CORE, and SNCC were central to advancing the work of the NAACP.

By the 1940s, the NAACP youth groups expanded to nonviolent direct action activities, such as voter registration and the desegregation of public facilities (movie theaters, skating rinks, and eating establishments).[4] In the mid-1940s, voter registration activities increased among NAACP youth groups. After the NAACP's legal victory in *Smith v. Allwright* in 1944, which outlawed the all-white primary in the south, youth councils and college chapters accelerated their work in this area. They set up voter registration clinics to instruct blacks on how to register and vote, and they held mock elections to further explain the voting process.[5] Although blacks turned out to vote in large numbers, they were met with resistance from southern whites who were committed to maintaining the subordination of blacks and the racial status quo of the south. Historian Patricia Sullivan maintains, "When the NAACP won a Supreme Court ruling that struck down the 'White only' Democratic primary in 1944, southern blacks turned out to vote in numbers not seen since Reconstruction, sparking a reign of terror in the Deep South."[6] Although the white power structure violently resisted change, black youth grew more determined to make America live up to its ideals.

Additionally, the youth councils and college chapters led protest demonstrations against Jim Crow–segregated facilities. In 1943, the NAACP college chapter at Howard University desegregated the Little Palace Cafeteria in Washington, D.C., via picketing and sit-in demonstrations.[7] In fact, Howard's NAACP chapter was among the first youth groups to initiate sit-in demonstrations as a strategy to break down Jim Crow segregation. In 1948, the youth council of East Chicago, Indiana, launched a successful six-week boycott that desegregated the American, the Vic, and the Indiana theaters—all theaters that profited from black patrons.[8] Not only did NAACP youth groups attack public accommodations, but the college chapters at predominately white universities and colleges waged successful campaigns to eliminate segregation practices on campuses. During the 1940s, black youth were increasingly admitted to predominately white colleges and universities outside of the south; however, these students found themselves excluded from most campus organizations and activities. As a result, college chapters launched successful campaigns against "racial bias clauses" of clubs, sororities, and fraternities that excluded blacks. Similarly, NAACP college chapters were successful in ending segregated housing both on and off campus.[9] Through these college chapters, black students were able to break down blatant racial discriminatory practices at predominately white colleges and universities.

Although they enjoyed a measure of success in dismantling discrimination in public accommodations and on college and university campuses during the 1940s, the NAACP youth councils and college chapters also suffered from allegations of Communist infiltration. During this period, the federal government took measures to crack down on Communist organizations. All Communist organizations, or allegedly Communist organizations, were considered subversive and un-American. As Mary Dudziak notes, "Following WWII, anything that undermined the image of American democracy was seen as threatening world peace and aiding Soviet aspirations to dominate the world."[10] Seeking to avoid such labeling and affiliation with Communists, the

NAACP national headquarters closely policed its member groups. Although there were Communist Party members within NAACP youth councils and college chapters, they were never in the majority. Allegations of communist domination were unfounded. Such allegations surfaced when young people resisted the senior branch officers' control over their youth program. The young people preferred to use nonviolent direct action tactics to break down racial discrimination; oftentimes, the older members were reluctant to use such tactics and preferred litigation. If the youth resisted, then officers of the senior branch would allege that Communist members had influenced them. This accusation became a common tactic used by senior branch officers to discredit youth programs they did not endorse. Although not all senior branches preferred litigation over nonviolent direct action tactics to confront white supremacy, growing discord between the old and the young forced the national office to take the youth programs more seriously.

During the 1950s, the NAACP youth helped to successfully desegregate public schools in the south. After the landmark court case *Brown v. Board of Education* in 1954, many youth participants involved in school desegregation were members of the NAACP youth councils. Josephine Bradley, who was the first black person to desegregate Greensboro High School in Greensboro, North Carolina, was a student leader of the Greensboro Youth Council.[11] The black students who desegregated Central High School in Little Rock, Arkansas—affectionately known as the "Little Rock Nine"—were affiliated with the Little Rock Youth Council. For example, Minnijean Brown, who was expelled from Central High after confronting a bully who tormented her, was instrumental in organizing the NAACP Youth March for Integrated Schools in 1958. Thousands of youth demonstrators converged on Washington, D.C., calling on the federal government to support the United States Supreme Court's decision banning segregation in public education. During the late 1950s, many of the pioneers of school desegregation cases belonged to NAACP youth councils, paving the way for black youths to have access to educational resources they had been denied under the "separate but equal" system.[12]

As civil rights activities in the South accelerated, youth councils and college chapters played major roles in eroding segregation in public accommodations. Prior to the mass southern student protest demonstrations of the 1960s, NAACP youth groups launched successful campaigns that ended segregation in some public accommodations. In 1955, after waging a two-year campaign, the Dallas, Texas Youth Council, under the direction of its fearless advisor, Juanita Jewel Craft, forced the Texas State Fair officials to end "Negro Day" and open the amusement rides at the fair to black people. In 1958, the Wichita, Kansas Youth Council's sit-in demonstrations, under its advisor, Rosie Hughes, and President Ronald Walters, desegregated the Dockum Drug Store chain. The desegregation of Dockum Drug Store led to the desegregation of other businesses in Wichita, Kansas. Similarly, under the leadership of Clara Luper, youth advisor, and fifteen-year-old Barbara Posey, youth council president, the Oklahoma City Youth Council's sit-in demonstrations desegregated several major chain stores, such as Kress and H. L. Green. In fact, these sit-ins placed the NAACP youth councils at the forefront of the first wave of nonviolent direct action protests that took place well before the Greensboro sit-in demonstration of February 1960. These protest demonstrations were highly influenced by the Supreme Court's ruling that declared segregated schools unconstitutional in *Brown v. Board of Education* (1954) and the success of the Montgomery Bus Boycott (1956), which ended segregated seating on city buses in Montgomery, Alabama. Most of all, the protest demonstrations of the NAACP youth chapters were influenced by the determination of blacks to break down the racial barriers in society that relegated them to second-class citizenship.

As the civil rights movement expanded during the 1960s, sit-in demonstrations and selective buying boycotts became popular protest strategies to end discrimination in public accommodations and employment. At the forefront of these protest demonstrations were NAACP youth councils and college chapters. In 1960, four students from North Carolina A&T University in Greensboro, North Carolina, staged a sit-in protest at Woolworth Department Store. Two of the students, Ezell Blair and Joseph McNeil, were student leaders within the Greensboro Youth Council.[13] Having gained significant leadership experience as youth council leaders, Blair and McNeil rallied students at the university and surrounding schools to protest the discriminatory practices of several major chain stores in Greensboro. The sit-in demonstration launched by these four students at Woolworth created a chain reaction. Sit-ins spread across the state and throughout several other southern states. While the sit-ins were a popular direct action strategy to combat discrimination, selective buying was another method. Nationally, these NAACP youth chapters sparked boycotts against businesses that discriminated in public accommodations and hiring practices. Suffering economically from these "withhold patronage" campaigns, many businesses ended their discriminatory hiring practices and began to hire blacks in clerical and sales positions.[14]

Although official NAACP youth groups did not participate in the Freedom Rides, some youth chapter members did test the Interstate Commerce Commission's (ICC) ruling (which outlawed segregated travel) and demonstrated against segregated public transportation facilities. In 1961, members of the Clarksdale Youth Council in Clarksdale, Mississippi, tested the validity of the ICC ruling by using the "whites only" waiting area to purchase train tickets to Memphis.[15] That same year, the Albany Youth Council members, assisting SNCC's efforts to end Jim Crow practices in Albany, Georgia, participated in demonstrations to desegregate local train depots and other segregated public facilities.[16] Additionally, several NAACP college students on their way home for summer break rode buses and trains to test the validity of the ICC ruling.[17]

As direct action campaigns accelerated across the south, the relationship between the NAACP national office and SNCC became tenuous. The association maintained that SNCC was "raiding" its youth groups for members. SNCC, born out of the sit-in demonstrations that erupted across the South in 1960, was an independent student-led organization unaffiliated with the older civil rights organizations.[18] Influenced by the group-centered leadership political ideology of civil rights activist Ella Baker, SNCC subscribed to a more democratic governing structure.[19] Unlike SNCC, the senior branches and the national office of the NAACP controlled the youth councils and college chapters' program and activities. During the 1960s, some youth became dissatisfied with the NAACP national office and senior branches' bureaucratic ways and quit the organization. Some joined SNCC because it was less bureaucratic and the young people controlled their programs. In fact, during the Freedom Summer Voter Registration Project in Mississippi in 1964, which was sponsored by the Council of Federated Organizations (COFO), many youths abandoned the NAACP and joined other civil rights organizations. They complained that the association's programs were too heavily manned, which meant that the national office had to approve all activities carried out by the youth councils and the college chapters.[20] The senior branches and national office's unwillingness to relinquish its heavy policing of student-based projects ultimately made other civil rights organizations more attractive. Although some youths withdrew their membership, others remained and pressed the NAACP national office to give youth members more control over their programs and activities.

Restructuring its youth work during the mid-1960s, the association took the initiative to make its programs more relevant to the needs of inner-city communities. While northern NAACP branches had been at the forefront of the fight to combat social ills in urban slums for years, the national office decided to make it one of the central focuses of its youth program during the mid-1960s. In the summer of 1965, the association's youth work spread to inner cities throughout the United States. For instance, to improve the quality of life for poor and underprivileged blacks, the association's youth chapters became involved with the Community Action Project (CAP). CAP, one of Lyndon B. Johnson's antipoverty programs created during the mid-1960s, focused largely on education, housing, and employment issues faced by inner-city residents. These programs helped to make local residents aware of the resources available to improve their living conditions.[21] Overall, through CAP, NAACP youth chapters played an important role in aiding the poor and underprivileged and advancing the association's work to eradicate urban slums across the United States.

Chapter one examines the formation of a national youth movement in the NAACP under the leadership of Juanita Jackson. Situated within the framework of a broader American youth movement launched in the 1930s by mostly white-dominated youth organizations, this chapter reveals how youth campaigns to combat socioeconomic and political problems of the Great Depression and to protest Nazism and Fascism created a space for black youth to criticize the dismal race relations in the United States. Focusing on the NAACP youth movement's organizational structure and national objectives, this chapter examines how the movement was organized and discusses the strategies and campaigns employed by NAACP youth groups to break down racial injustices during the late 1930s.

Chapter two explores how the Second World War created a platform for youth, particularly black youth, to protest colonialism, imperialism, and racism (at home and abroad), highlighting the international contours of youth activism on the NAACP youth movement's fight for human rights within the context of World War II antiracist propaganda against Nazism and Fascism. Secondly, highlighting the role of Ruby Hurley as national youth director, this chapter discusses the challenges that confronted a burgeoning NAACP youth movement, as Hurley sought to enjoin the program activities of the youth councils and college chapters in a more collaborative way. Lastly, this chapter explores the impact of the *Smith v. Allwright* decision, which outlawed the all-white primary in the South and accelerated voter registration activities of the NAACP youth chapters.

Chapter three examines the activism of the NAACP youth groups during the post-World War II era, discussing direct action tactics such as "withholding patronage" campaigns and early desegregation efforts by the youth councils and college chapters against public accommodations. Secondly, this chapter examines the role of the NAACP college chapters in breaking down discrimination on the campuses of predominately white colleges and universities. Lastly, this chapters examines the internal and external factors such as allegations of "Communist domination," friction between the NAACP youth groups and the national office and the senior branches, and the steps taken by the national office to address these concerns.

Chapter four explores the NAACP youth's participation in public school desegregation efforts after the *Brown* decision and the violent opposition they encountered in their effort to integrate public schools in the South. For example, this chapter highlights the courageous efforts of the Little Rock Nine to desegregate Central High School in Little Rock, Arkansas, and Josephine Bradley's courage to integrate Greensboro High School in Greensboro, North Carolina. Additionally, this chapter discusses the murder of Emmett Till and NAACP youth chapters' protests and demonstrations to bring about justice on his behalf. It also examines the Montgomery Bus Boycott and the role NAACP youth played in this event. Lastly, this chapter reveals how Till's death and the bus boycott provided the impetus for mass civil rights campaigns across the nation, especially in the south.

Chapter five examines the NAACP youth councils' and college chapters' participation in the sit-in demonstrations of the late 1950s and the 1960s and the impact these demonstrations had on local communities. A discussion of NAACP youth groups' early activism in the previous chapters establishes a foundation for the argument that NAACP youths were early initiators of direct action nonviolent activities and that their activism created a framework for SNCC political activism during the 1960s. The NAACP groups played an important role in the early sit-in demonstrations and withholding patronage campaigns during the late 1950s and the 1960s to dismantle discrimination in public accommodations and employment. Indeed, such activities established a model for youth activism in other civil rights organizations.

Chapter six discusses the expansion of the NAACP youth chapters' direct action programs under the leadership of national youth director Laplois Ashford. It also explores the national office's conflict with youth chapters and how the bureaucracy of the national office led some NAACP youth to join SNCC (which was less bureaucratic and run mostly by other youths) and measures the association used to combat this problem. Lastly, this chapter examines the administration of NAACP national youth director Eugene Hampton and how the NAACP sought to make its youth work more relevant to urban slum communities across the United States. This aspect of the NAACP's work was largely influenced by Lyndon B. Johnson's antipoverty programs of the mid-1960s.

The Epilogue provides a summary of the legacy of the youth councils and college chapters up to 1965 and shows how the NAACP youth chapters made vital contributions to the fight for civil rights across the United States. The conclusion contends that the national office's bureaucracy hampered the effectiveness of the NAACP youth movement. Although the national office's bureaucracy stifled youth programs at times, the successes of the NAACP youth councils and college chapters' direct action programs *revise* the general history of the NAACP as an organization that worked solely through the court system to secure civil rights for black Americans.

Moreover, while fraught with internal and external problems, the NAACP Youth and College Division still played a vital role in the fight for civil rights. And the youth movement that began in the 1930s established what would become a long tradition of youth activism in the post-WWII decades. Although recording the *entire* history of the NAACP youth organizations in this one book is impossible, the pages that follow capture the successes, failures, and challenges of the NAACP youth councils and college chapters at the national, state, and local levels, and offer an analysis of their activism and contributions to black Americans' struggle for racial equality.

Chapter One

"Ours Is an Immediate Task": Juanita Jackson and the Origins of the NAACP Youth Movement

During the era of the Great Depression, American youth joined and formed an expanding array of organizations, tackling problems of widespread poverty and protesting racial bigotry at home and increasing militarism abroad. Propelled by the rise of fascist and racist tyranny in Italy, Germany, Japan, and other nations on the international scene, American youth organizations, including the American Student Union (ASU), the American Youth Congress (AYC), National Council of Methodist Youth (NCMY), Southern Negro Youth Congress (SNYC), the Young Men's Christian Association (YMCA), Young Women's Christian Association (YWCA), Young Communist League, and Young People's Socialist League, sought to address the dismal state of black-white relations at home. A disparate group of young American activists—Socialists, Communists, liberals, pacifists, Christians, and civil right advocates—linked its fight against white racist practices at home to the broader international fight against the spread of Nazism and Fascism.[1] These young people longed for a more egalitarian society at home and abroad—and, in this spirit, a national youth movement within the NAACP was reborn and situated within the context of the 1930s youth movements.

Commenting on the American student movement of the 1930s, historian Robert Cohen writes, "The movement encouraged students to identify with the working class rather than the upper class, to value racial and ethnic diversity instead of exclusivity, and to work for progressive social change."[2] As a former student leader and organizer, Juanita Jackson used her astute leadership abilities and personal charisma to create a successful youth movement within the NAACP, in which nonviolent direct action protests were common. During her tenure as national youth director, Jackson saw the NAACP establish youth councils and college chapters in 30 states and 128 cities throughout the United States.[3] Jackson's success in building a vibrant national youth movement within the NAACP can be attributed to her organizing and activist skills, themselves rooted in a legacy of nonviolent direct action activism well established in her family, the Baltimore community, and the African American protest tradition. This chapter examines Jackson's leadership in the formation of a national youth movement within the NAACP between 1935 and 1938, focusing on the activism of the youth councils and college chapters.

In a memorandum to the NAACP Board of Directors dated February 2, 1933, Walter White, executive secretary, bemoaned the lack of a definite program and activities for what were called the "junior branches." "One of the greatest weaknesses of the Association's program," White declared, "is the lack of a definite program for activity by the junior branches and younger people. Many of our branches are officered by loyal and faithful but elderly people, who in an uncomfortably large number of instances, discourage initiative on the part of young people."[4] Although they provided an outlet for youth activism, the NAACP junior branches and college chapters were poorly organized and understaffed, lacked sufficient funding, and had no nationally coordinated youth agenda. Given the lobbying efforts of Jackson and others for a national youth program for the NAACP, at the twenty-sixth annual convention—held in St. Louis, Missouri, in July 1935— the board of directors voted to restructure its youth division.[5] This restructuring of youth work led to the establishment of the NAACP "Youth and College Division" in March 1936, with Juanita Jackson as national director.

"Mobilization! Legislation! Litigation! Education! The Ballot!" expressed Jackson's sentiment toward civil rights activism. Born in Hot Springs, Arkansas, on January 2, 1913, Juanita Jackson grew up in Baltimore, Maryland. She earned a bachelor of science in education in 1931 and a master's degree in sociology in 1935 from the University of Pennsylvania, where she was an active member of the Alpha Kappa Alpha sorority.[6] Jackson's activism began at age eighteen, when she founded and became president of the City-Wide Young People's Forum of Baltimore in 1931 as an organization to address the problems confronted by Baltimore's black youth.[7] The City-Wide Forum, which was held on Friday at the Sharpe Street Memorial Methodist Episcopal Church, brought together hundreds of youths from various socioeconomic and religious affiliations, including Methodist, Episcopal, Baptist, and African Methodist Episcopal.[8] Forum activities also helped to revive the inactive Baltimore NAACP branch.[9]

The Forum provided outlets where young people discussed and addressed the socioeconomic ills that crippled progress for black Baltimoreans. Jackson organized a weekly lecture series that brought Mary McLeod Bethune, W. E. B. Du Bois, Ralph Bunche, Nannie Helen Burroughs, Charles Wesley, Walter White, and other black leaders of Baltimore to speak on civil rights and other issues important to African Americans. Forum members attended movies together, held oratorical contests, and provided musical entertainment for the city's youth.[10] In 1933, the forum launched its "Buy Where You Can Work" (also known in some cities as Don't-Buy-Where-You-Can't-Work) campaign to protest the discriminatory practices of white businesses. Although their patrons were mostly African Americans, these white-owned businesses only hired white employees. For example, the local A&P grocery store did not hire black workers, because the manager believed that the white employees would quit. Given the store manager's discriminatory policy, Forum members picketed the store, and most African Americans refused to shop there. After a few days, reeling from the economic losses due to the boycott, the owner decided to begin hiring black workers.[11] The "Buy Where You Can Work" campaign became a popular nationwide strategy to defeat discrimination in northern and midwestern cities. Forum members also attacked Jim Crow practices and campaigned for black employment in libraries, welfare agencies, and schools. As Jackson explained, in the 1930s "in Baltimore we were totally segregated. We lived in court-enforced racial ghettos. We couldn't be firemen. We couldn't be policemen. . . . We couldn't be social workers."[12] By 1934, the Forum's protests and demonstrations led the Enoch Pratt Free Library to sponsor training programs for potential black employees and convinced the Baltimore Relief Commission to hire five black social workers.[13]

At the 1934 national conference of Methodist youth in Evanston, held in Evanston, Illinois, Jackson was elected vice president of the "National Council of Methodist Youth." At the conference, she urged young people individually and collectively to protest the practice of lynching, but also to oppose Jim Crow practices at restaurants and other public accommodations in the city of Evanston. The following year, she was offered a position with the NAACP as special assistant to Walter White; and, in 1936, she was appointed the national youth director. Jackson later recalled, "Walter White, the executive secretary of the NAACP, asked me if I would come to the national office in New York City to develop the youth program of the Association. I did. For three years, I traveled all over this country, but mainly in the South, organizing young people, challenging young people that this is America, this is a democracy."[14]

Having come from a family committed to the advancement of black civil rights, Jackson became involved in activism early. Her mother, Lillie Jackson, was active in the Baltimore NAACP for years before she was elected president of that branch in 1935. She served as branch president for thirty-five years. One of Lillie Jackson and the Baltimore NAACP's greatest civil rights victories was the equalization of pay for black teachers in the local public school system, an effort that was part of a larger campaign launched by the NAACP national office in the mid-1930s to end inequity in teacher salaries.[15] Because white teachers' salaries were significantly higher than similarly qualified black teachers in Baltimore, the NAACP filed a lawsuit against the school board.[16] Jackson recalled, "We could be teachers, but the school system was totally segregated. There was a colored school administrative building in the heart of the ghetto manned by a director of colored schools. The colored and white teachers had separate, segregated meetings."[17] Because she and her mother valued education and believed it should be first rate, they fought tirelessly against the inequalities that black youth suffered in public education. Moreover, Lillie

Jackson firmly believed that young people should participate in—and could lead—movements for social and economic change.

Having served as president of the City-Wide Young People's Forum and as vice president of the National Council of Methodist Youth, Jackson was connected to a larger American youth movement and the issues that confronted youth in general, which prepared her to take on the youth work for the NAACP. On June 30, 1936, at the NAACP annual conference held at the Sharpe Street Methodist Episcopal Church in Baltimore, Maryland, the youth division made its debut.[18] Singing the Challenge Song, led by Juanita Jackson's sister, Marion Jackson, the young people joined together in a melodious tune that asked the following:

> Should we sit idly by and sigh,
> While lynching rules the land
> And thousands suffer agony
> From Jim Crow's cruel hand?
> Shall we allow rank prejudice
> To thwart our destiny?
> No! With the N.A.A.C.P.
> We'll fight for victory.[19]

At that same meeting, Walter White announced to the NAACP's national conference that he was delighted that Jackson would be serving as national youth director of the organization's youth division. White declared,

> One of the greatest weaknesses of the [NAACP] is that we have not yet learned to have, or at least have not had, an intelligent, well integrated young people's program for the twelve million Negroes in America, seeing the importance of doing something about segregation, lynching, and disfranchisement, etc. I do not mean young Negroes only, but an organization of youth—one which does not ask any favors, one which will see things clearly and to fight with all the vigor we have in our beings. We had no such program. We are very much interested in having a young woman like Juanita Jackson with us in the office in New York. There are some of us who think it be the best thing to integrate the youth into a different organization or group. They have a zeal, a zest and fighting spirit which some of the older people in the Association do not have. . . . We have made mistakes, but we are looking to you young people to help us map out a program which will make the N.A.A.C.P. the kind of militant, uncompromising, fighting organization that you and I want it to be.[20]

White's appointment of Jackson as the national youth director was beneficial and timely for the establishment of a national youth movement within the NAACP. Her task in restructuring the existing, but moribund, junior organizations and establishing a national youth program was quite formidable.

As newly appointed national youth director, Jackson eliminated the junior branches and reorganized the youth division into "junior youth councils," "youth councils," and "college chapters." In restructuring the youth division, Jackson's primary goal was to attract a larger group of young people to the NAACP's work. Whereas the junior branches had restricted the membership to young people from fourteen to twenty-one years of age, the new youth divisions expanded that range. Under the new constitution (adapted from the framework that governed the senior branches), junior council membership was opened to young people twelve to fifteen, whereas youth council membership was for teenagers and young adults aged sixteen to twenty-five. At age twenty-six, membership was transferred to the senior branch.[21] Membership in college chapters was open to any student aged sixteen to twenty-five, enrolled in a college or a university. Officially setting up a junior council, youth council, or college chapter required twenty-five dues-paying members. Half of the membership dues would be sent to the national office, while the other half remained with the youth organization.[22] As an interracial organization, the NAACP held membership open to young people of all racial and ethnic groups.

The new directives issued by the national office spelled out the relationships and connections among the various programs pursued by the senior branches, junior councils, youth councils, and college chapters. The NAACP junior and youth councils were tied to the senior branch and were supervised by a senior advisor from the branch, while the college chapters fell under the jurisdiction of the national office's youth division. The programs initiated by the junior and youth councils first had to be approved by the "youth work committee," consisting of the presidents of the junior and youth councils and their senior advisors, and then passed on to the senior branch executive committee for final approval. The college chapters' programs had to be approved by the college administrators and the national office.[23]

The directives and guidelines also provided a broad outline for the national youth agenda for NAACP junior and youth councils and college chapters. Jackson believed that it was important to prepare African American youth to become future leaders within the organization, their communities, and the larger society, and her youth initiatives became integral to the NAACP's activities and objectives. Centering the youth program upon the initiatives coming out of the national office, Jackson sketched out five major objectives for the NAACP's youth work. These objectives included educating young people about the economic, political, and social problems confronted by black people; cooperating with and supporting the national office in its campaign for equal educational and employment opportunities, civil liberties, and antilynching legislation; developing knowledge and appreciation of African and African American history and achievements; promoting intelligent and militant youth leadership; and fostering interracial understanding, cooperation, and education.[24] African Americans could achieve these objectives through the ballot, the courts, the enactment of legislation, interracial organizations, and by educating themselves and the public.[25] Whereas these objectives provided guidelines for youth work, most of the programs sponsored by the NAACP youth councils and college chapters in the late 1930s focused on four specific areas: equal educational opportunities, employment opportunities, civil liberties, and antilynching legislation.

With regard to the internal governing structure, the NAACP modeled its youth organizations after the senior branches, whose elected offices were president, vice president, secretary, assistant secretary, and treasurer. The youth council president served as a representative for the council's youth at the monthly meetings of the local senior branch. He or she was also appointed a member of the local branch's executive committee, along with two other youth council members, to foster cooperation and participation. The adult member of the senior branch, who served as the youth council's advisor, acted as a liaison between the two groups. Juanita Jackson believed that to promote effective collaboration and to ensure a sense of belonging, the junior and senior members needed to be aware of each other's work and goals. She also believed that the life of the community was enriched when younger people and older people worked together to advance NAACP work in the fight for equal rights.[26]

Juanita Jackson encouraged youth organizations to build their membership by having dances, popularity contests ("Mr. and Miss NAACP"), cookouts, and other social activities to attract young people to the group. She recommended that official meetings be short and include light refreshments, and even encouraged the councils to hold meetings in their homes, where the environment would likely be more comfortable.[27] Jackson believed that all youths in the community, regardless of class, race, or religious orientation, should be recruited to NAACP membership. Although she believed that all youths mattered, the youth program was centered on addressing the depressed social and economic conditions facing black youth.

As national youth director, Jackson worked diligently to mobilize youth in a crusade for black civil rights. "Our fight is against lynching," Jackson declared, but it is "for educational equality, for economic justice, against discrimination in the courts, for the right to vote, [which] mainly concerns our youth. It is they who will reap the benefits of our endeavors, or face the brunt of increased prejudice."[28] Ever mindful of the importance of the struggle for civil rights, she believed that black youth, in particular, should be at the forefront of this struggle and have its voice heard in improving its own plight. "Ours is an immediate task," she noted. "Lynchers strike without warning. Jobs are few and far between. Relief is inadequate. Families are in need. . . . Thousands of youth are illiterate. Discrimination and segregation are on the increase. We cannot lose a moment. We must not falter a step. *We must march forward!!*"[29] Jackson believed that the young people in the NAACP should keep everyone in their communities on high alert about the problems African Americans faced. She also urged black youth to mobilize other young people to participate in the fight for social justice.

The NAACP first mobilized the youth to campaign in favor of antilynching legislation, because white racial violence threatened African Americans, regardless of age, social class, or education. From its inception, the NAACP worked to bring national attention to lynching and mob violence through investigations and by compiling and publishing statistics on lynching, holding conferences and mass meetings, and producing educational and other materials for distribution to the public.[30] Beginning in the post-World War I era, the NAACP lobbied for federal antilynching legislation. In 1934, Colorado's Edward Costigan and New York's Robert Wagner introduced the Costigan-Wagner Anti-Lynching Bill in the United States Senate. Walter White and other NAACP officials testified before a Senate Judiciary subcommittee on behalf of the legislation. In his testimony, White offered evidence of 5,053 lynchings in the United States since 1882; he noted that 3,513 of the victims were black. NAACP director and attorney, Arthur Spingarn, pointed out that since 1899, state and local authorities prosecuted less than 1 percent of these crimes.[31] The testimonies of White and other NAACP officials helped to convince the majority of the members of the Senate Judiciary subcommittee to vote in favor of the bill, but southern Democrats blocked it on the Senate floor.[32]

NAACP officials launched a "rigorous campaign for public support" of the Costigan-Wagner bill again in 1935, publishing articles in *The Crisis* magazine, circulating petitions, and even mounting an art exhibition on lynching that year at the Arthur U. Newton Galleries in New York City.[33] Juanita Jackson declared, "The masses of Americans, black and white, are unconcerned about the growing mob violence exhibited in this country. We must wake them up. We must let every American citizen, even to the most remote hamlet, know that young America does not want lynchings, will lead the protest against them, will fight for anti-lynching legislation to prevent them, and for a new social order that will eliminate them."[34]

The Costigan-Wagner bill was reintroduced in each session of Congress— and, in 1937, the NAACP youth councils and college chapters launched their first nationwide campaign to gain support for the measure. Underscoring the significance of this first nationwide antilynching campaign, J. G. St. Clair Drake, chairman of the Anti-Lynching Planning Committee, created a study guide, "For a Lynchless America," to ensure that NAACP youth was fully informed and educated about the horrors of lynching. The antilynching campaign was launched on February 12, 1937, on Abraham Lincoln's birthday, because "The Great Emancipator" symbolized a spirit of freedom and democracy. Juanita Jackson believed that February was the appropriate month, given the celebrations of Lincoln's, Frederick Douglass's, and George Washington's birthdays.[35] Throughout the entire month, NAACP youth organizations nationwide held antilynching demonstrations, which included educational programs, rallies, marches, and parades. In Cleveland, Ohio, the NAACP youth council secured the support of writer and artist Langston Hughes for its public program; and the performance of Hughes's play *Scottsboro Limited* became the highlight of the activities.[36] At many of these antilynching protests, NAACP youth wore black armbands as a sign of mourning for those who had been murdered. They sold "Stop Lynching" buttons to influence public opinion in favor of federal antilynching legislation and raised funds to support the NAACP's fight against lynching. That year, NAACP youth chapters raised $869.25 from the sale of antilynching buttons and contributed $337.98 to the association's antilynching fund. Furthermore, they visited their elected representatives' offices to lobby for the Costigan-Wagner Anti-Lynching bill. By 1938, the NAACP youth chapters, with support from the senior branches, held demonstrations in seventy-eight cities across the United States to raise awareness about the crime and horror of lynching.[37]

Juanita Jackson used radio broadcasts to spread her antilynching message. In 1937, she convinced the National Broadcasting Company to air a fifteen-minute radio address by Senator Robert Wagner on the need for federal antilynching laws. Senator Wagner condemned lynching as barbaric: "The crime of lynching is to my mind one of the most threatening [to society.] . . . Not only does it represent violence and intolerance and hatred at its highest peak . . . but moreover in 11 cases out of 12 it is directed against that very race which Lincoln released from physical bondage. Every time that a Negro perishes by rope or at the stake, the Emancipation Proclamation is suspended and the Fourteenth Amendment is blotted from our sacred law."[38] Local NAACP youth councils also made great use of radio programming; for example, the Boston Youth Council, through its bimonthly radio broadcasts, publicized the horrors of lynching and promoted support for antilynching legislation.[39] Radio was an effective medium to publicize the inhumanity of lynching to a larger audience and to spread the message to remote parts of America.

NAACP youth councils and college chapters also rallied young people in the AYC, ASU, SNYC, YMCA, and YWCA to pass resolutions, send telegrams, and write letters to their congressmen to support the Costigan-Wagner Anti-Lynching Bill.[40] For example, the ASU, one of the largest national student organizations, cooperated with NAACP youth chapters and supported their programs. In 1937, three ASU delegates, including Molly Yard, the organization's secretary, attended the Youth Section of the NAACP annual conference in Detroit, Michigan to show support for the association's youth program and to build a broad base youth coalition.[41] As an organization that represented all of America's youth, ASU included a civil rights agenda in its program and provided a platform for African American youth to mount its fight against racial oppression. Formed through a merger of the National Student League and Student League for Industrial Democracy in 1935, ASU represented "The Student and Minority Races," and supported freedom of speech, antilynching legislation, and the abolition of poll taxes. ASU leaders protested Jim Crow practices and condemned the use of quotas to limit the number of African American and Jewish students admitted to many private and public colleges and universities.[42]

Complementing the activism of these predominantly white youth organizations, the Southern Negro Youth Congress worked closely with NAACP youth councils and college chapters, taking an active role in challenging the racial injustices characteristic of the Jim Crow South. The National Negro Congress (NNC) had emerged in 1936 as an important civil rights organization, and the SNYC developed out of the NNC under the leadership of several young black activists, including Louis Burnham (who served as field secretary for ASU), James and Esther Jackson, and Edward Strong (who served as vice chairman for the American Youth Congress). The SNYC embraced a broad civil rights agenda that targeted citizenship rights, equal educational opportunities, youth employment, and health issues. The SNYC's principal advisor was Charlotte Hawkins Brown, founder and president of the Palmer Memorial Institute in Sedalia, North Carolina. Brown urged southern black youth to unite in the struggle against the racial injustices they suffered, asserting, "The time has come when Negro youth in no uncertain terms, but without flare or trumpet, should let the world know they prefer death to slavery or injustice."[43]

Often mirroring the work of NAACP youth chapters, the SNYC led campaigns for a federal antilynching bill, organized voter registration campaigns, led anti-poll tax demonstrations, and campaigned for the rights of black industrial workers.[44] According to Dorothy Burnham, the wife of SNYC founder, Louis Burnham, the two groups had similar objectives and waged cooperative campaigns in the fight for black civil rights in the South. NAACP groups and the SNYC worked jointly setting up voter registration campaigns. They also joined the Congress of Industrial Organizations and other labor organizers in the South in the late 1930s and early 1940s and supported interracial unionizing so sharecroppers and tenant farmers could bargain effectively against plantation owners for a decent wage and security.[45]

In addition to campaigning for antilynching legislation, NAACP youth groups organized rallies and protests over the extreme racial inequalities in public education. The NAACP's national educational program pursued six specific objectives: equal lengths of school terms for black and white public schools; equal pay for black and white teachers with the same qualifications; equal school transportation for black and white students; equality in school facilities and equipment; equal per capita expenditures for black and white public education; and equal access to publicly funded graduate and professional schools.[46] During the annual "American Education Week," held each November, Jackson mobilized the NAACP youth to protest racial inequities in public education. In November 1936, in Baltimore County, Maryland, for example, NAACP youth mobilized to protest educational inadequacies in a school district that had eleven public high schools, none of which was for black youth—even though African Americans comprised 9 percent of the total population. Believing high schools for blacks to be an unnecessary expense, white school officials argued that there was no need to build them, because so few were qualified for secondary education. African American students in Baltimore County who wished to go to high school had to pass the county's "special examination" to be eligible for tuition assistance to enroll in one of Baltimore City's all-black junior and senior high schools.[47]

This special examination was designed to be extremely difficult to pass. At the beginning of the 1935–1936 school year, after receiving failing grades on the special examination, Margaret Williams and Lucille Scott let their parents know that they would try to enroll in Baltimore County's all-white Cantonsville High School in September 1935. When the teenagers met with Daniel Zimmerman, the Cantonville High School principal, he refused to admit them. Soon after, Williams and Scott convinced their parents to file a lawsuit against the Baltimore County School Board. On March 14, 1936, NAACP attorney Thurgood Marshall filed the lawsuit, *Williams v. Zimmerman,* against Baltimore County, demanding that public high schools be opened for African American students. The NAACP lawsuit prompted Baltimore County school officials to increase tuition assistance to black youth attending the Baltimore City high schools, and they even covered some transportation expenses.[48]

Lucille Scott was allowed to pass the special examination and received tuition assistance to enroll in Booker T. Washington Junior High School and Frederick Douglass High School in Baltimore City, from which she graduated in 1941. Margaret Williams graduated from St. Frances Academy, a private comprehensive elementary and secondary school operated by the Oblate Sisters of Providence, the Roman Catholic Order of African American nuns, founded in Baltimore in 1829. The NAACP lost *Williams v. Zimmerman,* but to avoid further litigation, the school board opened three high schools for black students in Baltimore County by the 1938–1939 academic school year.[49] Williams and Scott's ordeal made very clear the obstacles and inequities that black students faced in Maryland in the late 1930s. But conditions were much worse in the Deep South states.[50] In Baltimore County in the late 1930s, the NAACP and Thurgood Marshall set out to force the county to provide high schools for black students that were comparable to those for white students—but not to desegregate the public schools. By pushing the county to uphold the "separate but equal" doctrine of *Plessy v. Ferguson* (1896), Marshall wanted to demonstrate how expensive maintaining a dual system of *equal* public education would, in fact, be.

The NAACP youth groups found some success in their local battles against racial discrimination and inequalities in public education. In Houston, Texas, in 1937, after several demonstrations drew attention to the large number of automobile accidents that had occurred near black public schools, the Houston Youth Council was able to get traffic officers stationed in these areas.[51] On the national level, many of the history and other textbooks used in public school classrooms throughout the nation misrepresented and distorted African American and American history, and therefore many youth chapters targeted public school systems that used these textbooks. In July 1938, at the twenty-ninth annual NAACP conference, social reformer Charles Edward Russell, one of the organization's founders, decried the "Mistreatment of the Negro in Public School Textbooks," and denounced at least seventeen specific textbooks that included numerous distortions and racist information about African American life and history. Russell urged the young people of the association to challenge the "anti-Negro propaganda" found particularly in history textbooks used in U.S. public schools. For example, *Nation's Progress,* a history textbook written by Eugene Colligan and Maxwell Littwin, maintained that the "Klan was organized against foolish Negroes and their evil leaders." Another history textbook, *History of the American People,* authored by David Muzzey, contended, "the rule of the Negro and his unscrupulous carpetbagger and scalawag patrons was an orgy of extravagance, fraud and disgusting incompetence."[52]

As a response to Russell's challenge, during the 1938–1939 school year, NAACP youth chapters launched a nationwide project to survey history textbooks used in local public school districts. Their aim was to identify history textbooks that promoted racist propaganda and/or distorted African and African American history, and to demand that these books be removed from use in classrooms. The NAACP youth groups published their survey findings in local daily and weekly newspapers and in *The Crisis* magazine. Members also attended school board meetings, where they demanded the use of textbooks that offered fair and accurate representations of African Americans, such as Carter G. Woodson's *The Negro in Our History* and W. E. B. Du Bois's *Black Reconstruction.*[53] The Fisk University NAACP chapter in Nashville, Tennessee was one of the first youth groups to respond to the appeal to examine public school textbooks for the distortion of facts about black Americans. The Fisk chapter also launched a book drive to secure books that depicted blacks in a positive light for the library at Pearl High School, one of Nashville's first black high schools.[54] This project became part of an ongoing campaign by NAACP youth to end the use of textbooks containing "anti-Negro propaganda." Juanita Jackson knew that exposing the pernicious practices and racial discrimination found in public school systems was not enough—it was equally important to arm black youth with accurate knowledge about its history and cultural heritage.

The NAACP stressed the importance of black youth taking pride in its heritage, and Jackson committed to fostering cultural pride among NAACP youth. Jackson compiled a bibliography of scholarly and popular works that dealt specifically with African American history and culture, including works by Woodson, W. E. B. Du Bois, James Weldon Johnson, Mary McLeod Bethune, Monroe Work, and others that served to educate young people about Africans' contributions to world and US civilization.[55] Jackson also urged NAACP youth to contact its local libraries to request that they purchase more books by and about African Americans. In rural areas without libraries, NAACP youth groups collected books and magazines and made them available to the young people and adults.[56]

In the late 1930s, the NAACP youth movement's greatest successes in the educational arena came in the fight for equal access to publicly funded graduate and professional schools. NAACP youth understood that the lack of educational opportunities served as a formidable obstacle to black educational and social advancement. In September 1936, the NAACP executive secretary, Walter White declared, "It is no secret to intelligent Americans that Negroes of the United States have had many chains fastened by race prejudice to their limbs in their struggle for existence. . . . In no field of human endeavor have these chains been more binding than in education. Negro Americans have had to pay the same tax rate as everybody else—the one manner in which Negroes have never been discriminated against. But in all southern and many border states, Negroes have been barred completely from tax-supported graduate and professional schools."[57] Donald Murray's lawsuit against the University of Maryland Law School in the case of *Murray v. Maryland* in 1935 paved the way for NAACP lawyers Charles Hamilton Houston and Thurgood Marshall to challenge the lack of graduate and professional educational opportunities for African Americans in most southern states.

In the *Murray* case, the Maryland Court of Appeals ruled in favor of Donald Murray, finding that under the "separate but equal" doctrine, the state of Maryland had to provide black residents equal access to a graduate and professional education. Thus, state officials either had to build a law school for African Americans or admit Murray to the University of Maryland Law School. He was admitted to the university's law school—an NAACP victory that challenged the absence of publicly supported graduate or professional education for black students in other southern and border states.[58] The victory not only exposed the educational inequalities that African Americans suffered, but also inspired young people to support the association's lawsuits to end discrimination in education. During American Education Week in 1936, youth councils and college chapters used a skit (created by the national office) based on the *Murray* case to educate local black citizens about the NAACP's initiative to end inequality in education. They also held a series of national youth mass meetings to protest educational inequalities. That same week, Walter White's radio speech (aired by Columbia Broadcasting System) further informed the general public about the NAACP's goal to eradicate educational inequalities. To the credit of the NAACP, on June 4, 1938, Donald Gaines Murray received his law degree from the University of Maryland, becoming the first African American to graduate from the institution.[59]

Although the *Murray* case established a precedent, the legal counsel had another hurdle to confront. In many southern states that denied African Americans admission to all-white public graduate and professional schools, some black students received tuition assistance to attend out-of-state universities. As a result of the NAACP campaign for educational equality, states such as Virginia, West Virginia, Georgia, Missouri, Oklahoma, Kentucky, Texas, and Tennessee provided out-of-state tuition assistance. Underscoring the progress of the NAACP in its fight for educational equality, Joel E. Spingarn, president of the organization, remarked, "We have fought for the education of youth, to get them into colleges and we are now making, through Charles H. Houston, our Special Counsel, and his assistants, a tremendous effort to permit colored youth to go to any college they want to go wherever they are. And where we are not winning we are making states pass laws giving colored students sums of money to secure their education elsewhere if they cannot secure it in the state university of that state."[60] Although the NAACP was able to get several states to provide tuition assistance, this tuition assistance rarely covered the student's living expenses, and the eligibility requirements were often arbitrary.[61] Ultimately, the NAACP challenged the legality of out-of-state or "out-of-county" tuition assistance to black residents.

In December 1938, Charles Houston and Thurgood Marshall won a major victory in *Missouri ex rel. Gaines v. Canada* when the United States Supreme Court ruled that the University of Missouri had to admit Lloyd Gaines, a black student, to the University of Missouri Law School or open a professional law school for African Americans in the state he wished to study law.[62] For Juanita Jackson, NAACP's victories in *Murray v. Maryland* and *Gaines v. Canada* provided the impetus for black youth to continue its fight for equal educational opportunities. "[U]nder the Constitution," Jackson declared, "as Charles Houston taught us, and as my mother put it, 'We've got to take the white man's law into the white man's court and tell him to obey.' That is what we did."[63] Supporting the NAACP fight for educational equality, youth councils and college chapters across the country raised funds through local dances, sold Christmas seals, and solicited donations in their communities. For example, the Boston Youth Council raised fifty dollars to support the NAACP campaign for educational equality.[64] Jackson knew that offering black youth equal educational opportunities was crucial to its success in a society that discriminated and afforded limited opportunities because of race.

Whereas they centered most of their efforts on antilynching and public educational inequities, NAACP youth organizations also protested the economic and employment conditions for black youth. Alarmed by the steady rise in youth unemployment and juvenile delinquency, President Franklin D. Roosevelt's New Deal administration launched the National Youth Administration (NYA) in 1935, with Aubrey Williams as director, to address the plight of youth during the Depression and to offer solutions to the problems that accompanied idleness and the absence of work.[65] The NYA, the Federal Emergency Relief Administration (FERA), the Civilian Conservation Corps (CCC), and the Works Progress Administration (WPA) provided work relief jobs to 110,000 undergraduates and graduate students. The NYA provided over four hundred thousand jobs to high school students and other young people.[66] Although the NYA and other New Deal youth programs tried to combat unemployment and poverty, many youth criticized their operations, especially because the demand for jobs far exceeded the supply. For instance, during the height of the Depression, five to eight million youths between the ages of sixteen and twenty-five were unemployed. The NYA could only provide economic assistance to a half million.[67] Formed in 1934, the American Youth Congress (AYC) "advocated for millions of underprivileged young Americans—blue collar workers, blacks, the unemployed, and needy students."[68] Through AYC, black and white youth mobilized to confront the socioeconomic ills that plagued its generation. AYC student leaders publicly criticized NYA relief programs and believed that the NYA was inadequate to fix the economic problems they suffered. Historian Robert Cohen asserted, "The Youth Congress deemed the NYA far too limited and underfunded to provide a realistic solution to the economic problems confronting young Americans."[69] Protesting the inability of the NYA to resolve its socioeconomic ills, youth campaigned for an American Youth Act that would provide federal aid to *all* needy youth between the ages of sixteen and twenty-five. These students believed that they could win support for the legislation in Congress, but it was not passed. Cohen maintained, "The American Youth Act represented so radical an expansion of federal aid to youth that it stood little chance on Capitol Hill."[70] However, the legislation did bring national attention to the

"Ours Is an Immediate Task"

economic conditions of a younger generation and forced the NYA to address the social ills that youth faced.

Poverty, social inequalities, and violence throughout the world during the Depression years drove many young people into the arms of fascist and racist movements. "We have come to grips with the problems of insecurity, education inequalities, political injustices, and mob violence. We are aware of the long arm of poverty, Jim Crowism, lynching and oppression," Juanita Jackson observed, "as [they seek to] tighten [their] fascist hold upon twelve millions Negro Americans. Remember, it is not enough to awaken; it is not enough to understand. We must act—and act now."[71] Given that African Americans—and black youth in particular—were suffering more than others from the depressed economic conditions, President Roosevelt offered Mary McLeod Bethune, president of Bethune-Cookman College, an appointment within the NYA in 1936 as the director of the "Division of Negro Affairs," where she would oversee the administration of educational and jobs programs aimed at black youth.[72]

In most instances, before the creation of the Division of Negro Affairs within the National Youth Administration, particularly in the southern states, New Deal youth programs provided limited opportunities for black youth. However, programs put in place through the Division of Negro Affairs at the state and local level provided jobs for teachers and young people in black settlement houses, libraries, YMCAs, and the YWCA, and provided adult educational classes to bring about black youth participation in its national programs. Juanita Jackson and other NAACP officials saw Bethune's NYA division as beneficial because it sought to address the problems confronting black youth, particularly the lack of educational and employment opportunities.[73] By creating the position of "state administrative assistant" staffed by capable black professionals, the NYA greatly increased black youths' participation in the NYA and other New Deal programs at the state and local levels.[74]

While tens of thousands of black youths benefited at some time from NYA programs, they suffered disproportionately from the economic depression and still faced discriminatory treatment, even in New Deal programs. Cohen contended, "The Youth Congress leaders took the NYA to task for its 'complete lack of democratic administration. They charged that too little was being done to see that the NYA did not discriminate against blacks."[75] Bethune understood this problem and complained about the inequitable treatment of black youth to NYA director, Aubrey Williams. Commenting on her 1936 appointment, Bethune observed, "It is about time that white folks recognize that Negroes are human too, and will not much longer stand to be the dregs of the work force."[76] Historian B. Joyce Ross remarked, "as NYA Director of Negro Affairs . . . in so many instances she [Bethune] was forced to accept not only separate, but also less than equal consideration for her people. The root of the problem was the failure of national NYA administrators, even in the wake of demands of the Director of the Division of Negro Affairs and the resolutions of black conferences, to apply fully the principle of federal auspices of racial equality at the state and local levels."[77] Evidence indicates, however, that Bethune's lobbying and administrative efforts led to increased federal aid to improve educational and employment opportunities for black youth within the Civilian Conservation Corps as well as in the NYA.[78]

Given the high levels of unemployment, Jackson believed it was important that the NAACP youth connect its activism to the organized labor movement that had succeeded in gaining the legal right to collective bargaining for wages and working conditions with the passage of the National Labor Relations Act—or "Wagner Act"—in 1935. The Committee on Industrial Organizations, which broke away from the American Federation of Labor (AFL) in 1935, became the Congress of Industrial Organizations (CIO) in 1938, and began unionizing efforts among automobile, steel, clothing, and other industrial workers. At the same time, the CIO, under the leadership of mine workers' leader John L. Lewis, supported the NAACP's civil rights activism, including the push for antilynching legislation.[79] Juanita Jackson believed that supporting workers' rights could result in positive social and economic changes for black workers in general and southern black sharecroppers in particular. For example, she praised the activities of the Cleveland, Ohio, Youth Council that observed "National Sharecroppers Week" in 1938 by sponsoring an educational meeting and a benefit dinner to raise funds to support black sharecroppers. Like other major cities such as New York, Chicago, and Detroit, Cleveland had become home to black southerners fleeing the oppression of Jim Crow and the exploitation of sharecroppers in the South. Because southern migrants in Cleveland maintained connections with family members back home (and as some of them joined the NAACP), the Cleveland NAACP branch became sympathetic to the plight of sharecroppers in the South and felt compelled to support them. Andrew M. Fearnley writes, "For migrants who traveled North and settled in Cleveland understood, the Association was both a conduit for their journeys, and a means of staying in touch with, and often protecting, those who stayed behind."[80]

Leading the Cleveland's branch efforts to support southern sharecroppers was the youth council. Beatrice Avery Bates, youth council president, believed that awareness about the plight of black sharecroppers in the South was of the utmost importance. On March 6, 1938, W. O. Walker, the Cleveland NAACP Branch president, seeking to better inform youth council members about black sharecroppers' struggles in the South, gave a lecture at their meeting and educated them about the circumstances faced by the black sharecropper population and the purpose of the Southern Tenant Farmers' Union (STFU).

Commenting on the significance of Walker's lecture, Adelia Bradley, corresponding secretary of the Cleveland, Ohio, Youth Council, wrote, "Mr. Walker devoted his talk to the subject of the plight of the sharecroppers and the purpose of the Tenant Farmers' Union. He gave a graphic picture of the condition of the sharecropper in the South, his home life, his economic predicament, his lack of educational facilities, and the difficulty faced by union organizers in carrying on their work." At the end of the lecture, Walker commended the youth council members for supporting the sharecroppers and urged them to continue their work.[81] The following week, on March 12, Howard Kester, one of the founders of the STFU, gave the keynote address at the benefit dinner sponsored by the youth council for the sharecroppers. The program focused on the organizing activities of the farm workers union and on the campaign of intimidation and violence against sharecroppers who sought to unionize. Not only did the Cleveland Youth Council raise funds to support sharecroppers, but individual NAACP youth councils and college chapters also subscribed to the STFU official publication, *Sharecroppers' Voice,* and observed "National Sharecroppers' Week."[82]

Influenced by the activism of Ella Baker, former executive director of Young Negroes Cooperative League and NAACP field secretary, Juanita Jackson urged youth councils and college chapters to support southern sharecroppers and encouraged them to set up "buying clubs" and "youth cooperatives" in their local communities to ease the economic burdens created by the Depression. Baker's support for cooperatives stemmed from her family's farming background. Historian Barbara Ransby maintains, "The cooperative ethos that permeated Baker's childhood was deeply implicated on prevailing notions of family and community; it connoted groups of individuals banding together around shared interests and promoting a sense of reciprocal obligation, not of individualism and competition."[83] Speaking at the 1936 NAACP annual conference in Baltimore, Maryland, Baker explained to the young people how the consumer cooperative movement began, and why it was important. Baker asserted, "In theory Consumers Cooperative merely eliminates profit that goes to the middleman. It is a movement that says profit goes to the consumer. . . . Consumers Cooperative, in its simplest form, is simply a method by which the profit that goes into the hands of the middleman, especially in America, comes into the hands of the consumer."[84] Because of economic hardships, Jackson believed that the cooperative movement offered great possibility as an alternative economic adventure and a possible solution to the current economic crisis. Defined by President Franklin Roosevelt's Committee on Cooperative Enterprise in Europe, a cooperative was an enterprise that "belongs to the people who use its services, the control of which rests equally with all members, and the gains of which are distributed to the members in proportion to the use they make of its services." In other words, "consumers supply the capital, run the business, use the service of the business, and receive the gains of the business."[85] In 1937, Seaton Manning, a young social worker and Harvard graduate, conducted a course on consumer cooperative for members of the Boston Youth Council. As educational chairman of the Boston Youth Council, Manning wanted to educate the youth about the cooperative movement and to show how it could be a partial solution to the economic woes black people were suffering during the Depression. Under Manning's leadership, the Boston Youth Council set up a buying club, selling stockings and other student products. Jackson believed that cooperatives and buying clubs connected the NAACP youth chapters to labor activism and campaigns to alleviate hunger and poverty in their communities. She wanted NAACP youth to be informed about the economic alternatives that buying clubs and cooperatives offered, and she wanted them to be cognizant of the hardships that tenant farmers, sharecroppers, and other southern black workers faced and the conditions their children and families endured.[86]

Similar to the "Buy Where You Can Work" campaigns organized by Baltimore's City-Wide Young People's Forum in the early 1930s, the Plainfield, New Jersey NAACP Youth Council led demonstrations in 1937 to get the A&P Grocery Stores in black neighborhoods to hire black workers. That same year, the Gary, Indiana, Youth Council led protests against neighborhood businesses with no black employees. As a result, Gary's youth council succeeded in getting thirty-five blacks employed as clerks in fifty of the stores it boycotted. And to make sure that the business owners fulfilled their promise, members of the youth council checked on the stores every two weeks and reported on the conditions they found.[87] Juanita Jackson understood that these protest activities organized at the local level strengthened and legitimized young people's commitment to civil rights activism within their communities.

Jackson urged NAACP youth chapters to set up "citizenship training schools" in many southern black communities. Supporting the work of the NAACP to educate blacks about their voting rights, the local youth councils and college chapters organized many of these schools. These schools offered a series of programs to prepare black southerners to register and to vote. Juanita Jackson promoted these citizenship schools, because she understood that accessing the ballot remained critical for African Americans to improve their economic plight and political powerlessness in the United States. Members of NAACP youth councils and college chapters canvassed their local communities, appealing to nonregistered voters to attend the training classes.[88] Such voter registration activity could be difficult and even dangerous in parts of the rural South due to potential economic or physical reprisals from powerful whites. African Americans who challenged the status quo in the rural South risked being fired, evicted from their homes, or even targeted for mob violence and lynching. These social and economic realities made enlisting in contemporary battles for social justice a daunting prospect for black southerners.[89]

Protesting legal injustices and police brutality against black youth, NAACP youth chapters organized a vigorous campaign to secure the freedom of the Scottsboro Boys, who had been wrongly convicted. In June 1936, delegates from the youth chapters at the NAACP annual conference, held in Baltimore, Maryland, pledged that they would not stop fighting until the Scottsboro Boys were set free. On March 25,1931, nine young black males had been arrested in Paint Rock, Alabama for allegedly raping two white girls, Victoria Price and Ruby Bates, on a freight train headed for Memphis, Tennessee. Twelve days later, the Scottsboro Boys were tried and convicted. Although no substantial evidence existed, the girls' words alone were enough to convince an all-white jury that the young men were guilty. After all, many white southerners believed that these black young men were "savages" and "brutes" who had committed an unspeakable act—a crime against southern womanhood. All the defendants except one (twelve- year-old Roy Wright, the youngest of the defendants) were given death sentences. None of these young men was over the age of twenty. Historian Rebecca de Schweinitz contends, "Prosecutors and the white southern press described the nine defendants as men, savage and sexual, unquestionably capable and so probably guilty of heinous crimes against southern womanhood."[90]

During the 1930s, black men, "regardless of their innocence, had little hope of eliciting public sympathy and less hope of finding justice," especially if they had been accused of raping a white woman.[91] Indeed, the Scottsboro Boys, because of their alleged crime, were presumed to be guilty and viewed as men. In the minds of many white southerners, these boys embodied the age-old racist stereotype of the black man as hypersexual, lustful brute. Demonized, they stood little chance of securing justice in the South. At no point did the prosecution call into question the sexuality of the young women. Historian Patricia Sullivan states, "A confident Victoria Price, aged twenty-one, and a hesitant Ruby Bates, aged seventeen, reconstructed their accounts of what happened on the train. The women differed on key points, but they were spared rigorous cross-examination. Two doctors who examined Price and Bates said that both women had been sexually active during the previous twenty-four hours, but there was no evidence of a violent assault. Ruby Bates recanted her testimony two years later, saying that she and Price had lied about the rape; they had not had any contact with the men on the train.[92]

Even after Bates's confession, the Alabama penal system did not overturn the rape conviction, and the Scottsboro Boys were not released from prison. As Mel Watkins aptly puts it, "The boys had become pawns in a larger struggle between liberal, progressive forces and the conservative, racist forces of regional southern politics."[93] The Scottsboro ordeal represented all that could go tragically wrong with the United States justice system. De Schweinitz asserts, "Police harassed them; the courts, as civil rights groups charged, legally lynched them; and jailers beat them. These 'nine negro children grow[ing] to young manhood in jail,' defenders argued, represented the 'shame of America.'"[94]

By 1936, the Scottsboro Boys had been incarcerated for five years for a crime they had not committed. On November 20, 1936, Juanita Jackson, along with Dr. E. W. Taggart, president of the Birmingham, Alabama NAACP, and Laura Kellum, secretary of the Birmingham Youth Council, visited the Scottsboro Boys at the Jefferson County jail in Birmingham, Alabama. Jackson delivered to them a pledge of support from thousands of young people throughout the United States. At the urging of the national youth director, members of the youth councils and college chapters wrote personal letters to the Scottsboro Boys. For example, the Fisk University NAACP College Chapter sent "a flood of greeting cards" to the young men, assuring them that NAACP youth would be relentless in its fight for their freedom. On December 22, Kellum, along with other members of the Birmingham Youth Council, visited the Scottsboro Boys and brought them decorated gift baskets containing "nuts, fruits, stationery, and cigarettes" for Christmas.[95] The young men were delighted with their gifts and praised the youth group for its continued support. In addition to the letter-writing campaign, NAACP youth groups launched a legal defense fund to provide financial support for the Scottsboro Boys legal team. For instance, the Houston, Texas, Youth Council contributed five dollars toward the defense fund, and the Montgomery, Alabama, and West Virginia youth councils contributed two dollars each.[96] The following year, NAACP youth councils and college chapters organized a massive letter-writing campaign to members of Congress to protest the all-white jury's conviction of the Scottsboro Boys. The NAACP youth chapters continued their protest of this legal injustice; nonetheless, the young men were not all released from prison until years later.

In 1938, Houston, Texas, Youth Council secured the freedom of Christal Gibson, a graduate of Wheatley High School, who had been brutally beaten by an off-duty police officer and falsely charged for disorderly conduct. Upon learning of Gibson's ordeal, youth council members obtained the legal assistance of W. Jay Johnston, a prominent white attorney and chairman of the Houston NAACP Branch Legal Redress Committee. Johnston succeeded in getting the charge dropped against Gibson, and the chief of police ordered that the offending officer be suspended for ten days.[97] The Houston Civil Service Commissioner, Jesse E. Moseley declared, "There's too much of this sort of thing going on in the police department. I think ten days is a short layoff for an offense of this kind." Shortly after the incident, an editorial in the May edition of the *Houston Defender* stated, "even the suspension of a white police officer for taking advantage of or beating and maltreating a Negro is something new and novel in Houston, and shows that times are really changing here."[98] The fight to free Christal Gibson in Houston and the Scottsboro Boys in Alabama connected the NAACP youth to social activism in a more personal way. In these efforts, NAACP youth witnessed firsthand the injustices and dangers that black youth faced in the 1930s. At the same time, participation in collective campaigns, programs, and other forms of community activism served to attract more young people to the work of the NAACP youth movement.

In 1938, Juanita Jackson married attorney and civil rights activist Clarence Mitchell, who served as director of the NAACP Washington Bureau.[99] After marrying, she resigned from her position as national youth director for the NAACP. Executive director Walter White and others tried to persuade Jackson to stay, but her mind was made up; "I resign my post to marry my prince."[100] The decision to forego career plans after marriage was not uncommon among highly educated professional women in the 1930s. As Juanita Jackson Mitchell points out, "In those days [there] was a different conception, women left [jobs] to marry" and raise a family.[101] Historian Barbara Ransby contends that Jackson's mother's beliefs about marriage might have also influenced her decision. Ransby maintains, "She [Lillie Jackson] did harbor some very conventional notions about marriage and the proper role of married women. Her status as Mrs. Jackson was important to her, a value she passed on to her daughter Juanita."[102] Although Juanita Jackson Mitchell embraced "conventional notions about marriage and the proper role of married women," she did not fully abandon her work as an activist. Mitchell remained committed to youth work and civil rights without the title or organizational post.[103]

While the Great Depression and the rising tide of Fascism in the 1930s largely influenced American youth's consciousness about racial injustices at home and abroad, the inequalities and racial injustices that African Americans suffered served as the catalyst for the revitalization of the NAACP national youth movement. Juanita Jackson remained a source of empowerment for these youth as they struggled against the socioeconomic structures of Jim Crow segregation and white racism. Jackson knew that if the voices of black youth were to be heard, they must be heard through their own movement. She firmly believed in the young people's ability to effect social change. "[I]n spite of their contemplation of a world full of [antithetical] interests and destructive social practices," Jackson declared, "the youth of today still have a vision. . . . May their idealism, energy, and enthusiasm be increasingly harnessed to the work of our organization."[104]

Juanita Jackson's passion, zeal, and activism established a legacy of leadership and dedication that influenced later national youth directors. James H. Robinson, Jackson's successor as national youth director, continued her legacy and advanced the fight for civil rights during the years when Fascism and Nazism began to tighten their hold over Europe, and after the United States had entered World War II. Juanita Jackson had launched an NAACP youth movement that continued to contribute mightily to black social and political activism into the postwar years and in the early years of the modern civil rights movement.[105]

Chapter Two

To "Keep Our Vision Unclouded": War and Democracy

A year before the United States entered the Second World War, the NAACP leader, Walter White, had envisioned a world free from racial bigotry and social injustice. In 1940, at the First Annual NAACP Student Conference, White remarked, "We must keep ourselves free from bitterness and hatred, and keep our vision unclouded as far as it is possible to do so, because we can never build a democracy for Negroes or whites, but for all of the citizens of America." For White, this war would have special significance. The defeat of Fascism and Nazism would mean victory against totalitarianism abroad—and against racism at home, and would represent the first step toward the liberation of *all* oppressed people. So he hoped. White believed the destiny of mankind to be inextricably linked to the elimination of Fascism, Nazism, and racism, and he called for international democracy, maintaining its necessity for global peace. Even as racism was unsettling America and the world, White cautioned black youth not to become cynical but rather to embrace a vision of the world not tainted by racism. His idealism was unrealistic in the face of the grim realities that black youth faced during and after the Second World War. This chapter explores how the Second World War created an international discussion among youth concerning colonialism, imperialism, and racism, and how that discussion influenced the NAACP youth in particular to link its fight for civil rights to the global struggle for self-determination and human rights. Additionally, this chapter examines the NAACP youth's disillusionment with America's practices of democracy during the Second World War and the members' fight for *full* democracy at that time. Lastly, this chapter captures the association's efforts to enjoin the college chapters and the youth councils' activities in a more collaborative way as its youth divisions expanded greatly during these years.

On August 16, 1938, youth from the United States and from around the world met at Vassar College for the convening of the Second World Youth Congress.[1] Attendees shared the idealist belief that world peace could, indeed, be achieved. "Despite mounting international difficulties, despite wars being waged, young people the world over look hopefully to the future. They refuse to submit to prevalent pessimism and insist on continuing their efforts to build a peaceful civilization."[2] These words graced the cover of the pamphlet for the Second World Youth Congress. Although some Americans questioned the motives of this conference, this mixed cadre of youth gathered at Vassar College to foster a better understanding of youth from different cultures and religions and to search for viable alternatives to war.[3] In a statement refuting the National Catholic Welfare Conference's position that the World Youth Congress was irreligious and communistic, Betty Shields-Collins, Second World Youth Congress international secretary, commented, "Some of the aims of the World Youth Congress are to unite young people of all faiths, promote their constant collaboration on all issues affecting their general welfare and erase existing prejudices."[4] Although Communist students may have wielded great influence at the gathering, the conference was far from communistic and irreligious. The Second World Youth Congress provided an opportunity for youth from around the world to seek solutions for world peace and to work toward eradicating social injustices. Eleanor Roosevelt delivered the keynote address for the opening session of the conference, urging youth to discard narrow-mindedness and to embrace tolerance. The First Lady believed that recognition and acceptance of differences, and the self-determination of nations, were essential to preserving peace.[5] Her persuasive and affable personality made her well respected among most American youth, as she became their liaison in Washington, campaigning for legislation that would help to improve their overall plight.[6] Although it set the tone for the conference, Mrs. Roosevelt's presence did not overshadow the youth's discordant voices on the issue of war.

The thin thread of anti-fascist unity, rooted in the Oxford Pledge (which condemned all wars as imperialistic), splintered as youth began to question whether war was necessary to stopping the spread of Fascism and Nazism. Youth groups, such as the Youth Committee Against War (YCAW), the National League of Methodist Youth, and the Young People's Social League (YPSL), opposed war at all cost and urged delegates at the conference to endorse the Oxford Pledge. Unlike those in the National League of Methodist Youth and the YPSL, YCAW members were strictly pacifists. Because of the rapid spread of militarism and totalitarianism, youth groups that had once endorsed the Oxford Pledge—such as the American Youth Congress, the American Student Union, the Southern Negro Youth Congress, the NAACP, and the Chinese, and the Spanish delegations—now called for collective security. Collective security (vaguely defined at the Vassar Conference) supported concerted military action on the part of nonbelligerent nations to prevent the spread of Fascism and Nazism and economic assistance for victims of such aggression. The policy of collective security, which stood in stark contrast to the Oxford Pledge, allowed youth who had been antiwar to reconcile their belief that war would prevent the spread of totalitarianism. Many youths who were antiwar (and who opposed another world war) believed an age-old historical assumption that the First World War was waged to advance the capitalistic and imperialistic interests of plutocrats; the Second World War would be no different.[7] Through much debate and the dispelling of myths, youth at the Second World Youth Congress reassessed this age-old assertion and this oversimplification of the historical connections between these two wars. As a result, the conference ended with the majority of the youth signing the Vassar Peace Pact (which called for collective security).[8] The YCAW opposed the Vassar Pact because it represented the disingenuous political maneuverings of Communist students (guided by the Comintern) who had once supported the Oxford Pledge but now called for collective security.[9] Although it was correct in its observations about the political maneuvering of the Communist students, the YCAW was shortsighted in its belief that isolationism was a viable solution to world peace.

The position of collective security expressed in the Vassar Peace Pact had more than mere abstract political meaning for NAACP youth and other non-white youth at the Second World Youth Congress. Having witnessed Italy's invasion of Ethiopia in 1935 with no sanctions from the international community or the United States—only public condemnation against such aggression—black youth gladly endorsed the Vassar Peace Pact.[10] For many black youth, the looming war against Fascism provided a possible vehicle to eliminate racial bigotry and social injustices around the world. In their estimation, the defeat of Fascism abroad meant the defeat of racial inequality at home.

At the Second World Youth Congress, African American youth became better acquainted with the global injustices that imperialism and racism inflicted on the world. As white and nonwhite youths from countries under colonial and dictatorial regimes shared their stories, they personalized the horror of imperialism and racism. For black American youth, these stories were reminiscent of—and similar to—the social conditions they suffered in the United States, particularly in the South. Detailing the activities of the Second World Youth Congress, Virginia E. Anderson, the Brooklyn, New York NAACP Youth Council delegate, highlighted the plight of youth in other countries. In her report on the Second World Youth Congress, she noted how she spent long hours with these youth delegates discussing the predicaments they faced in their countries. Anderson asserted, "During the congress session I was able to talk to some of the delegates who had come from countries where the system of imperialism ruled, others where there was a fear of dictatorships being established, and still others where dictator rule had been established."[11] For example, a youth delegate from India believed that with the international cooperation of youth and other governments, imperialism could be dismantled in India. This kind of optimism and idealism exhibited by youth at the conference gave Anderson inspiration and hope, for she believed that black youth could overcome the problems they suffered.

While discussing the problems of black youth with several delegates, Anderson realized that youths from other countries were familiar with the atrocities that blacks suffered in the United States, namely, lynching. These youth declared that such evil cast a great shadow over American society. Her discussion with youths from countries under colonial and dictatorial regimes revealed that they were well aware of the negative effects of racism and colonialism. For many youth, particularly Anderson, the Second World Youth Congress brought greater awareness of the global struggle against imperialism, racism, and colonialism, and revealed that the fight for human rights must be linked to the struggles of all oppressed people. Furthermore, this conference indicated that the struggle for full citizenship rights waged by black youth in the United States was not an isolated struggle, and that youth under colonial and dictatorial regimes faced similar oppression. The egalitarian and congenial atmosphere that Anderson experienced at the Second World Youth Congress provided determination that the fight for human rights must prevail.

Almost a month following the closing of the Second World Youth Congress conference at Vassar College, the NAACP youth division underwent a leadership change. In September 1939, the NAACP Board of Directors appointed James H. Robinson as the acting national director, replacing Juanita Jackson, who had resigned her post to marry civil rights attorney Clarence Mitchell.[12] Jackson's keen leadership had established the NAACP youth movement nationally, and Robinson assumed the grand task of furthering the association's youth work. Born in Knoxville, Tennessee, on January 24, 1907, Robinson's family had migrated to Cleveland, Ohio during the early years of his youth. During the 1930s, he transferred to Lincoln University after completing his freshman year at Western Reserve University. While at Lincoln University, Robinson pledged Alpha Phi Alpha Fraternity, Incorporated and was a member of the American Youth Congress. After becoming involved with the work of the NAACP, he reorganized Lincoln University's NAACP chapter and remained active in the association's youth work.[13]

In 1935, Robinson graduated from Lincoln University as valedictorian of his class. That same year, Robinson was elected to the NAACP National Board of Directors as a special representative for the youth division. Also, after graduating from Lincoln University, Robinson prepared for the ministry and enrolled in Union Theological Seminary, graduating in 1938. While at Union Theological Seminary, he worked with the Neighborhood Union Center for two years as director of boys' work.[14] Upon graduation in May from the Union Theological Seminary, he was appointed minister of the Morningside Presbyterian Church (which he renamed the Church of the Master) in Harlem, New York, and was ordained in June of that same year. Robinson reorganized Morningside Presbyterian Church into the Church of the Master and founded the Morningside Community Center, which provided a host of services to Harlem's inner-city residents.[15] Though he assumed the position as acting director within the association, Robinson was still deeply committed to his ministerial work.[16] His years of work with the Union Neighborhood Center, the Morningside Community Center, and leadership within the NAACP college chapter at Lincoln University amply prepared him for the role as the NAACP national youth director. The real test to Robinson's leadership skills came when the local Greenville, South Carolina NAACP and the fledgling youth council decided to initiate a mass voter registration drive in that city.

In 1938, blacks in Greenville, South Carolina, under the leadership of James A. Brier, a schoolteacher, established a local NAACP branch. The Greenville branch brought together blacks from across class lines to address racial discrimination that relegated them to second-class citizenship. Peter Lau asserts, "By the beginning of 1939 the NAACP had become a critical organization in black Greenville, bringing black men and women together in a collective effort to raise issues of concern to the city's black residents and to formulate a means to address them."[17] For example, black leaders petitioned the city council for funds for a park and public housing for black residents; however, the city council resisted their demands. After the city council blocked funds for the park and public housing, the local NAACP and black citizens launched a mass voter registration campaign, which had started out as an underground movement to register blacks to vote.[18]

By May 1939, the Greenville NAACP branch set up voter registration schools, where young people in the branch's youth council assisted. The nineteen-year-old William Anderson, president of the Greenville Youth Council, "held two community forums on 'Youth and Democracy.'"[19] Greenville's white community did not become aware of the voter registration activities in the black community until early July. On July 5, J. C. Williams (from the Workers' Alliance) and Anderson led a group of blacks, mostly women, down to the local courthouse "to obtain voter registration certificates" and to the city hall to get their names on the "city's voter registration polls." The next day, the city's newspaper, the *Greenville News,* reported that fifty-seven blacks had registered to vote in the upcoming general election. The story in the *Greenville News* outraged local whites. The local white newspaper headlines publicized the violent intentions of the Ku Klux Klan.[20] Whites in Greenville were committed to maintaining the racial subordination of blacks. Lau contends, "In the days and months that followed, the response of Greenville's white residents to the voter registration drive suggested the degree to which the black insurgency represented a challenge to a world ordered by hierarchies of race and gender—that is, by white male supremacy."[21] Blacks in Greenville suffered from violence and economic reprisals from local white citizens who tried to thwart any effort by blacks to eliminate the barriers that relegated them to second-class citizenship.

Since Reconstruction, the Ku Klux Klan and local whites had used violence, intimidation, and economic reprisals to render black voters politically powerless in Greenville, South Carolina. Anderson believed it was important that blacks vote to change the course of politics in that city. As voter registration activities increased among black residents in Greenville, so did retaliation from local white citizens. That summer, local authorities arrested Williams three times on trumped-up charges, and the Ku Klux Klan visited him while he was incarcerated in the local jail. Jerry Owens, who worked as a bootblack, was also arrested for attempted rape, after he supposedly propositioned a white waitress at one of the city's cafés. Allegedly, days before his arrest, Owens, who was illiterate, had joked with his white customers about the mass voter registration efforts that black people had launched in the city.[22]

Similarly, because of his political activism, youth council president William Anderson was also convicted on trumped-up charges of disorderly conduct and breach of peace. Prior to his arrest, Anderson, who worked as a janitor at the local white junior high school, had allowed three white boys to use the school's telephone. When a white woman filed a complaint that someone at the school had tried to court her daughter over the telephone, the local authorities accused Anderson of making the call. The real culprits, however, were the three white boys. Local white citizens rumored that Anderson had telephoned a fifteen-year-old white girl and tried to arrange a date with her. They reported the incident to the police, who questioned, beat, and jailed Anderson.[23] Although he denied the charges, Anderson was not believed by the local authorities. In recounting the ordeal, Anderson shared the chilling words of the arresting officer: "You're the kind of Negro I would rather kill than to take to jail and when we get through with you, you will not be able to use a telephone."[24] Fortunately, this young man did not perish at the hands of the local authorities, as so many others did for challenging the South's established social system. However, the authorities did place Anderson under a five thousand dollar peace bond and sentenced him to serve thirty days or pay a one thousand dollar fine.[25]

Upon immediate notification of the horrific episode, the national office of the NAACP came to his defense. Acting Youth Director James Robinson appealed to the youth councils and college chapters to raise funds for Anderson's release. He asked the youth to also raise funds for Anderson's defense and to write letters to the Civil Liberty Division of the Justice Department to protest this horrible crime. The responses from the association's youth councils and college chapters were remarkable. The youth chapters additionally staged mass meetings and rallies, and raised $258.79 to assist with Anderson's $1,200 bail. Because of the widespread publicity given to the case by the Greenville Youth Council and the national office, the plaintiff dropped the charges for fear of the girl's identity being exposed. Despite investigating the incident, the Department of Justice claimed that it could not do anything because it was a municipal—rather than a federal—matter.[26] Sad to say, blacks received this

To "Keep Our Vision Unclouded"

type of runaround from officials at the local, state, and federal levels. In a letter written to the NAACP youth chapters concerning Anderson's ordeal, James Robinson stated, "It has been definitely established that William Anderson was framed not only on the occasion on which we appealed to you for funds, but on two subsequent occasions, and that these were attempts to intimidate him and the other members of both our branch and the youth council who worked with him in order that the very effective fight they were waging for the rights of Negroes at the polls might be curtailed."[27]

Anderson, like many black southerners who challenged the South's age-old practices, suffered at the hands of white supremacists. Several weeks prior to his arrest, Anderson and the local NAACP had initiated a voter registration drive to register blacks for Greenville's municipal election to be held in September of that year. Most of Greenville's blacks were not registered to vote, and the local KKK used force and intimidation to maintain the status quo. Anderson decided to challenge this practice. The Greenville Youth Council was very active in its community, with the voter registration drive epitomizing its level of commitment. While Anderson and the thirty-one other members of the youth council worked to register blacks for the upcoming election, the KKK prepared to unleash its assault on the nineteen-year-old youth council president. Buoyed by the trumped-up charges brought against Anderson and the violence he had suffered at the hands of the police, the Klan plotted to destroy Anderson's reputation and teach him not to challenge local practices. Apparently, Anderson had established a fine reputation in the community among both blacks and whites, and this ordeal was orchestrated to have the community—not to mention his peers—lose faith in him. Nevertheless, deeply committed to the struggles of his people, Anderson believed that it was his responsibility to fight for social equality. In a letter to Robinson thanking him for the support he had received from the other NAACP youth and the national office, Anderson asserted, "My executives may rest secured that I will always be race conscious and will fight to the end for its benefit. I will never surrender."[28]

Anderson's level of dedication exemplified the resilience and determination of other black activists like him—and those who had preceded him. His ordeal underscored the danger that youth council members faced as they worked to register blacks to vote in the South. However, Anderson understood that his fight for equal rights represented more than the advancement of the association's work; it was about accountability to the race. The activism of the youth council and the local NAACP branch inspired black Americans to continue to challenge Jim Crow segregation and racial discrimination. Lau maintains, "Across the nation, the black struggle for voting rights in Greenville and the violent efforts to suppress it served as a rallying cry. In South Carolina the voting rights movement in Greenville helped provide a crucial impetus for the formation of a statewide NAACP that would help coordinate NAACP activities across the state and spur the massive growth of branches membership during the 1940s."[29]

That year, in 1939, following Anderson's fiasco, the Second World War commenced in Europe. The war came as no surprise—many had watched the militarism of Germany mushroom. As European countries waged war against each other, the United States formulated a policy to remain neutral, while the federal government cut vital social programs in order to increase military appropriations. In March 1940, prior to the U.S. entrance into the Second World War, the first annual student conference of the NAACP convened at Virginia Union University.[30] Delegates at the conference were mostly college students from black and white colleges and universities, while a small delegation of youth councils also attended. During the conference, delegates addressed a gamut of issues that involved the black youth struggle for full democracy. NAACP youth went on record opposing the Roosevelt administration's cutting of vital social programs to expand the military budget. They denounced Roosevelt's military spending policy and condemned the war by drafting the "Peace Proclamation of Negro Youth." The peace proclamation established the NAACP youth as the first black youth organization to officially oppose the war. The declaration stated, "Be it resolved that the Student Conference of the N.A.A.C.P. call for the immediate preparation and mass distribution of an appeal to the Negro youth of the nation to join in the fight for peace as a concrete contribution to the campaign against the warmakers, to be known as the 'Peace Proclamation of Negro Youth.'"[31]

Perhaps the only true pacifist at the conference, James Farmer gave a stirring speech against the war. A member of pacifist groups, such as the Fellowship of Reconciliation, the YCAW, and the Congress of Racial Equality, Farmer denounced all wars as imperialistic and serving the greed of the rich. He asserted that the war in Europe was a fight among imperialists, part of a longstanding practice of the ruling class's battle for capitalist gains, and that American youth had nothing to gain from supporting the war. For Farmer, the only way to create world peace was to replace nationalism with internationalism.[32] Whereas Farmer's position left no room for ambiguity, the "Peace Proclamation of Negro Youth" did not specifically restrict NAACP youth from supporting war. The proclamation called for peace, but these youth really meant that they opposed going to war if they were not going to enjoy full democracy at home.[33] Blacks were tired of being treated like second-class citizens—and tired of fighting for a country that did not fight for them. The persistent question many blacks asked was, why fight a war abroad for democracy when there is no democracy at home? Contrary to the position taken earlier in the proclamation, at the outbreak of war, the NAACP went on record supporting U.S. involvement. These youths, like other NAACP leaders, believed that the war against Fascism and Nazism would illuminate the nation's peculiar democracy

To "Keep Our Vision Unclouded"

and force the United States to do right about its race problems at home. When the United States entered the war on December 7, 1941, after Japan attacked Pearl Harbor, NAACP youth hoped that this war would bring full democracy to all Americans.

Keenly aware of the inequalities for blacks in the New Deal programs—and having confronted these inequalities before—NAACP youth hoped that the war would create new economic opportunities for them. Despite their shortcomings, the NYA and the CCC did offer a modicum of relief to black youth. However, NAACP youth continued to call on the federal government to make the practices of the NYA and the CCC more equitable. Most NYA and CCC projects were segregated. Black youth complained about the differences in the educational courses and facilities set up for blacks and whites. For example, the Kansas City NYA made courses such as automobile mechanics, automobile electricity, automobile body and fender work, air communications, sheet metal and woodworking available for young white males. On the other hand, young black males only had courses available in building maintenance and repair, which simply meant janitorial work. Young black females confronted a similar situation. Courses for young white females consisted of office work (typing and filing), commercial food services, alteration, and remodeling—while young black females had classes in alteration, remodeling, and personal grooming.[34]

Similarly, the CCC, which provided conservational work relief for young men between the ages of eighteen and twenty-five, discriminated against young black men. The CCC director, Robert Fechner, doggedly defended segregation, claiming that the CCC treated black and white young men no differently; however, under Fechner's tenure, fewer blacks gained supervisory positions. In 1939, out of the 150 camps, only two company commanders were black. Additionally, out of the twenty-five thousand supervisors and fifteen hundred camp superintendents, a mere five were black.[35] Sensing that these practices greatly disadvantaged black youth—making it virtually impossible for them to be competitive in the job market—Walter White complained to NYA director Aubrey Williams. He noted that if this problem persisted, employers would be able to deny black youth jobs based on inadequate training.[36] National Youth director, Madison S. Jones, who succeeded James Robinson, also found serious problems with the conditions that black youth experienced at NYA facilities in Champaign-Urbana, Illinois. Jones pointed out the lack of courses and equipment for black youth and failure of the classes in preparing black youth for the job-related needs of that community.[37] Eradicating these blatant discriminatory practices became a top priority for the NAACP youth councils and college chapters.

When college chapters and youth councils convened at the Third Annual Student Conference, held on November 1, 1941, at Hampton University in Richmond, Virginia, discussions concerning economic opportunities and training for black youth took center stage. A decade earlier, the association had only a nominal link to labor-related concerns, supporting the legal cases of the Southern Tenant Farmers' Union and contributing financially to the plight of sharecroppers. During the 1940s, however, the NAACP developed a substantial relationship with the labor movement, openly denouncing the marginalization of blacks within labor unions and the workplace.[38] Indeed, youths who gathered at this conference already knew about the labor conditions under which blacks suffered and were prepared to discuss ways they could make good on President Roosevelt's promise to improve labor conditions for blacks. Months before, A. Philip Randolph had threatened to launch a March on Washington Movement (MOWM) to open up employment for blacks in the defense industry and to confront the industry's discriminatory practices. The NAACP national office went on record as one of MOWM's primary supporters, and the NAACP youth councils and college chapters had readied themselves to participate in the march as well. Convinced that a demonstration of this magnitude would generate bad publicity against his administration at home and abroad, Roosevelt issued Executive Order 8802, which outlawed discrimination in the defense industry and established the Fair Employment Practice Committee (FEPC).[39] Commenting on the MOWM in his closing address at the Third Annual Student Conference, White asserted, "It took the threat of a March on Washington to galvanize our government into action and to get the President to issue the executive order banning discrimination in the defense orders and to set up a committee on fair employment practice to investigate and eliminate such discrimination."[40]

Although White recognized glaring discrepancies in American democracy, he still had faith in the possibility of blacks gaining full democratic rights. When the *Pittsburgh Courier* dubbed the "Double V Campaign" as victory against racism at home and the evil forces of Fascism and Nazism abroad, White embraced such idealism with an air of expectancy. Emulating White's optimism, NAACP youth chapters showed their support for the campaign. For example, the Toledo, Ohio, Youth Council participated in Ohio's gigantic statewide Double V campaign. Youth council members sold pins, buttons, and stickers to support the war.[41] White admonished NAACP youth not to believe the foolish propaganda put forth by some blacks that "they hope Hitler wins because he will teach white Americans what it means to suffer from oppression." White maintained, "This is both silly and dangerous. . . . I urge you to read Hitler's *Mein Kampf.* . . . If Hitler wins there will be no schools like Hampton Institute, no organizations like the National Association for the Advancement of Colored People."[42] The association denounced anti-Semitism as insidious and as a perpetuation of racial hatred. White passionately believed in the ideals of democracy and the brotherhood of humankind. Furthermore,

To "Keep Our Vision Unclouded"

he also believed that democracy must become the earnest possession of all people around the world. Therefore, he warned the youth not to embrace the vileness of racism or to isolate their plight in the United States from the predicament of all oppressed people around the world. White's sentiments actually echoed what Virginia Anderson had discovered almost three years earlier while attending the Second World Youth Congress as an NAACP youth delegate; according to White, the fight for democracy must be a fight for all oppressed people.

That year, the NAACP youth chapters waged successful campaigns protesting labor discrimination against blacks. In Tulsa, Oklahoma, the Tulsa Youth Council, along with the senior branch, successfully picketed a bombing plant and got the company to allot 20 percent of its jobs to local black Tulsans. This same youth council demonstrated against the Pepsi Cola plant, which resulted in the plant's hiring of a black person. Mary Pittman, a youth council member, remarked, "In the Pepsi Cola project we did not get a man to serve on a delivery truck but we got one to work for Pepsi Cola, selling this pop, and he makes more than those in the delivery service."[43] The San Antonio, Texas, Youth Council, through a letter-writing campaign, forced a local newspaper to correct an advertisement that read, "Nigger in the wood pile cutting down prices."[44] These campaigns exemplified the ardent fight of NAACP youth to advance the association's fight against racism and labor discrimination. That same year, the NAACP youth movement inaugurated the first annual essay contest and the national "American Negro Youth Week," to be observed annually in April. The essay competition, held from February 1 to April 1, offered high school and college youths a chance to display their knowledge on topics relevant to the work of the association and black history. That year's essay theme was "What Negro Youth Expects [sic] from National Defense." Prizes totaled three hundred dollars, with the first-place prize at one hundred and fifty dollars, the second-place prize at seventy-five dollars, and the third-place prize at twenty-five dollars. The national office considered the money a form of scholarship assistance.[45] During "American Negro Youth Week," the NAACP celebrated achievements of black youth and focused attention on its needs and aims through programs and activities in the church and the larger community. That week, the youths also selected a big project to tackle; they gathered information on the participation of blacks in the defense industry. The project proved successful, as they received a terrific response.[46] Perhaps, for the youth, the most exciting activities were Parade Day and Social Activity Day. Through such activities, the NAACP youth councils and college chapters attracted other youth to the work of the association.

The Second World War moved NAACP youth to greater activism—and led many youths to be drafted into the war. WWII had a tremendous impact on the lives of black youths. Drafted black youth trained in segregated camps, which were often hostile environments. The NAACP condemned the United States Army for maintaining racial segregation at military training camps. During the war years, NAACP youth councils and college chapters assisted the national office by compiling the grievances of soldiers in training camps in their vicinities. These younger NAACP members exposed the ways in which black soldiers suffered physical violence at the hands of their commanding officers and, at times, experienced mob violence from local whites near training camps. The NAACP National Office, in turn, used the data collected by the NAACP youth councils and college chapters to expose the abuse blacks soldiers faced and to appeal to President Roosevelt to investigate these injustices. In 1942, the New York City youth councils distributed flyers at the Joe Louis-Buddy Baer fight, publicizing the United States Navy's policy of relegating blacks to cooks and mess boys. The Flint, Michigan, Youth Council investigated local defense plants' discrimination against blacks, collected books for soldiers, and held demonstrations for the "Mixed Brigade, Second Front." Additionally, the Washington, D.C., Youth Council established a soldier's welfare funds project. [47] This activism grew partly out of the personal loss these youths suffered, as the United States military drafted their friends and other youth council members into the war. The Philadelphia, Pennsylvania, Youth Council initiated a letter-writing campaign to keep in touch with members who had been drafted into the war—and paid their membership fees.[48] The war changed the lives of most Americans, as many families suffered losses with increased combat casualties. NAACP youth certainly bore the brunt of this tragedy as well. The Philadelphia Youth Council letter-writing campaign personalized and humanized the tragic reality of war. That same year, several youth councils protested Mississippi senator Theodore Bilbo's racist position on the anti–poll tax bill and a federal antilynching law.[49] NAACP youth realized that the absence of free elections in the South permitted the likes of Bilbo to remain in office. During the next several years, NAACP youth councils and college chapters would stage rigorous voter registration campaigns to mobilize southern blacks against such political repression.

In 1943, NAACP youth work underwent a significant transition. Madison Jones, former national youth director, resigned in order to become the executive secretary of the Bridgeport, Connecticut YMCA.[50] That year, Ruby Hurley was selected national youth director. Born in Washington, D.C., in 1913, Hurley had attended Miner Teachers College and the Robert H. Terrell Law School. Having become involved with the association's work in 1939, she had assisted with reorganizing the local Washington, D.C., branch of the NAACP. In her mid-twenties when her work with the association started, Hurley ultimately gave thirty-nine years of her life to the organization's work.[51]

Hurley's appointment reflected the NAACP's commitment to giving young men and women equal opportunity to serve as national youth director. Of the four directors appointed up to that point, two had been men. The association's first national youth director, Juanita Jackson, established a legacy that, as a woman, Hurley could follow with pride. Although the NAACP showed no preference in appointing women or men as national youth director, this egalitarian practice was not pervasive in the organization. Historian Barbara Ransby asserts, "In the NAACP, as in other political organizations, women were indispensable but underappreciated. The association had never elected a woman as its executive secretary, and women were often excluded from the informal inner circle of decision makers. . . . Women's contributions had to be acknowledged, even if they did not translate into formal positions of power."[52] Indeed, Jackson's and Hurley's contributions as national youth directors would have a lasting impact on the youth work of the NAACP.

Like Jackson, Ruby Hurley was passionate and adamant about her work as National Youth director. Commenting on the importance of the work of youth councils and college chapters, Hurley asserted, "The NAACP has been the voice of the repressed Negro for 34 years. We have made ourselves heard in the past and we shall continue to be heard in the future. . . . It is your job to mobilize all of the Negro youth in your communities into the rank of the NAACP. . . . so that we may ultimately attain our goal of true democracy and complete emancipation."[53] Over the years, she developed a great rapport with the youth, at times developing personal relationships or sharing her frustrations about the work. Indeed, Hurley developed a more intimate relationship with the youth than her previous colleagues had. In numerous letters, Albert Henderson, president of the Ohio State Youth Conference, addressed Hurley as "Chief" as a term of endearment—just one example of the many letters youths wrote to Hurley that read like a letter to a friend.[54] Under Hurley's tenure, which lasted eight years, the number of youth councils and college chapters increased. In 1943, when it appointed Hurley as national youth director, the NAACP had 123 youth councils (82 active) and 24 college chapters (17 active). When Hurley left office in 1951, the NAACP had 336 active youth councils and 88 active college chapters.[55] Indeed, Hurley's leadership ability as national youth director did not go unnoticed.

In Hurley's service as national youth director, White recognized her ambition and hard work. Sensing a need to strengthen the association's work in the South, White sent Hurley to Birmingham, Alabama, in 1951 to coordinate campaigns for new branches as the southeast regional director. Hurley's work in the Deep South brought her into closer contact with the grim plight faced by black southerners. Commenting on her life in Birmingham, Hurley asserted, "I had a tremendous personal job to do in getting over the trauma of moving from New York to the South. . . . I had not had the experience of living in a completely segregated society where everything was segregated by law. . . . I point out always . . . I found that on the statute books were city ordinances which included one that said that Negroes and whites could not play checkers together."[56] Indeed, Hurley discovered the North's marked difference from the South, with its strange racial system and Jim Crow laws.

As southeast regional director, Hurley investigated the despicable crimes committed against blacks who confronted the South's discriminatory racial and social system. She recalled the brutal murders of Reverend George Lee and Lamar Smith, who had been gunned down because they defiantly resisted whites by registering blacks to vote in Mississippi. Referencing Lee's murder, Hurley maintained, "I will not be able to forget how the whole lower half of his face had been shot away. A man killed because he, as a minister, said that God's children had rights as God's children and as American citizens."[57] Even more widely reported, the brutal murder of the fourteen-year-old Emmett Till fell to Hurley for investigation. Hurley described how she had to disguise herself in cotton-picking clothes and secretly go from plantation to plantation to gather information on Till's death because blacks feared (for their own lives) to talk to her as an NAACP representative in plain clothes.[58] Langston Hughes, commenting on the association's remarkable work, said of Hurley, "On the national staff of the association too, there are people whose tasks are often too dangerous for comfort, whose jobs require the greatest tact, bravery, mental agility and ordinary common sense. Ruby Hurley, a handsome and dynamic woman, shows no fear when she gets off a plane at a southern airport to take a local bus to a remote hamlet New Yorkers never heard of, where mobs have just roamed the streets smashing the windshields and slashing the tires of all Negro-owned cars or stoning churches and homes."[59] Although some of his description of the association's work bordered on sarcasm, Hughes knew and well understood the grave dangers Hurley faced as she advanced the work of the association in the Deep South.

Not only was Hurley instrumental in investigating hate crimes committed against blacks, but she also advanced the association's fight for educational equality after the *Brown* decision. Hurley assisted in the drive to register Autherine Lucy as the first black student to attend the University of Alabama. Facing an angry white mob, she stood at Lucy's side as she entered the university.[60] At the personal risk of her own life, Hurley advanced much of the work of the association. Because of Hurley's courage and tenaciousness, White knew she would be perfect for the job as southeast regional director. Looking back over her life some years later, and reflecting on her work with the association, Hurley commented, "But for the grace of God, I couldn't have done it, because there were days when if I had any sense, I'da been scared. But I never let myself. I didn't get scared. . . . I was mad."[61] This kind of audacity propelled the efforts of the NAACP—but Hurley's heroism has still received little attention from historians and scholars.

To "Keep Our Vision Unclouded"

Hurley's appointment as national youth director in 1943 greatly benefited the association's youth work. Because the youth work lay dormant for almost six months after Madison Jones had resigned, Hurley's immediate task was to revitalize that effort. During that year, she devoted much of her time to visiting inactive youth branches and to assisting in establishing new ones. Within that year, Hurley chartered twenty-three youth councils and five college chapters.[62] That year, many of the programs carried out by the youth councils and college chapters were educational, focusing mostly on the work of the association—with some exceptions. The Albany, Georgia, Youth Council secured a swimming pool and recreational center for blacks. The West Philadelphia Youth Council, after having held meetings with the manager of the F. W. Woolworth store to get young black girls hired in the store—and being turned down—picketed the store for its discriminatory practices. These direct action activities and others accelerated under Hurley's administration. To increase enthusiasm for its youth work, the following year, the NAACP inaugurated the Ike Smalls Award (a silver cup) to honor the work of the most outstanding youth council and college chapter.[63]

Hurley believed that growth in the association's youth work depended on the effective collaboration of youth councils and college chapters. The lack of cooperation between the college chapters and the youth councils in advancing the national youth agenda was obvious. Although sporadic collaborative activities had occurred with the youth councils, college chapter activities were somewhat isolated from the general youth work. The college chapters really did not have a visible presence in their respective communities. Furthermore, concerns existed about the college students' lack of participation in their local youth councils when they returned home from college during the summer break. Hoping to address this challenge, the association, at the Fifth Annual Student Conference, held on October 29, 1943, at Lincoln University in Chester County, Pennsylvania, passed a resolution, which established the student conference for the benefit of the youth councils and the college chapters.[64] Under Robinson's tenure, in 1940 the NAACP inaugurated its first annual student conference, which was held at Virginia Union University in Richmond, Virginia.[65] Prior to creating the annual student conference, college chapters and youth councils met in separate sessions at the association's annual meeting, held in late June. By the time the NAACP selected Robinson to head up its youth work, the youth division had grown tremendously and was nationally recognized. Before Jackson had resigned her post, the time allotted at the association's annual meeting was really not sufficient for the youth to meet and discuss its problems. Furthermore, concerns were growing over the lack of representation for college students at the association's annual conference. Upon closer examination of the problem, the association discovered that the low attendance of college youth at the association's annual meeting was because colleges and universities had adjourned for the summer, and students—having returned home—were scattered about the country.[66] Additionally, no real collective effort was being made on the part of college chapters at their respective schools to send representatives to attend the annual meeting. Like most college students, members of the college chapters were eager to get home to enjoy summer break.

Because they were absent from the annual conference, many college students missed out on valuable information that could further the association's youth work. To address this challenge and to boost the morale of college youth, the association reasoned that a separate conference for college students would be beneficial. The student conference would allow college youth to get the pertinent information it needed to advance the association's youth work—and the conference would revitalize the NAACP college division. Annual student conferences provided a venue for college students to address issues relevant to the advancement of the association's youth work on college campuses and in their communities.

Although the youth work of the college division and of the youth councils was different, both entities were linked to a national youth agenda. Youth councils and college chapters were responsible for advancing the four main objectives of the national office, which were to secure (1) equal educational opportunity, (2) equal economic opportunity, (3) civil liberties, and (4) anti-lynching legislation. Although these four objectives standardized the youth agenda, the national office did not stipulate how the college chapters and the youth councils should go about achieving these aims. There were some fundamental differences. In terms of organizational structure, college chapters were composed only of college youth, whereas the many youth councils comprised high school students, college students, and recent college graduates. However, it was not uncommon for youth councils to be composed largely of high school students.[67] Whereas youth councils reported to their local senior branches, college chapters were under the jurisdiction of the National Board of Directors.[68] Programs initiated by the youth councils had to be approved by the youth work committee (composed of the presidents of the junior and youth councils and their senior branch advisors), then submitted to the executive committee of the senior branch for final approval. The college programs had to be approved by the national office and college administrators.

Unlike the youth councils, college chapters had the additional burden of being subjected to college administrators (who, at times, restricted programs for fear of losing financial support for the school). Oftentimes, such limitations, in turn, constrained the work of college chapters within their communities, thus alienating them from the local people. Although they were grassroots entities, youth councils had a better chance of getting the community to cooperate with their programs; the college chapters did not always enjoy the same level of support. College chapters were extended into the community via the college. Because many youths who attended colleges and universities were not always from that city or town, they were not familiar with their respective college or university's local problems and were not as invested in solving them. For the most part, the local people viewed them as outsiders, and they had to work harder to gain the trust of the community. Lastly, not all NAACP college chapters were on black campuses; the association had expanded its youth work to white colleges and universities.[69] On these campuses, youth experienced a backlash from administrators who restricted programs that they considered too militant. For example, most white college administrators discouraged youth from challenging segregation practices on campus (that is, in housing, clubs and Greek-letter organizations).[70] In many ways, the challenges faced by youth councils and college chapters were different.

Although the student conference was composed mostly of college youth, some youth council members were represented at these annual conferences. Whereas the rationale for creating a separate student conference for the college chapters was to identify its disparate work and to accommodate students who could not attend the association's annual meeting, it did not benefit the advancement of youth work as a whole. Indeed, the separate student conference inadvertently privileged recognition of the youth work of the college division over that of the youth councils, whereas the work of both groups was equally important.

While the work of college chapters had come under scrutiny, not all were inactive in their respective communities. In 1943, the Howard University's NAACP chapter took an active role in the association's fight against segregation and established the NAACP as one of the first student organization to stage sit-ins. [71] A show of direct action began when Howard University's students became fed up with the day-to-day humiliating practices of segregation they confronted when they frequented businesses in the downtown section of the nation's capital. Pauli Murray, a law student at Howard who had three years earlier tried to desegregate the University of North Carolina Law School, helped to organize these campaigns. In fact, young women like Murray, Marianne Musgrave, Ruth Powell, and Juanita Marrow provided much of the leadership for the Committee on Direct-Action, under which the students operated to coordinate the demonstrations.[72]

Interestingly, all students who participated in the demonstrations had to sign a consent form, pledging to conduct themselves nonviolently. Students carried signs with slogans such as "Our boys, Our bond, Our brothers are fighting for you, Why Can't We Eat Here?" That year Howard University's NAACP students desegregated the Little Palace Cafeteria.[73] Before they went home for the summer break, the students made plans for a second demonstration to take place that fall semester at a restaurant beyond the school's vicinity. However, when activities got underway in 1944, they were quickly stopped. Howard's president, Mordecai Johnson, maintained that college policy prohibited students from engaging in direct action protest. He even threatened to suspend the NAACP and the students if the activities did not cease.[74] Aware that the majority of the school's funding came from the federal government, the students grudgingly complied with Johnson's position.[75] Although the demonstration against Little Cafeteria had not received a rebuke from Mordecai Johnson (largely because he claimed he was unaware of such activity), this second one did.[76] Perhaps, as Flora Bryant contends, Johnson did not protest earlier demonstrations because the restaurant was in a black neighborhood.[77] Because the second protest was outside the college's vicinity, Johnson feared that such a demonstration could arouse disgust from the white community and result in loss of funds for the school. Most of Howard's funding came from the federal government, and he did not want to jeopardize the school's relationship with conservative congressmen and risk cuts to Howard's liberal funding.[78] Johnson, like many other presidents at historically black colleges and universities who feared the loss of funds for their schools, quelled direct action civil rights protest activities. The position taken by Johnson and the obstacles that the students encountered from the administration foreshadowed obstacles students would encounter in the 1960s. Furthermore, the demonstrations carried out by Howard University's NAACP chapter characterized and set a precedent for much of the large-scale student activity waged two decades later.

By 1944, the association's fight for civil rights expanded to the fight for human rights. At the Wartime Conference held on July 12, 1944, in Chicago, Illinois, the previous civil rights platform (which was limited to equal educational and economic opportunities, civil liberties, and anti-lynching) was greatly expanded to include affordable healthcare, low-rent housing, full employment, voting rights, and self-determination of colonial peoples.[79] In many ways, these new measures reflected the association's intensified efforts to wipe out discrimination and segregation. For example, the association condemned restrictive covenant housing clauses and protested the lack of affordable housing for low-income families. Lauding its legal victory in *Smith v. Allwright*, which outlawed the all-white primary, the association denounced the poll tax as an obstacle to blacks' ability to vote in the south. Furthermore, the association called for an end to the Red Cross's segregated blood plasma policy and segregated practices in the military. The NAACP also denounced colonialism and called for the self-determination of "colonized" people.[80] This broad agenda transformed and catapulted the association as a major civil rights organization at home—and established it as an international organization in world affairs.

To "Keep Our Vision Unclouded"

Months following the Wartime Conference, the sixth annual youth conference (formerly known as the annual student conference) opened at Virginia Union University with a fiery and a provocative keynote address given by Congressman Adam Clayton Powell Jr. of New York. Powell challenged the youth to continue its fight for full democracy despite the formidable obstacles it faced. Illuminating the current race relations, he compared the racial terror that the blacks suffered at the hands of the Ku Klux Klan to the tactics practiced by Hitler. Powell further commented, "[W]e can have no V-Day in Europe and in the Pacific unless we have a V-Day at home."[81] His words captivated the youth members and compelled them into action. At this conference, the NAACP youth drafted resolutions modeled after ones adopted at the earlier Wartime Conference.

Whereas the national office was slow to embrace a human rights agenda, the youth councils and college chapters had called for such a broad agenda as early as the late 1930s. Being affiliated with other international youth organizations and having attended international youth conferences (the World Youth Congresses), youth council and college chapter members understood the advantages of linking their local struggles to the global fight for human rights. At the annual youth conference, they called for an end to all discriminatory practices at home and abroad and for full access to their nation's resources. Although most of their resolutions reflected the resolutions that the national office had adopted at the Wartime Conference, some resolutions dealt specifically with the plight of youth. For example, the youth passed a resolution affirming its commitment to international youth organizations (such as the World Youth Congress) to fight for full participation of youth in government, world peace, and democracy. Domestic resolutions called for federal aid in education, the incorporation of black history into the nation's educational curriculum, and the end of discrimination in education.[82]

Hoping to strengthen the local and national direct action demonstrations of the youth councils and college chapters, Hurley implemented a session that discussed "Protest and Pressure Techniques for a Mass Organization."[83] While direct action tactics had been inaugurated under Jackson's tenure, Hurley hoped to greatly advance the youth work through such measures. Much of the history on the NAACP has cast the organization as guided by a narrow scope of legalism as the exclusive route to achieving civil rights, but the activities of the youth councils and college chapters reveal a different story. The national office was not opposed to direct action but believed that such programs should be carefully planned and organized, and coordinated with the local branch and the national office so that they were not carried out in a helter-skelter fashion. This bureaucratic position (which stifled some activities) would create friction between the national office and the youth division. The association, however, did encourage direct action programs in states where civil rights statutes outlawed segregation. During the late 1940s, youth councils and college chapters initiated widespread campaigns that targeted public businesses and facilities that violated these statutes (see further discussion on these campaigns in chapter three).

In 1944, the youth councils and college chapters launched rigorous voter registration campaigns, demonstrated against segregation in public places, and addressed crime in their neighborhoods. Only Georgia and South Carolina allowed eighteen-year-olds to vote. In light of this fact, the Savannah, Georgia, Youth Council held a voter registration campaign registering eighteen-year-olds to vote.[84] Similarly, the Virginia State College NAACP chapter cooperated with the Virginia State Voters League to register twenty-one-year-olds to vote. Like the Howard NAACP college chapter, the Bryn Mawr, Pennsylvania, and the Centralia, Illinois, youth councils led demonstrations against segregated establishments. The Centralia Youth Council integrated the auditorium at the local high school in its community. The Flint, Michigan, Youth Council wrote letters to its commissioners protesting criminal activities in the vicinity of schools. As a result, the city commissioners padlocked four establishments.[85] Indeed, these campaigns highlight the ambition and determination of these youth to assist in the fight to resolve local issues plaguing their communities. Additionally, the NAACP youth worked nationwide for the passage of a federal anti–poll tax and the establishment of a permanent Fair Employment Practice Committee (FEPC). Youth councils and college chapters wrote letters to their local and national congressmen urging them to abolish the poll tax and to support Executive Order 9463 (amending Executive Order 8802), calling for a permanent FEPC to combat the discriminatory hiring practices in labor and governmental agencies.[86] Although lobbying efforts for these two measures continued for two decades, 1944 marked a great turning point in the work of the association. Hurley, in a memorandum to Walter White, made this observation of the association's youth work: "My feeling is that this is the beginning of our Youth Work taking on the true aspect of a movement. The young people are anxious to work and my program for the coming year must be more defined and broader in scope."[87]

In August 1945, the Second World War ended. Festive parades were organized throughout the country to celebrate the soldiers' return. The streets were filled with jubilation: Tunes of marching bands, flags waving, and a multitude of people—husbands and wives, fathers and mothers, sons and daughters, brothers and sisters, cousins, friends, and lovers—rang out loud cheers to welcome the soldiers as they paraded down American streets. This festive spirit marked the beginning of a new era, as the United States celebrated the triumph of democracy over totalitarianism and militarism. The Germans and the Japanese had been defeated. This moment was particularly poignant for black veterans, who had returned from fighting abroad. Blacks, who had

served their country and risked their lives to achieve democracy abroad, returned home with a renewed and optimistic spirit that their country would
make good on its promise of democracy. At the close of World War II, the
United States, however, stood at the crossroads as millions of blacks remained
on the fringes of American democracy.

Months after the war, youth from around the world gathered in London,
England, on October 29, 1945, for the convening of the Fourth World Youth
Congress. More than six hundred delegates from sixty-three nations met to
discuss issues relating to peace and democracy in the postwar world. The
United States' delegation included five black youths: Esther Cooper (SNYC),
Russell Jones (National Intercollegiate Christian Council), Alexander Mapp
(National Urban League), Olivia Pearl Stokes (The Baptist Christian Center), and Gloster B. Current (NAACP). Like the conference's other attending
youths, who had witnessed a Second World War tear the world apart, this
black American delegation hoped for a postwar world free of bigotry and racial prejudice. With great expectancy, they passed resolutions calling for full
employment, equal educational opportunity, the end to all forms of Fascism,
the self-determination of all subjugated peoples, and the international cooperation of youth through cultural exchange and travel, to name a few. Current
maintained that the essence of the conference's resolution was predicated on
the idea that "you needed our efforts to make war and win victories for the
allies, now use us in a constructive way to keep peace and bring about understanding."[88] These youths took the position that it was now their government's
turn to allow them the opportunity to share in the process of legislating their
realities. However, these youth embraced an idealism that far exceeded the realities of the postwar world that they would inherit. But they were undaunted
in their fight.

A month later, Current gave a report on the Fourth World Congress at the
seven annual youth conference that had convened at Wilberforce University in
Wilberforce, Ohio. His report was received with much enthusiasm, confirm-
ing as it did that the association's youth work was aligned with the international work of other youth organizations. Like the youths who had gathered
at the Fourth World Youth Congress, the NAACP youth was also prepared to
cash in on its nation's promises of democracy, having supported and fought
in a war for democracy. Historian Charles Wesley, president of Wilberforce
University and former president of Alpha Phi Alpha Fraternity, Incorporated,
challenged the youth to push forth in the fight for democracy and to confront
the obstacles that impeded that progress. Commenting on the youth's constant
fight for democracy, Wesley asserted, "'Our great task remains.' I want you to
leave here with a crusading idea. . . . It is our hope that youth will challenge
those things which affect our social stamina."[89] Challenge they did! NAACP
youth continued to fight for full access to America's democracy. Various youth

councils and college chapters held voter registration drives. That year, Morehouse College established an NAACP Intercollegiate Council, which registered eighteen-year-olds to vote. Paine College waged a similar voter registration campaign. Not only did Association youth launch widespread voter registration campaigns, but it also challenged discriminatory practices against blacks at local recreational facilities and schools. The River Rouge, Michigan, Youth Council, with the aid of the senior branch, succeeded in getting school officials to allow blacks to swim in the pool at the local school in their community.[90] These kinds of victories, although small in scale, epitomized the work of the youth councils and college chapters in the association's long and arduous fight for democracy.

In 1945, as the NAACP youth members and their leaders stood at the crux of American democracy, they realized one thing: They had effected change in their local communities. And that alone prompted celebration; however, the association knew that its larger battle remained to force the nation to practice *true* democracy. Having formulated a national agenda that called for human rights, the association worked to advance this agenda during the late 1940s and mid-1950s, implementing measures to involve youth councils and college chapters in the process. Indeed, youth councils and college chapters pushed for full democracy, launching campaigns against segregation practices throughout the United States. In the midst of this fight for full equality, however, the NAACP youth councils and college chapters would confront internal problems that would test the very foundation of the youth movement. Friction between youth members and the national office—and friction between the youth members and the senior branches—began to eat away at the youth movement and limit its effectiveness.

To "Keep Our Vision Unclouded"

Chapter Three

To Finish the Fight:
"Freedom from Fear!"

As youth gathered on November 21, 1946, at the eighth annual youth conference held at Dillard University in New Orleans, Louisiana, Judge Hubert Delany delivered his provocative keynote address, "Freedom from Fear."[1] Judge Delany challenged the youth to lay claim to its rights guaranteed under the United States Constitution. He asserted, "The time has come for us to do something about the status of second class citizenship. It is criminal to think that our boys went abroad to fight for democracy and cannot find it here at home."[2] Judge Delany's expression echoed the sentiments of the majority of youth and adults assembled at the conference. For most black Americans, the time had come for the nation to make good on its promise of democracy. Disillusioned by the nation's promise of democracy after the First World War, blacks did not accept the nation's empty rhetoric this time. They decried the status of second-class citizenship and launched a full-scale frontal assault against racial discrimination. In many ways, the mass mobilization campaigns of black Americans to secure *full* democracy shortly after the Second World War marked the beginning of a new era in the fight for civil rights.[3] This chapter examines how activities within the NAACP youth movement accelerated greatly after the Second World War. Illuminating the youth movement's intensified efforts to secure equality and to wipe out segregation, this chapter also explores the organizational challenges that the youth division confronted. Lastly, this chapter highlights the Cold War's impact on—and particular challenges for—the NAACP youth movement.

Youth at the eighth annual youth conference heard the powerful and evocative keynote address of Judge Delany, and the passionate and tragic story of Sergeant Isaac Woodard. Although Judge Delany's keynote address was moving, Woodard's speech was more poignant. This twenty-seven-year-old World War II veteran had suffered an unspeakable horror on February 12, 1946. Having been released on an honorable discharge seven months earlier from Fort Gordon in Augusta, Georgia, Woodard boarded a Greyhound bus home to North Carolina. At one of the local stops before Batesburg, South Carolina, he asked the bus driver for permission to use the restroom, and the driver grudgingly consented. Unbeknownst to Woodard, the bus driver had called ahead to the local authorities in Batesburg to inform them that there was an unruly passenger on the bus. In Batesburg, South Carolina, Lynwood

Shull, the chief of police, forced Woodard off the bus and severely beat him in his uniform and charged him with disorderly conduct.[4] The assault left Woodard blind.

In his speech at the eighth annual youth conference, Woodard stated, "I wouldn't want what happened to me to happen to anyone, black or white. Unless we all get together now before it is too late there are going to be others like me."[5] Notably, he had not committed any verbal or physical act of aggression against the bus driver. He had only asked to use the restroom. As a result of the lobbying efforts of the NAACP, President Harry S. Truman ordered United States Attorney General Tom Clark to launch a federal investigation of the matter. Having examined the core facts, Attorney General Clark brought charges against Shull; however, on November 2, 1946, he was found innocent in a federal court trial in Columbia, South Carolina, after an all-white jury deliberated for only thirty minutes.[6] Many other WWII veterans throughout the nation suffered similarly despicable acts at the hands of white supremacists bent on maintaining a racial hierarchy that subordinated blacks.

A month after Shull's acquittal, Truman issued Executive Order 9808, establishing the President's Committee on Civil Rights (PCCR) to investigate race conditions within the country. In many ways, Woodard's tragic misfortune influenced that decision. Appalled by the tragedy that had befallen Woodard, and hoping to secure the political support of the black community, Truman knew that something had to be done to improve the racial climate of the nation. Several months later, in November 1947, the PCCR produced a report, *To Secure These Rights,* outlining specific recommendations for improving the country's race conditions. Among its other proposed measures, the report called for the end of segregation in the military, abolition of the poll tax and discriminatory voting practices, and antilynching legislation.[7] The NAACP heralded *To Secure These Rights,* which consisted of thirty-five recommendations, as a significant step in the right direction in the fight for civil rights. Indeed, the report echoed sentiments that the association had expressed long before President Truman's executive order established the committee. Whereas *To Secure These Rights* set historic precedent (as Truman was the first president to go on record endorsing civil rights), the grassroots organizing efforts of the NAACP and other civil rights organizations led to the eradication of many of the discriminatory practices outlined in the report.

Prior to the end of World War II, the NAACP had undertaken efforts to assist returning veterans in readjusting to civilian life. One of the many problems black veterans encountered was securing benefits under the Servicemen's Readjustment Act (commonly known as the G.I. Bill of Rights). Passed in Congress in 1944, the G.I. Bill of Rights provided educational and job training, loan security for homes, farms, or businesses, and twenty dollars per month in unemployment payments to veterans.[8] However, discrimination prevented or interfered with many black veterans enjoying these benefits. In addition, the military did not adequately provide information about all the provisions outlined in the bill to black veterans. Supporting the national office's initiative to aid veterans, members of the youth councils and college chapters familiarized themselves with the provisions of the G.I. Bill of Rights and set up veterans committees to provide valuable information to veterans about their rights and benefits. Through the efforts of the NAACP youth chapters, many young black veterans took advantage of the educational benefits under the G.I. Bill of Rights. For example, in 1945, out of the 418 students enrolled at Morehouse College, 25 of the students were veterans who took advantage of the G.I. Bill. Similarly, at Hampton Institute, of the one thousand students enrolled, at least forty of them were veterans.[9] Additionally, black veterans started the NAACP college chapters at Cornell University, Long Island University, and Columbia University.[10]

Youth councils and college chapters not only set up veterans committees, but they also adopted resolutions and wrote letters to President Truman and congressmen, urging the expansion of benefits under the G.I. Bill and the passage of legislation to end discrimination in the military. At the eighth annual youth conference, the youth passed a resolution calling for the expansion of the bill to include "Liberalized benefits for disabled veterans and their dependents," minimum unemployment benefits of twenty-five dollars per month, and the withholding of G.I. Bill funds from educational institutions that practiced discrimination. Additionally, the conference passed a resolution condemning Jim Crow practices in the military as "undemocratic and in strict violation of the rights of minority groups."[11] The resolution asserted, "We deplore the repeated attacks that have been made by southern representatives and senators on the performance and valor of Negro servicemen who served their nation honorably and loyally in World War II. . . . We urge the introduction and passage of legislation specifically forbidding segregation and discrimination in the armed forces now."[12] These resolutions expressed the NAACP youths' sensibilities and profound respect for the sacrifices that veterans made for their country. Indeed, the Korean Conflict, which erupted shortly after World War II ended, brought to bear greater sensibilities toward the sacrifices of soldiers in the midst of Jim Crow practices in the military.[13]

During the Korean Conflict, youth councils and college chapters mobilized their antisegregation campaigns around the slogan "Smash Jim Crow for the Heroes in Korea." College chapters of the association distributed approximately thirteen thousand surveys to black males on thirty-four campuses at black colleges to get their responses to the Randolph-Reynolds Proposal, which urged young black men to resist the draft because of segregation in the military.[14] Out of the 13,000 surveys distributed, 2,200 were returned from twenty-seven of those thirty-four campuses. The survey revealed that 24 percent of the respondents said it would register, 23 percent of the respondents maintained that it would register but would not serve if called, 14 percent of the respondents contended it would refuse to register, and 39 percent of the respondents were not sure. The results of the survey are intriguing. Whereas the largest percentage of black males was not sure, the percentage of males who said it would register for the draft was almost equal to the percentage of those who would register but refuse to serve if called. In many ways, the survey revealed that black youths would fight for their country, but did not want to fight as second-class citizens, humiliated by the practices of segregation. Indeed, Isaac Woodard's tragedy was a constant reminder of what Jim Crow symbolized and what their sacrifices meant—second-class citizenship.

Determined to "Smash Jim Crow for the Heroes in Korea," Ruby Hurley urged the youth councils and college chapters to continue their mobilization efforts. Youth members launched a mass letter campaign urging congressmen to ratify legislation to abolish segregation in the military. They also raised funds to support the legal defense of black soldiers who had been court martialed.[15] Influenced by the mobilization efforts of the association and the upcoming presidential election, in July 1948 Truman issued Executive 9981, outlawing segregation in the military.[16] Although President Truman outlawed segregation, he did not take steps to see that the mandate was immediately enforced. At the tenth annual youth conference, held in St. Louis, Missouri, in 1948, NAACP national youth director, Hurley, commended President Truman for his executive order but urged him to take further steps to eradicate segregation in the military. She asserted that discrimination could never be eliminated as long as segregation existed.[17] In a letter to President Truman, Hurley discussed a passionate resolution that NAACP youth had adopted at the conference. The resolution stated, "We call upon the Commander-in-Chief to issue an executive order immediately eliminating segregation in all branches of the armed forces; and, we demand that cabinet members and other officials who persist in promoting the concept of racial segregation be removed from office. We pledge ourselves to wage a ceaseless campaign to accomplish these ends."[18] Although black soldiers continued to experience vestiges of segregation during the Korean Conflict, segregation was eventually phased out.

Intensifying its campaign to wipe out segregation, and understanding the vital role that youth councils and college chapters would play in this process, the association inaugurated on April 10, 1947, the first annual youth legislative conference, which was held at Howard University in Washington, D.C.[19] The NAACP opened the conference to all youths who shared the association's aims; however, it was mostly attended by NAACP youth.[20] Hurley believed that the legislative youth conferences would provide NAACP youth with valuable leadership training for political and social activism. Youth council and college chapter members were familiarized with the political processes of government and the association's legislative program. The association's legislative program (which reinforced its human rights agenda) called for antilynching and anti–poll tax legislation, a permanent fair employment practice commission, low-rent public housing, rent control, school lunch program, federal aid to education, affordable health, and the abolition of segregation both in travel and in the nation's capital in Washington, D.C.[21] Hurley knew that it was crucial for youth to gain an understanding of the association's broad legislative agenda because it would ultimately play a crucial role in advancing the association's political program.

The first annual conference focused largely on the inner workings of Congress—how a bill is passed and effective lobbying strategies. The goal of the conference was to provide the youth both immediate hands-on experience concerning the political process and knowledge about the association's legislative program. All the bills discussed at the conference were those currently on the floor in Congress and related to the association's legislative agenda. Part of the conference's initiative was to provide youth an opportunity to visit the office of their respective congressmen and to discuss these measures while in Washington. The youth attended long sessions about the political process of government. Leslie Perry, administrative assistant in the Washington Bureau of the NAACP, described in great detail the various stages that a bill passes through before becoming law. George L. P. Weaver, executive director of the CIO Committee to Abolish Discrimination, discussed effective lobbying strategies, thus sharing valuable information with the youths about how to intelligently discuss their position on a bill and how to reply to typical responses received from their congressmen. Weaver's session (which was less intense) offered a little humor and hands-on experience. Youth participated in mock interviews, and impromptu skits introduced youth to congressmen who would take favorable positions on civil rights legislation—and those who would not. These skits addressed not only the rather straightforward comments from congressmen about a bill, but also their unfavorable responses. In one scenario, a congressman favored one aspect of a bill, but voted against it because he disliked the other provisions. After the mock sessions, the youths put their skills to the test the following day.

Having received valuable training, the youths visited the offices of their respective congressmen and key members of Congress. For example, a delegation visited the office of Republican senator Joseph Hurst Ball of Minnesota. Ball favored legislation to curb labor and supported abolition of the poll tax, but he opposed federal aid for the school lunch program because it infringed on states' rights.[22] Whereas answers from Senator Ball were straightforward, responses from Congressman Carroll Reese, chairman of the Republican National Committee, were evasive. Congressman Reese meandered on the issue of a permanent fair employment practice commission and maintained that federal legislation would be needed to abolish the poll tax. When asked about rent control, he confessed that he had not followed the issue closely.[23]

After meeting with various congressmen, the youth got a firsthand experience in politics. That night at the conference, they discussed their findings. The following day, the youth met, offered critiques, and made suggestions to improve the next conference. They discussed how the delegates did not know enough about the bills and that the delegations were too large. The youth members also felt they had not asked the appropriate questions—and conferred at length about how questions had arisen that the congressmen would not answer. Hurley recommended that the delegates send follow-up letters to the congressmen.[24] Although it had many shortcomings, the conference provided the youth with valuable knowledge, training, and experience concerning the processes of government. The closing speech from William Hastie, governor of the Virgin Islands, captured the sentiments of the conference, as he exhorted the youth to continue the fight for equality. He asserted, "You know that the efforts of 1870 were strangled by force and violence but I do not think that this time we will be strangled, and there is no way of stopping young people today throughout the country."[25]

The annual legislative youth conferences provided members of the youth councils and college chapters valuable knowledge and training about the political process of government—and afforded them an opportunity to meet notable congressmen and activists. Congressmen Adam Clayton Powell Jr. (Democrat, NY), John F. Kennedy (Democrat, MA), Kenneth B. Keating (Republican, NY), and Richard Nixon (Republican, CA) addressed the youth and provided valuable insight about bills in Congress. For example, at the second annual legislative youth conference, Kennedy presented the delegates with valuable information concerning the Taft-Hartley Bill, Federal Aid to Education, and Taft-Ellender-Wagner Housing bill (low-rent housing).[26] He expressed the importance of educating people (even congressmen) on these measures. Additionally, youth members received important information from social activists. Sarah H. d'Avila, executive director of the Committee to Abolish the Poll Tax, discussed the Anti-Poll Tax Bill and offered pertinent information on the bill and its status in Congress. Elmer Henderson, executive secretary of the National Council for a Permanent FEPC, discussed the history of the fair employment practice legislation and pointed out the need for the legislation.[27] These training sessions were enlightening, providing NAACP youth with instructive leadership training and experience that were transferable to work in their local communities.

Armed with sufficient knowledge about the association's legislative agenda, the youths informed members of their local communities about the importance of these measures. Indeed, they also intelligently discussed the bills, the voting record of congressmen, and what action was needed to get these measures ratified. Additionally, members of the youth councils and college chapters assisted the association in its letter-writing campaigns, urging congressmen to vote favorably for such measures. The annual legislative youth conferences gave youth members of the association the wherewithal to spring into action. Throughout the United States, youth councils and college chapters began challenging discriminatory practices within their communities, particularly in states that did not enforce civil rights laws.

By the late 1940s and 1950s, many northern, midwestern, and western states had ratified civil rights laws that outlawed segregation. For example, the state of Michigan ratified the Diggs Civil Rights Law (sponsored by Congressman Charles Diggs), which outlawed segregation practices. In 1947, the Detroit, Michigan NAACP Branch (after two years of litigation against the Bob-Lo Excursion Company) got the Michigan Supreme Court to uphold the Diggs Law. Legal action commenced after Sarrah Elizabeth Ray (along with several of her white classmates) boarded Bob-Lo's excursion streamer but was kicked off because she was black.[28] Similar incidents were happening to blacks in other states where civil rights laws had been passed. Commenting on the Detroit Branch's victory, Hurley urged youth chapters in states that had civil rights laws to challenge segregation practices.[29] In these states, the direct action activities of the youth councils and college chapters against businesses and public facilities that practiced segregation became prevalent. Initiated long before civil rights protests against segregation spread through the South in the late 1950s, this type of activism was a model for youth activists who would later perform similar demonstrations in the South.

In southern states, particularly in the Deep South, direct action organizing was undertaken with great caution, because that region had practically no civil rights laws banning segregation. Apart from voter registration campaigns, widespread direct action initiatives that attacked segregation were in states that had civil rights statutes that were not enforced. At the eighth annual youth conference, attorney Thurgood Marshall cautioned the youth about direct action programs in the South. Denouncing the proposal from radical groups in New York that the NAACP should apply Mahatma Gandhi's tactics in the South, Marshall contended, "In the deep South, any non-violence or civil disobedience movement executed on this pattern would bring violence on the part of local and state police which would result in the imprisonment of hundreds of young people and the death of scores, with nothing achieved except a measure of publicity."[30] In other words, the national office knew that legal recourse would be difficult because the young people would be willfully violating lawful statutes.

The NAACP hoped that it could achieve integration in the South without mass violence, death, and imprisonment. Marshall believed that if direct action tactics were to be carried out, they should be done within the confines of the law. His cautionary position, which expressed fear of violence, death, and imprisonment, partly explains the national office's position concerning direct action demonstrations in the South. A simplistic explanation would be that the association preferred litigation because of its long history of achieving victory through the courts. This rationale is partly true; however, it is far too easy an explanation. The cost of staging mass civil disobedience campaigns in the South was a major factor in the national office's cautionary position.

During the late 1940s and 1950s, the NAACP experienced financial difficulty due to membership decline, which resulted from the government's allegations that the association was a Communist organization.[31] In many southern states, affiliation with the association had grave consequences. Because some southern legislatures had passed laws classifying the NAACP as a subversive organization, membership in the organization could result in the loss of one's job. This consequence was particularly true for state employees. For example, in South Carolina, state employees were required to take an oath affirming whether they were members of the NAACP. Admitted members lost their jobs.[32] In Georgia, the state board of education adopted a resolution that banned teachers from joining the organization and threatened to suspend the licensure of those who remained in the association.[33] Some state employees who preferred their jobs removed themselves from the association. Undoubtedly, others simply hid their membership and remained in the association. Although how many chose to hide their affiliation is unknown, the association clearly experienced a decline in membership, which impacted its financial resources derived from membership fees.

In 1950, Walter White appealed to youth members to donate all they could to help with the organization's financial crisis. He asserted, "The Association is faced with a serious financial emergency . . . it is imperative we have your help. We are faced with a dangerous operating deficit which threatens . . . the whole national program."[34] Eighty-five percent of the association's income came from membership fees, and Walter White made constant inferences to the lack of funds to carry out the association's programs. In 1953, Herbert Wright, a World War II veteran and national youth director, sent a letter to youth councils and college chapters soliciting contributions for the organization's national budget. Wright commented, "The NAACP, contrary to popular belief, does not derive the major portion of its funds from foundations, corporations, or wealthy donors. In fact more than 85% of the association's budgetary requirements are secured from individual memberships recruited through youth councils, college chapters, and senior branches."[35] Because the bulk of the association money did not come from philanthropic organizations or wealthy patrons, the operation of its programs depended largely on income derived from membership. Certainly, a mass movement in the South could have bankrupted the organization.

The NAACP slowly moved to organize mass direct action campaigns in the South. Aware of the cost associated with ending racial segregation (bail, court costs, and other legal fees), the association launched the Fighting Fund for Freedom (FFF), designating it to provide the organization with the financial resources to legally challenge segregation. With this ambitious goal, the NAACP aimed to completely wipe out segregation by 1963 to coincide with the centennial of the Emancipation Proclamation.[36] The moral and legal factors—coupled with the lack of financial resources—may help explain why the association did not launch widespread civil rights activities in the South. Certainly, research has revealed that civil rights campaigns were costly. During the 1960s, when the civil rights movement climaxed in the South, groups such as the NAACP, SNCC, CORE, and SCLC were receiving large sums of money from wealthy white organizations to sustain their projects.[37] During the late 1940s and 1950s, the NAACP would not have been able to sustain a large-scale direct action movement in the South based on its financial resources. Understanding its precarious financial situation, the NAACP chose the route that posed the least resistance to widespread civil rights campaigns—challenging segregation in states that had civil rights laws that were not being enforced.

Although Marshall and the national office shared these views, youth in the association held the sentiment that large-scale direct action mobilization could bring about significant change in the South. They believed that through grassroots organizing efforts the local people would come to support their programs. To some extent, this assumption was naïve and prematurely conceived because no one fully anticipated the dynamics that came into play as the civil right movement culminated in the South. Fear of physical and economic reprisals kept many African Americans from supporting civil rights activities in their own communities. However, this fear did not let the national office off the hook. Because the association dismissed the idea of staging mass direct action demonstrations and presupposed what would happen, it could not know for certain whether or not the local people would have supported its organizing efforts. Because NAACP youth members wanted more direct action campaigns in the South, they criticized the national office's policy, which in turn led to friction among youth chapters, senior branches, and the national office. Many youth members wanted the association to become more flexible and less bureaucratic toward their programs.[38]

Supporting the association's initiative to get civil rights laws enforced, youth councils and college chapters launched campaigns against businesses and facilities that violated their state civil rights laws.[39] These campaigns not only exposed flagrant violations of the law, but they also educated local citizens concerning their rights under these laws. Youth councils and college chapters targeted recreational facilities, movie theaters, eating establishments, and barbershops in an effort to end segregation in their local communities. In

1948, the East Chicago, Indiana, Youth Council initiated a program to eliminate segregation in its local theaters. Members of the youth councils organized their campaigns along these lines: arbitration, legal action, and picketing. After getting approval from the youth committee of the senior branch, youth members contacted the owners of the Broadway, American, Vic, Indiana, and Garden theaters to see if they would eliminate their segregation policy. The owners of American Theater refused to end their segregation policy until the other theaters changed theirs. The owner of the Garden Theater never responded to the correspondence except to claim that he was too busy to discuss the matter. Because the Vic and Indiana theaters belonged to a national chain, youth council members were unable to speak with the owners; however, the district manager maintained that segregated seating at the Indiana Theater was due to the acoustics (making the claim that black patrons could hear better on the far right side of the theater). Youth council members told the manager that such a response insulted their intelligence and, if segregation practices were not ended, legal action would be taken. The manager complied, ending twenty years of segregation at the Indiana Theater.[40]

The Vic Theater (belonging to the same chain) refused to desegregate. On December 8, 1948, two youth council members, Wendell Campbell and Charles Brown, patronized the Vic Theater; they purchased tickets and tried to sit on the left-hand side of the theater (the white section) but were refused seating. They complained to the manager, but he brushed them off. The following dialogue was exchanged between a councilor and the manager:

> Councilor: We would like to know why we can't sit on the left-hand side of this theater. Manager: What's wrong with these empty seats on the right? Councilor: Well, I have a bad left eye and I can see the picture better from the left side of the show. Manager: If you look at the back of your tickets you will see that the management reserves the right to tell the holder where he shall be seated, and I say you have to sit on the right-hand side or take your money back and leave. Councilor: What are your reasons for segregating? Is it because some colored people conduct themselves in a disorderly manner in your show? Manager: No, in fact, some of our best patrons are colored. Whenever such disturbance takes place, the colored are usually the first to demand that the disturber be thrown out. Councilor: Are you aware that the Civil Rights Laws of Indiana prohibit segregation in the theaters and that you are subject to fine or jail sentence? Manager: Did you come here looking for trouble? If so, I have other things to do. All I know is that when I took over the management of this

theater I was given orders to seat the colored people on the right-hand side. Here is your money back.[41]

After leaving the theater, the youth informed attorney W. Henry Walker, legal redress chairman, about the incident. Campbell and Brown filed a lawsuit against the theater at the behest of Walker, and the youth council decided to picket the theater. Ten days later, youth council members organized picket lines in front of the theater. The manager of the theater called the police; however, the police did not arrest the protestors because they were picketing within the confines of the law. Youth council members passed out thousands of pamphlets asking citizens to cooperate with their efforts to desegregate the theater. The NAACP youth called upon other organizations within the community to assist with these efforts. Cooperation from the community was great. After two weeks of picketing, the youth council's efforts impacted the nightly profits of the theater, which dropped from two hundred dollars to fifty dollars. Of the community organizations that collaborated with the youth council, the Jessie Gerring Post (Veterans of Foreign Wars) and the CIO provided much support. For example, the CIO printed all of the leaflets free of charge and sent members to the theater to protest the policy.[42] As a result of the picket line, on January 28, 1949, the owner met with the youth council and offered a compromise. The owner maintained that if the youth ended the picket lines, he would allot 80 percent of the seats to black patrons. Appalled by the owner's response, the youth council members promised to continue to picket until all seats were desegregated.

Angered by the youth members' response, the owner replaced English-speaking movies at the American Theater with Spanish movies and showed black movies only at the Broadway Theater (which was not segregated). Although the owner hoped this move would end the picket lines, the plan backfired. Youth members began picketing the Broadway Theater. The picketing was successful in lowering profits to ten dollars that night. Determined not to desegregate, the owner started showing Spanish movies at this theater as well. Not to be outflanked, youth council members picketed the theater using Spanish placards and distributed Spanish leaflets. When he realized that the youth were not going to go away, the owner decided to desegregate the American Theater. On January 29, 1949, the campaign came to an end after six weeks of picketing—even in inclement weather when the temperature had dropped to near or below zero. On February 7, 1949, the Vic Theater desegregated and settled the lawsuit out of court with Campbell and Brown.[43] The lengthy campaign waged by members of the East Chicago, Indiana, Youth Council against the segregated movie theaters represented the concerted efforts of the youth council and the local community to change a practice that humiliated segments of its population. Additionally, the campaign showed the youth council's ability to collaborate with other organizations to wage a successful campaign to stamp out discrimination in its community.

In a similar vein, members of the NAACP chapter at Pennsylvania State College (Penn State) staged a mass demonstration to end the discriminatory practices of the state college's six barbershops that refused service to black students. Black students at the university had to travel twenty-eight miles to Tyrone to get a haircut because of the local barbershops' policy.[44] The incident ignited after local barbershops refused a haircut to Mitchell Williams, a member of the Penn State track team and organizer of the school's NAACP chapter.[45] Fed up with the state college barbershops' discriminatory practices, the Penn State NAACP chapter created a committee (which included five black students) to test five of the six barbershops—Smith, Hartman, Martin, Kreamer, and Cassidy—to determine attitudes of the barbers toward cutting black people's hair.[46] In each test case, barbers politely refused service to the black students. One of the local barbers explained, "Not that I've got anything against them myself, mind you! But it's the trade you got to be careful of. You know, a lot of people wouldn't come in here if they saw a nigger in the chair."[47] However, William Meeks, Penn State NAACP chapter president, noted that none of the white patrons left when black students had gone in to barbershops to inquire of service.

Under Meeks's leadership, on December 10, 1948, the students mobilized against the barbershops. Meeks asserted, "Our fight is not primarily against the barbers. It is, however, against racial discrimination, which in the case of State College, is prevalent in the barber shops."[48] That following day, the NAACP chapter staged a rally on Old Main (campus plaza), attracting over three hundred participants.[49] With placard signs in hand and chanting "Jim Crow must go," students marched past the barbershops and through the town square demanding an end to the discriminatory practices.[50] At the height of the boycott, there were twelve picket lines and no fewer than fifty students picketing. The Bucknell University NAACP Chapter supported the Penn State initiative. Penn State chapter members were not only able to get other chapters in the vicinity to cooperate with their program, but they also recruited the campus faculty. Such esteemed professors as Clarence Anderson, Rabbi Benjamin Kahn, Scott Keyes, David McKinley, and Robert Hollis supported the students' cause.[51] Indeed, the support from faculty and students helped to sustain the chapter's endeavor. Because the students protested within the confines of the law, little hostility came from the local citizens. With the exception of one picketer being pushed (by a man who worked across the street at the Hartman Electric Company), the boycott continued without incident for four consecutive days.[52]

While it did not end discrimination at the barbershops, the boycott did win the support of local citizens. By 1949, with the support of local citizens, the students raised over eighteen hundred dollars and established a barbershop that serviced all clients.[53] The boycott awakened the sensibilities of the local citizens—and of individuals outside of the campus community. Bucknell University's student paper published a letter from a local barber, George Yoder. Yoder insisted,

> The incident of the Negro who was denied a haircut in the State
> College Barber shop is particularly interesting because it comes
> so near home. . . . Whether or not to cut a Negro's hair or shave
> him has never been a problem in my business. More than four
> years ago I made it known that I would be happy to serve Ne-
> groes going to college here or any other Negro or foreign persons.
> . . . In short, I am sure that no business will ever suffer through
> the application of Christian principles of that business.[54]

Yoder's letter expressed the sentiments of students of the Penn State chapter and of those who supported their campaign. No lawsuit could be filed against the barbershops because Pennsylvania's civil rights statutes did not include barbershops, but the boycott did awaken the local community and surrounding populations to the inhumanity of segregation. This incident also prompted the association and local citizens to mobilize for state civil rights statutes to include barbershops. The boycott of the state college barbershops symbolized more than the students' fight to get a haircut at the local barbershop. The boycott revealed their fight for human dignity and their sincere efforts to be fully integrated into all aspects of campus life at white colleges and universities. Indeed, the boycott revealed the racial barriers that black students had to surmount at white colleges and universities to achieve as men and women within a society that considered them second-class citizens.

During the late 1940s and 1950s, a small percentage of black students was being admitted to white colleges and universities, mostly in northern, Midwestern, and western states.[55] The NAACP served as a clearinghouse for white colleges and universities seeking to admit black students, and the national office maintained a list of the colleges and universities that sought to recruit black students. Furthermore, the association encouraged members of youth councils to apply to white schools. For example, in 1951, the national office sent information to the youth councils informing them about educational opportunities at the University of Rochester. The role of the NAACP was evident in that the letter stated that students interested in applying could notify Miss Audrey Ramm, chairman, NAACP Education Committee at the school.[56] Perhaps she unofficially recruited for the school or held some influence in the admission office. Whatever the case, the association endorsed black students attending white schools because it believed this route was a way to break down segregation. The national office of the NAACP also assisted in securing scholarships. The NAACP never established a scholarship fund for black students (mainly because it contradicted its interracial principle), but it did cooperate with the National Scholarship Service and Fund for Negro Students (NSSFNS) to get scholarships for black youths. The NAACP youth director, Herbert Wright, also assisted the agency in surveying the "racial policies and attitude" of faculty, students, and administrators of southern colleges and universities toward black students.[57] Founded in 1948, NSSFNS, under Richard Plaut, executive vice-chairman, wanted to increase opportunities for blacks to attend white schools. In 1952, the NSSFNS awarded 160 scholarships to black students totaling $67,900 to attend Amherst, Barnard, Bryn Mawr, Columbia, Colgate, Princeton, Yale, and Vassar, to name a few.[58] The NSSFNS played a significant role in aiding black students to attend white colleges and universities. Although white schools offered some form of financial assistance to black students, such funding was not always enough to cover all educational expenses. As a result, many youth turned down acceptance to these schools. Nonetheless, the NSSFNS helped black students surmount one of their many obstacles in acquiring an education.

Although some white colleges and universities admitted black students, these students were not fully integrated into all sectors of college life. Black students complained of isolation because segregation practices excluded them from many of the social clubs and Greek letter organizations on the campuses. Yet, black students did manage to create some semblance of college life by establishing their own social clubs and fraternal organizations. For many black students, the NAACP chapters provided the only outlet for social activities. Through the NAACP chapters and other interracial organizations, like the National Student Association (founded in 1947), they could break down discriminatory practices on their campuses and integrate into campus life.

Because social organizations were the most workable entities through which to facilitate integration into campus life, black students targeted discriminatory practices within these organizations. NAACP chapters launched campaigns against campus clubs and Greek letter organizations to remove discriminatory clauses from their charters. For example, the University of New Mexico's NAACP chapter waged a successful campaign against all fraternities whose constitution or bylaws of the parent organization discriminated on the basis of race or religion.[59] Similarly, Columbia University's NAACP chapter launched a campaign to get white fraternities and sororities on their campus to eliminate bias clauses.[60]

Although many colleges and universities admitted black students, they did not always provide them with housing. When institutions did provide housing, black students were segregated from the white students. Although these states had civil rights statutes that prohibited segregation in the renting or selling of houses, these measures were not always enforced on college and university campuses. For example, the Housing Bureau at the University of Wisconsin referred black students to the Groves Co-op and the Doxey (off-campus houses). When white students inquired about taking up residence at these two houses, administrators steered them to other locations, telling them that being at these two houses was not desirable.[61] With respect to dormitories, some college officials justified the policy of placing students of the same race in rooms together because the application asked the student to indicate a roommate choice. At the University of Wisconsin, the student board against discrimination worked to get the wording changed to read "any particularly qualities you desire in a roommate."[62] Through concerted efforts, students at the University of Wisconsin were able to get the administration to enforce nondiscriminatory practices on campus. As a result of the campaigns initiated by NAACP college chapters during the late 1940s, college campuses eliminated segregation in dormitories and student organizations and fully integrated black students into campus life.

Acting upon the report of the president's Commission on Higher Education, issued December 11, 1947, which called for state legislation banning discrimination in educational institutions, the association endorsed the commission's efforts.[63] Building upon the legal victories of the late 1930s, the association played a significant role in eroding discrimination in higher education. During the late 1940s, Ada Sipuel and George McLaurin applied for admission to the University of Oklahoma Law School and the University of Oklahoma, respectively. Hoping to maintain a dual system of education for blacks and whites, the state of Oklahoma created a law school at Langston University. The NAACP challenged the state's decision by arguing that the Langston University Law School was not equal to the University of Oklahoma Law School. Arousing international attention, students from Great Britain supported Sipuel's case. In a letter to the American Embassy in London, the National Union of Students (representing roughly fifty thousand students) protested the University of Oklahoma's practice. W. Bonney Rust, president of the National Union of Students, asserted, "We would like to express the grave concern of the N.U.S. at the news regarding Ada Sipuel. . . . I am asked to convey to you the strong feeling raised by these reports among students in my country. We have always considered that an essential part of education is to study alongside other people. To deny this educative factor to a person because of his race appears both indefensible in itself and unworthy of the tradition of the great American people."[64]

Because of the NAACP youth division's affiliation with international student organizations, students abroad were both aware and supportive of its aims to purge segregation in the United States.[65] In 1949, the Supreme Court ruled that Sipuel should be admitted to the law school. Sipuel's case provided the precedent upon which NAACP attorneys could argue George McLaurin's case against the University of Oklahoma before the Supreme Court. McLaurin, a retired teacher, had decided to go back to school to earn his doctorate. The university admitted him but segregated him from his fellow classmates. In 1950, the Supreme Court ruled against the Oklahoma Board of Regents and asserted that the enrollment of McLaurin at the University of Oklahoma on a segregated basis was unconstitutional.[66]

Similarly, Herman Sweatt successfully challenged the segregation practices of the Law School at the University of Texas at Austin. Like Oklahoma, the state of Texas hoped to maintain its dual educational system. In 1947, rather than admit Sweatt to the University of Texas Law School (UT), the state of Texas established the Texas State University for Negroes (Texas Southern University).[67] Ironically, the same year Sweatt challenged segregation at the school, the NAACP established a chapter there, making it the first chapter chartered at a white institution in the South.[68] Jack Graham, president of the UT NAACP chapter, and other chapter members supported Sweatt's admission and the association's efforts to break down discrimination at the school.

NAACP youth, attending the ninth annual youth conference held in 1947 at the Antioch Baptist Church in Houston, Texas, and the UT NAACP chapter picketed Texas State University's creation of the State University for Negroes and its refusal to admit Sweatt to UT Law School.[69] Commenting on the law school built for black students, Hurley argued, "Certainly the state officials aren't interested in integrated education when they set up schools such as this law school and that state university in Houston for Negroes, which in my estimation isn't a university at all."[70] In 1950, the Supreme Court ruled that the University of Texas had to admit Sweatt. The Sweatt case, like the McLaurin and Sipuel cases, was a landmark victory for the association in its fight against segregation in higher education. The Supreme Court's position validated the association's belief that segregation policies breed prejudice. Commenting on the Supreme Court's decision in these cases, Thurgood Marshall declared, "The complete destruction of all segregation is now in sight."[71] Indeed, these cases established the precedent for the *Brown Decision* (1954).

In attempts to further break down segregation at white schools, the association helped black professors to secure employment at these institutions. The NAACP compiled a list of qualified black professors and disseminated the list to white colleges and universities urging them to hire black professors. The NAACP chapters at white schools aided this initiative. They also pushed for campus administrators to hire black faculty. For example, the Cornell NAACP chapter was successful in getting the school to hire Gertrude Rivers in the music department. Rivers had served as chairperson of the membership committee of the Cornell chapter.[72] By 1948, approximately sixty black faculty members taught at white institutions, such as Harvard University, Smith

College, the University of Chicago, Southern California University, Roosevelt College, Wayne State University, New York University, and Columbia University.[73] Activism on the part of NAACP college chapters greatly aided in the erosion of segregation at white colleges and universities.

While many youth councils and college chapters actively engaged in breaking down segregation in states that had civil rights laws—and at white colleges and universities—others led efforts to gain equality in the educational facilities in their communities. In 1946, the Lumberton, North Carolina, Youth Council launched a campaign to improve the educational facilities in Lumberton. Members of the youth council mailed letters to the city officials complaining about the unequal educational facilities for blacks; no officials responded. The youth council decided to stage a protest parade to awaken the sensibilities of the officials. This effort also failed to capture the attention of officials. Under the leadership of Cardelia Williams, a youth council member, the youth staged a mass demonstration that involved more than four hundred school children protesting the unequal facilities.[74] The Lumberton Youth Council's efforts to get equal educational facilities in their communities reinforced the association's position that southern states were not interested in maintaining equality under segregation. Indeed, this disparity—among many others—intensified the association's efforts to end segregation in public education.

Although the national office cautioned direct action campaigns in the South, many youth councils, like the Lumberton Youth Council, still demonstrated against segregation. During the early 1950s, under the leadership of Juanita Craft, youth advisor, the Dallas, Texas, Youth Council initiated activities to end discrimination at the Texas State Fair in Dallas. Not all youth advisors were as passionate and persistent as Craft about challenging segregation practices in the South. During World War II, Craft had been involved with the work of the association, serving as the Dallas NAACP membership chairman. By 1946, she became the youth advisor for the Dallas Youth Council. Under Craft's leadership, the youth council attacked local segregation practices at lunch counters, theaters, North Texas State University, and the Texas State Fair.[75] In May 1952, NAACP youth councils and college chapters, at the First Annual Texas State Conference on Youth and Human Rights held in San Antonio, Texas, adopted a resolution condemning the discriminatory practices at the state fair in Dallas. The resolution called for the cooperation of youth councils and college chapters in immediately beginning campaigns to eliminate Negro Achievement Day at the state fair, the only day blacks could attend the fair.[76]

Supporting the aims of the resolution, and disgusted with the segregation practices, Craft and youth council members began picketing Negro Achievement Day. For two years, the Dallas Youth Council picketed the state fair. The Dallas Youth Council secured the cooperation of the local black community and the Negro Chamber of Commerce, and was able to get Brigadier General Benjamin O. Davis not to show up on Negro Achievement Day to receive an award for his military feats.[77] In 1955, the boycott efforts waged by the Dallas Youth Council proved successful. The fair officials ended segregation on all rides and opened to black patrons on all days. Vestiges of discrimination remained at concession stands and other eateries, but segregation was eventually wiped out. The fight waged by the Dallas Youth Council symbolized the youths' efforts to make the association's youth program more relevant to their needs. It also revealed that local members knew what strategies worked best to resolve problems in their own communities. Although the national office cautioned against direct action, the Dallas Youth Council's efforts would be among many other direct action activities that increased in the South to challenge segregation during the mid-1950s.

Although they staged successful campaigns against segregation and discrimination during the late 1940s and 1950s, the youth councils and college chapters were fraught with internal problems that limited their effectiveness. Many of the problems that surfaced between the youth councils and senior branches resulted from desire on the part of the senior branches to control the youth's programs or from the lack of knowledge concerning the youth council's constitution on these matters. Many of these conflicts were silly, whereas others were heartrending. However, day-to-day operational issues could have been easily resolved if senior branch leaders possessed sufficient knowledge of the youth council's constitution; the situation concerning the Chicago Youth Council provides an excellent example.

In December 1947, the Chicago Youth Council held a meeting to elect officers for the upcoming year. Members of the senior branch thought that junior youth council members could vote in the youth council's election. A big ruckus resulted. The youth council members refused to allow the junior council members to vote in their election on the grounds that it was unconstitutional. Checking with the national office confirmed that junior council members could not vote in the youth council's election.[78] Almost a year later, another incident occurred concerning the election of officers. This time the conflict erupted because the advisor was ill-informed of the procedures regarding electing officers. The advisor told the youth council members that they had to postpone their election because the nominating committee had to be in session thirty days before the election. Eleanor Cunningham, secretary of the Chicago Youth Council, challenged this claim, asserting that no such policy was in place. Once again checking with the national office, she confirmed that, indeed, no policy existed.[79] When the election finally did take place, the youth had to sign an oath of loyalty to the NAACP and its government. Outraged by this nonsense, youth members contacted the national office again to inquire about the policy. Once more, no such policy existed.[80] Numerous problems plagued the Chicago Youth Council. Members lacked knowledge concerning the constitution, misappropriated funds, and worked in cliques, and conflicts occurred among officers. While the problems were numerous, the struggles faced by the youth council were often of the type endemic to organizational work. Thus, not surprisingly, such problems stifled the effectiveness of the organization within the community. Issues that plagued the Chicago Youth Council adversely affected its membership. The senior branch refused to accept that the relationship between the youth council and the senior branch should be reciprocal and not dictatorial.

Whereas the youth councils were under the auspices of the senior branch, the relationship between the entities was supposed to be reciprocal. Oftentimes the senior branch interpreted its position to mean that it could decide what the youth councils could or could not do. Commenting on the relationship of the youth council to the senior branch, Gloster B. Current, director of branches, asserted,

> The interpretation of "subordinate" creates friction at times. Some senior branches take the attitude that they have the power to dominate the youth, to tell them what to do, and to disagree completely with their program and activities. Particularly does friction arise over the types of entertainment to be sponsored by the youth council. For example, a dance. In the branch on whose Executive Committee there may be prominent church men opposed to social dancing, it will be very difficult for the youth council to sponsor in the name of the NAACP an activity engaged in almost universally by youth without incurring the objection and outright refusal of the branch to sanction this program. This type of negative interpretation of "subordinate" disrupts the program of the youth council and oftentimes prevents its growth–may even destroy it.[81]

This interpretation was a major problem for youth councils in Texas. The majority of the senior branches' presidents were preachers, which created a rift between the senior branches and the youth councils. Many of the presidents considered the dances sinful and would not sanction such programs initiated by the youth councils.[82] Through dances, youth councils attracted other youth to their program or raised money for their programs. In fact, the national office encouraged such activities. Many senior members saw themselves in a position of *in loco parentis* (that youth were subordinates and, as adults, senior members knew what was best for them). Hurley believed that the problem could be corrected if the youth councils and senior branches integrated more of their programs and if the older members became more accepting of the youth's programs.

During the late 1940s, senior branch members made allegations of Communist "domination" against youth councils and college chapters. Although known Communists were in the youth councils and college chapters, they were never in the majority or wielded significant power to control programs. If they were in the majority or in power, Communists never disclosed their identity. But because of the hierarchal structure of the association, remaining invisible would have been very difficult for them. Most of the allegations that surfaced concerning Communist domination had a lot to do with the senior branches wanting to control the youth councils and college chapters' programs. If the youth chose programs that the local branch or national office did not endorse, then allegations of Communist domination often surfaced. Historian Rebecca de Schweinitz understood, "Young people's willingness to consider and act on ideas and strategies that senior members considered too radical resulted in . . . more serious 'false accusations' on a number of occasions."[83] Officers of the senior branch employed this tactic to stifle direct action programs that they did not endorse. The known Communists in the youth councils and college chapters made it easy for local branch leaders to allege that Communists were influencing the youth programs when the youth did not heed their advice. The national office investigated these allegations but found them to be untrue. Known Communists remained in the youth councils and college chapters up until 1951, at which time the NAACP ratified a resolution banning Communists or those affiliated with communistic organizations from all of its member organizations.[84]

In November 1947, the Flint, Michigan, Youth Council decided to boycott the Flint Roller Drome, a skating rink. The boycott began because the owner would not allow black and white youth to skate on the same nights. Aware of the Diggs Civil Rights Law, which outlawed segregation, the youth decided to protest the owner's policy. The members of the youth council, aided by white students from the local high school, who patronized the skating rink, boycotted the Flint Roller Drome for three weeks. Refusing to cave in to the pressure to integrate, the owner created two private membership clubs to keep the youth from skating together. To combat the owner's tactics, the youth decided that they needed wider publicity. The youth council organized a committee to coordinate the activities and decided that the council should distribute flyers. The president of the Flint Branch, Elisha Scott (also an attorney), did not support the youth actions. He alleged that the plan was ill-advised and that the youth should not distribute leaflets.

Disagreeing with the senior branch president, they voted to distribute the leaflets. Vehemently opposed to the youth's decision, the president wielded accusations that Communists dominated the youth council. Although there were Communist and Socialist members, they were not in the majority. According to Vasolonyer Baxter, the youth advisor, the only professed Communist in the group was Lewis Baxter (her son), and there were only two Socialists. Nonetheless, the senior president claimed that Communists were dominating the youth and influencing their programs. The day following the vote, President Scott secured an injunction against the group on the grounds that it was illegally operating in the name of the NAACP. He further alleged that the youth council was filled with Communists and Socialists who were trying to stir up trouble in the city. A local Jewish attorney (whom the youth council had consulted for legal advice when the boycott commenced) informed them that Scott had issued an injunction against them and warned them not to distribute the leaflets.

Acting on Scott's allegations, the FBI began investigating some of the members. The next day, an article appeared in the local newspaper alleging possible Communist infiltration of the Flint Youth Council. The article maintained, "An officer of the National Association for the Advancement of Colored People here has also requested an investigation of the aims of the new arrivals who have succeeded in causing a split within the NAACP chapter."[85] After the issuance of the injunction and the newspaper article, the youth council appealed to the national office. The national office investigated the incident and determined that the primary reason for the friction between the senior branch and the youth council was that President Scott (and some of the senior branch board members) did not like the youth advisor. He had been trying to get Mrs. Baxter removed as advisor; however, the youths liked her and wanted her to remain as their advisor. Scott may have resented that the youth council sought outside legal advice about the boycott before discussing it with him. Lastly, this matter could have been prevented if President Scott had understood that the relationship between the youth council and the senior branch should be reciprocal and not dictatorial. In the final analysis, the association censured President Scott for his actions, vindicating the youth members.

Like the youth councils, the NAACP college chapters dealt with allegations of being dominated by communist members—and thus Communist ideology. Though it did not report to the senior branch, the college branch was subjected to college administrators, who at times sought to control the political activities of clubs and organizations on and off campus. In February 1947, allegations of Communist domination were made against the Cornell University NAACP chapter. To inquire about such allegations, Ruby Hurley wrote to Dr. Milton Konvitz, a professor at Cornell, to see if he knew anything about this situation. Hurley explained, "I am experiencing some concerns now as a result of a report that has come to our attention from several sources to the effect that Communists were beginning to infiltrate into the chapter. This fact in itself may not be too important as long as the chapter conforms to the policies of the Association. . . . We are anxious for the NAACP to function properly on Cornell campus and if there is anything amiss in the early stages, we might be able to take corrective measures before it is too late."[86] Hurley does not reveal the source of her information; however, the accusation followed the national office's discovery that Ferdinand Smith, the Jamaican born cofounder of the National Maritime Union—and a devout communist—was to speak at the university under the auspices of the Cornell chapter.[87]

Acting upon the information received in the national office, Hurley sent Madison Jones, former youth director, to investigate the matter.[88] Responding to the allegations, Walter Lewis, Cornell chapter president, wrote Hurley to clear up the matter. Lewis asserted, "I was quite surprised. . . . while we do have some members of confessed or questionable Communist party affiliations here at Cornell, I assure you that they are not in the majority and are not in a position to control the policies of this chapter."[89] F. L. Marcuse, faculty advisor, wrote Hurley criticizing the national office for acting on circumstantial information, and denounced notions of Communist domination.[90] Marcuse maintained,

Mr. Walter, president of the Cornell Chapter of the NAACP, informs me that there have been repercussions from the central office as a result of the Ferdinand Smith lecture. . . . I gather that you are worried about "Communist domination" on what basis this notion is founded I don't know nor am I interested. . . . The charge of Communist domination is ridiculous. I feel especially dismayed that thus accusation should originate from our own head office, since it seems to me that our Association if any should recognize the tactic for what its worth. I fully recognize the right of the central office to know what's going on in their branches, but I strongly resent the manner in which it was done on this occasion. . . . The resentment and friction which I note has been caused by this incident is regrettable since I feel, and believe you will agree, that problems of far greater urgency confront us to-day.[91]

After investigating the situation, the national office determined the allegations of Communist domination to be unfounded. Hurley apologized to the chapter's president, Walter Lewis, for acting on a rumor. Hurley stated, "I am sorry that my letter to Doctor Konvitz caused so much confusion. . . . Please do not be too concerned about this since we were making a routine inquiry following a rumor which came in through an outside individual."[92] The allegations made against the Cornell chapter resulted from the Ferdinand

Smith lecture. Because it hosted a Communist speaker, the chapter was labeled communist. As previously stated, when finding themselves unable to control the youth's programs, conservative NAACP adult leaders would concoct such an allegation. Although communist members were, indeed, within the Cornell chapter, they constituted a minority. If Communists did dominate the youth councils or college chapters, they did so without publicly disclosing their affiliation.

Concerned with growing friction among youth councils, college chapters, and the senior branches, Hurley took action. During her tenure, she had worked to adapt the national youth program to the needs of local youth councils and college chapters. Hurley constantly urged youth members to write to the national office to fill her in on their programs. She also encouraged youth councils and college chapters to set up state youth conferences so that they could coordinate their youth programs statewide and have greater input on youth work in their respective states. In 1949, the NAACP held eight state youth conferences; by 1953 it was holding thirteen state conferences.[93]

At the eleventh annual youth conference, held in Dayton, Ohio, youth delegates recommended that the National Planning and Advisory Committee (which was established in 1944 to assist the national youth director with planning and supervising youth programs) be organized along regional lines.[94] Under the new guidelines, two members would be elected by their regions to serve on the committee. Hurley believed that the National Planning and Advisory Committee (NPAC) would help the national office address the regional needs of the youth councils and college chapters. NPAC would allow the youth to have more input directing its programs. Because it served as a liaison for the youth councils and college chapters, NPAC was responsible for recommendations to the national office on how to improve the youth division. Members of the NPAC were to meet once a month with Hurley and discuss the association's youth work. Although this measure was put in place, many of the regional leaders did not take their responsibilities seriously. Albert Henderson, president of the Ohio Youth Conference, in a letter to Hurley, criticized NPAC leaders for their lack of concern toward the youth work of the association. Henderson commented, "I request the initiation of a drastic program to clean up the NPAC. We don't want to wait and hope for a better committee. Wait, you know, broke the wagon down. We don't believe that the NPAC was meant to be a disconnected group of individuals."[95] Henderson's sentiments reflected those of other NPAC members, such as Melusena Carl, Wendell Campbell, W. W. Law, and Aurelio Sterlings, who were dedicated to advancing the youth work of the association.

By 1950, NAACP youth membership had declined, the Annual Legislative Youth Conference and National Annual Youth Week had been discontinued, and the National Essay Contest no longer existed. Perhaps the only positive aspect in 1950 was the Mass Civil Rights Mobilization Campaign held in January in Washington, D.C., where the association tried to persuade the United States Eighty-First Congress to endorse a human rights agenda.[96] Apart from this campaign, enthusiasm for the association's work declined—largely because of the organization's bureaucratic ways. Youth members wanted to make the youth program more relevant to their local needs. They wanted to play a greater role in influencing the type of programs that the national office initiated. In December of that year, an Emergency National NAACP Youth Leaders Conference convened at Howard University to address ways to revamp the national youth program.[97] Hurley and youth leaders decided to dissolve the NPAC for ineffectiveness, and established an interim youth committee to coordinate the youth work of the association until the NAACP's annual convention.

At the forty-second annual NAACP convention in 1951, the National Youth Work Committee was established; its responsibility was to make recommendations to the national convention the following year on ways to improve the youth work of the association. That same year, Herbert Wright succeeded Ruby Hurley (who was appointed as southeast regional director) as the national youth secretary. Wright assumed the responsibility of restoring the vitality of the youth work that Hurley had so greatly advanced. That following year, at the forty-third annual NAACP convention, the National Youth Work Committee recommended partitioning the youth division into seven regions (each region having two youth leaders and one adult as representatives elected annually to the National Youth Work Committee). The National Youth Work Committee also recommended that the association employ seven field workers to assist the national youth director. The committee maintained that the deterioration of the youth division was due to the lack of administrative support to the youth director and the little say that the youth had in determining its own programs.[98] In 1953, at the association's annual meeting, the NAACP national office agreed that one field worker would be hired to assist Wright. Perhaps due to the lack of finances, an entire year passed before the association acted on this decision. After constant letters from youth members filled the national office urging the association to follow through on the committee's recommendation, the organization hired Muriel Gregg as national youth field secretary to assist Wright with the youth councils and colleges. Gregg, who had served as youth advisor to the Hartford, Connecticut, Youth Council, assumed her duties on May 16, 1955.[99]

By 1955, the NAACP youth movement began to turn around. After spending a month getting familiarized with the association's national work, Gregg commenced her work. From July 5 through 31, she toured Pennsylvania, visiting youth councils and college chapters to revamp the association's youth work. After the tour, Gregg made her recommendations to the national office. She surmised that there were five major problems stifling youth work in the state: (1) lack of leadership, (2) failure to create programs to interest young people and include other youth, (3) failure of adults in the youth councils to transfer to the senior branch, (4) failure of the branch to set up a youth work committee, and (5) lack of college chapters.[100] Gregg's report was teeming with recommendations to improve the youth work in Pennsylvania. She called for the integration of senior branches and youth councils' programs; greater emphasis on the role of youth in advancing its programs; the incorporation of more youth activities; and the integration of other youth groups, like the YMCA, into the youth councils' programs.[101] In August, Gregg toured West Virginia and Kentucky. After visiting these two states, she offered similar recommendations. Gregg's findings revealed what Hurley had highlighted years earlier: The association could have greatly strengthened its youth work had it acted years before. Gregg's most important recommendation was that the association grants youth greater autonomy over its programs.

Gregg's work with the association proved to be significant, but she resigned in October to marry. Before her resignation, Gregg had a disagreement with Wright about her October assignment in Chicago. According to Wright, after Gregg had completed her work in Cleveland, she had been asked to report directly to Chicago. Gregg claimed that that plan was not her understanding, and that she was not prepared to leave Cleveland and go directly to Chicago. In a letter to Wright, she contended, "It will be impossible for me to report directly to Chicago from Cleveland. Not having expected a change in dates, I will not come prepared for a stay in Chicago until the end of October."[102] Although Gregg went on to Chicago (without notifying Wright), Wright had already called and cancelled her trip. Once Gregg arrived in Chicago, the youth council president informed her that Wright had said she had resigned from her position. Gregg was infuriated, as she had not told him that she was resigning from her position.[103] The fiasco was a breakdown in communication—but because of the chaos and the back-and-forth bickering, she submitted her resignation on October 1, 1955. Gregg's work was vital to the NAACP; remaining on the staff would have benefited the association. Wright, in a letter to Gloster Current, commented that the association needed someone as efficient as Gregg but with a better personality.[104]

During the late 1940s and 1950s, the NAACP youth movement experienced successes and failures. Inspired by civil rights gains in the north, Midwest, and west, NAACP youth challenged racial segregation practices that sought to keep them second-class citizens. While the youth councils and college chapters in the North and Midwest played a vital role in advancing the association's youth work, the courageous feats of youth members in the South were equally important. Chafing under segregation, the Dallas Youth Council, under Juanita Craft's leadership, epitomized the local efforts of southern youth to resist segregation. Despite the NAACP's cautionary appeal against direct action in the South, the efforts of the Dallas Youth Council revealed that the national office did not always know what tactics worked best for the local people. Craft defied the association's bureaucratic ways and sought to make the youth movement more relevant to the needs of the local black people in Dallas. Although it ignored youths who persistently demanded to have more control over their programs, the national office could no longer do so when other less bureaucratic youth organizations exploded on the scene in the 1960s and provided an alternative to membership in the NAACP youth organizations.

Attorneys Thurgood Marshall (left) and Charles Hamilton Houston (right) with their client Donald Gaines Murray (center) during court proceedings, Maryland, 1935.

NAACP youth and delegates at the twenty-seventh annual NAACP conference held at the Sharpe Street Memorial M.E. Church Community House, Baltimore, Maryland, 1936.

New York City NAACP Youth Council members picketing to support antilynching legislation in front of the Strand Theater in Times Square, 1937.

Juanita Jackson (fourth from left), NAACP national youth director, visits the Scottsboro boys in prison, 1937. Also shown are Laura Kellum, secretary of the Birmingham, Alabama, Youth Council and Dr. E. W. Taggert (far right), president of the Birmingham NAACP.

Charlotte, North Carolina, NAACP Youth Council members with adult advisors, who are holding signs that read, "Join NAACP Youth Council," 1942.

Chicago NAACP Youth Council's float in the Bud Billiken Parade, Chicago, Illinois, ca. 1940s.

Detroit, Michigan, NAACP Youth Council members in a meeting at the Detroit NAACP branch office, ca. 1940s.

Judge William Hastie and Louisville, Kentucky, NAACP Youth Council members: L. N. Sedwick, Violet Beard, Katherine Burton, Minnie Harrison, Mary E. James, Lina Belle Laine, and Mary Anna Woolfolk, ca. 1940s.

NAACP youth marching with signs protesting Texas segregation laws. Houston, Texas, 1947.

Santa Clara, California, NAACP Junior Youth Council drummers and majorettes posed on steps in front of a church. Santa Clara County, California, ca. 1940s.

Arthurine Lucy (left) leaves federal court in Birmingham with her attorneys, Thurgood Marshall (center) and Arthur Shores (right), 1956.

Ruby Hurley (left), NAACP national youth director, Eleanor Roosevelt (center), unidentified man, and Walter White (right), NAACP executive secretary, at an NAACP program or meeting, ca. 1950s.

Flushing, New York, NAACP Youth Council baseball team, ca. 1950s.

NAACP Youth Council delegates from Indiana and Illinois, along with NAACP attorney Leslie S. Perry (left), meet with Senator Joseph Ball of Minnesota (center), who discussed his support for abolishing the poll tax, ca. 1950s.

Sit-in at Woolworth's department store in Greensboro, North Carolina, 1960.

Sit-in at a downtown department store in Nashville, Tennessee, 1960.

Chapter Four

"With All Deliberate Speed": School Desegregation, Emmett Till, and the Montgomery Bus Boycott

Two years had passed since the Supreme Court's ruling outlawing segregation in public schools. At the beginning of 1956, public school desegregation had not taken place in schools throughout the South. In fact, because of noncompliance from southern states, a year after the ruling, NAACP attorneys went back to court to press for immediate implementation of the ruling. However, the Supreme Court in *Brown II,* issued on May 31, 1955, ruled that desegregation should take place "with all deliberate speed."[1] According to Harvard law professor Charles Ogletree, the ruling did not obligate "federal courts to mandate that school districts formulate desegregation plans within any set time frame, and it did not set any time at which segregated schools would no longer be permitted."[2] This chapter explores the NAACP youth councils and college chapters' efforts to desegregate public schools after the *Brown* decision and the opposition these young people encountered. Additionally, this chapter discusses Emmett Till's murder and the Montgomery Bus Boycott, revealing how these events served as catalysts for a mass civil rights movement across the United States.

Although it proved to be a great year for the association's youth work, 1955 was also tragic. In March, Walter White died. Having served as executive secretary of the NAACP since 1931, White witnessed the association's successes and failures. White believed that the association would achieve full integration for blacks. He lived to see the Supreme Court's decision in *Brown v. Board of Education* (1954), which outlawed segregation in public education. On August 2, 1954, more than two hundred youths attended a gala to pay tribute to his outstanding leadership of the association. That night they honored both Thurgood Marshall and White for their work and legacy.[3] To honor the work of the association, youth members issued "An Appeal to the Youth of America," which called for uncompromised support to achieve the goal of integration.[4] In 1955, the association geared up its fight to implement the *Brown* decision. Vice President Richard Nixon, speaking at the second annual national legislative youth conference, heralded the Supreme Court's decision, maintaining that it was a significant step to breaking down prejudice and fear.[5]

In August of that year, another tragedy struck America. Fourteen-year-old Emmett Louis Till of Chicago was brutally murdered in Money,

Mississippi. Till's death symbolized the injustice and inhumanity of the South's racial segregation and white supremacy. On August 24, 1955, three days after arriving in Money, Mississippi, to visit his uncle, Moses Wright, Till supposedly entered the local grocery store and disrespected the owner, Carolyn Bryant. Bryant claimed that Till made ugly remarks toward her and whistled. Other accounts maintained that he only said, "Bye-bye Baby."[6] For those small words, days later, Till was lynched. His body was found in the Tallahatchie River severely disfigured with a cotton gin fan around his neck.[7] The following month, an all-white jury declared Till's alleged murderers, Roy Bryant and J. W. Milan, innocent.[8] Commenting on Till's death, Hurley asserted, "There is no question in my mind that [the two white men] . . . decided that they were going to 'get a nigger.' . . . And I always say, the Lord moves in mysterious ways [and] wonders to perform, because his body was not supposed to come up the way it was weighted down."[9] Milam and Bryant later sold their story to a reporter, William Bradford Huie, for four thousand dollars and confessed to having committed the murder.

To protest Till's death, youth councils and college chapters staged demonstrations calling for justice. They held rallies in cities such as Chicago, Newark, and New York. On October 16, 1955, youth councils and college chapters (in the northeastern region) held a rally at the Abyssinian Baptist Church, and Congressman Adam Clayton Powell Jr. was the keynote speaker. Powell castigated the Mississippi congressional delegation and called for justice.[10] Youth councils and college chapters mailed letters, petitions, and telegrams to President Dwight Eisenhower calling for justice; however, there was no justice in the murder of the fourteen-year-old Chicagoan. Till's death represented the travesty of the South's legal system, which so often failed to protect the lives of innocent African Americans against the violence of white supremacists—those who would stop at nothing to defend a southern way of life that subjugated and relegated blacks to second-class citizenship.

Because of widespread southern resistance to *Brown* and the murder of Emmett Till, the NAACP geared up for action. At the southeast regional conference, held in February 1956, in Charleston, South Carolina, one panel discussion focused on the role of youth in school desegregation. In efforts to speed up the implementation of the *Brown* decision, the NAACP urged parents and youth to support the Court's ruling.[11] Indeed, racial tension exploded in the South as young men and women challenged the South's segregated education system.

In 1952, Autherine Lucy applied to the University of Alabama and was accepted; however, after the university's officials discovered she was black, she was told that state law prohibited her from attending the school. With the support of NAACP attorney Thurgood Marshall, Lucy filed a lawsuit against the university. In October 1955, the Supreme Court ruled in her favor and ordered

"With All Deliberate Speed"

the university to admit her. On February 3, 1956, having braved a raging mob, Lucy became the first black to attend the University of Alabama.[12] Supporting Lucy's efforts, the NAACP youth division successfully secured a scholarship through the Jessie Smith Noyes Foundation.[13] This scholarship enabled her to attend the university. Although she did not have to worry about paying her tuition, Lucy did worry about white students' reaction to her presence. Committed to maintaining segregation at the university, two days after Lucy's admission, segregationists sparked a riot that rocked the campus. The rioters threw rotten eggs, hurled racial slurs, and tried to physically harm her. Some shouted epithets such as "Lynch the Nigger and Hit the Nigger Whore."[14] After narrowly escaping their attacks, Lucy was locked in Graves Hall for three hours until she was rescued by state troopers.[15]

As a result of the riot, the university's board of trustees voted to expel her, maintaining that it was for her safety and the safety of the other students.[16] Lucy had only attended the university for three days. Protesting her expulsion, the NAACP youth chapters called a meeting with national organizations and local groups operating at the university. Together they sent letters to their leaders to support Lucy's readmission. Additionally, these student groups sent letters to the student body president and other campus leaders urging them to protest the administration's decision to expel her.[17] As a result of these efforts, student officers passed a resolution calling for Lucy's readmission. Not only did the youth councils and college chapters play a key role in getting national youth groups to send letters to the university's president, but they also urged the governor, the president, and the United States attorney general to support Lucy's reinstatement.[18] Additionally, the World Youth Assembly passed a resolution condemning Lucy's expulsion and the discriminatory racial policies of the university.[19] Despite the efforts of the NAACP youth chapters and their ally youth organizations, Lucy failed to be readmitted to the university.

In Tennessee, the hard work of NAACP attorneys Z. Alexander Looby and Avon Williams led to school desegregation in that state. Upholding the *Brown* decision, on January 4, 1956, Judge Robert L. Taylor ordered the desegregation of Clinton High School in Clinton, Tennessee. Although there was local white resistance, Principal David J. Brittain complied with the judge's order. Historian Bobby Lovett documents, "In 1956, there were only sixty-seven Negro students in Clinton public schools, and CHS had eight hundred students." On August 27, 1956, twelve black students desegregated Clinton High School, which became the first public high school in Tennessee to desegregate. Regina Turner and Bobby Cain were among the twelve students who desegregated Clinton High School.[20]

A week before school was to start, Frederick John Kasper, a vowed segregationist and executive secretary of the Seaboard Citizen's Council of Washington, D.C., entered the town to provoke trouble. Lovett asserts, "Frederick

John Kasper was the most active of the segregationist leaders. . . . he hated Jews and Negroes, even though it had been reported that he had a Negro girlfriend." Edited by Horace V. Wells, who supported school desegregation efforts, the *Clinton Courier-News* described Kasper as the "'self-styled executive secretary of the White Citizens' Council.'" The *Clinton Courier-News,* urged "compliance with *Brown* and avoidance of any further pain for the community."[21] However, Kasper and other white segregationists ignored such "liberal" messages and used sexual and racial propaganda to incite fear in white parents around the issue of school desegregation. Historian Rebecca de Schweinitz writes, "In many southern communities that moved toward integration, white segregationists circulated fictitious rumors of blacks molesting white girls, beating teachers, or drawing weapons on white youth" to discourage school integration.[22] The night before the first day of school, Bobby Cain attended a Sunday evening service with his mother at Mount Sinai Church. Reverend O. W. Willis prayed that night for peace and safety for the youth who would desegregate Clinton High the next day. That night Cain remained restless in his bed, not knowing what to expect the next day.[23]

On August 27, 1956, the students, including Turner and Cain, integrated the school with little incident, although Kasper managed to recruit five local citizens to protest their presence. Because the press misrepresented the demonstration at the school (which only ensued for five minutes), the protest gained more supporters the next day. Reflecting on her participation in the desegregation of Clinton High School, Turner maintained, "I didn't want to go to Clinton High School in the first place, but I knew I had the right to be there and I wasn't afraid."[24] By the following school day, Kasper had convinced more local white citizens to support his efforts. Rallied by Kasper, fifteen local whites picketed the school carrying signs that read, "'We Wont [*sic*] Go to School with Negroes.'" Because of the demonstrations, the black students did not attend school that day. On Wednesday, August 29, the black students returned to school but not without incident. After lunch break, Cain responded to an attacker who had confronted him. As a result, he was placed in "temporary police protection," and the principal closed the school early for the students' safety.[25]

By the end of the week, the town was inundated with local white citizens protesting the black students' enrollment at the school, although "Superintendent Frank E. Irwin, School Board Chairman Chester E. Hicks, and Mayor W. E. Lewallen urged citizens to 'obey the law.'" Kasper and other white segregationists used fears of "interracial dating" and "miscegenation" to fuel the fire around school desegregation and to make the situation more explosive, knowing this propaganda would incite riots. The small town of Clinton was not equipped to handle the mob, so the mayor had to deputize some local citizens to restore order and peace. Parents of the students received telephone threats, and one of the students was attacked by the angry mob picketing outside the school.[26]

Hoping to restore peace, Judge Robert Taylor issued a restraining order against Kasper, the ringleader and inciter of the protest. Kasper ignored the judge's ruling and continued protesting at the school. Violating Judge Taylor's order to desist from picketing, he was sentenced to one year in jail. Released on bail, Kasper returned to Clinton High and resumed demonstrations.[27] On Friday, August 31, 1956, a big football game at Clinton High brought more segregationists to town; a rumor circulated that a cross burning would take place at half-time. Nothing happened. That Saturday, September 1, "more than four thousand people," including those outside of the county and state, "gathered around the courthouse, shouting that they wanted Kasper to speak." The inflamed crowd "rocked cars, destroyed property," and threatened a black US Navy serviceman, who had to be rescued by local police.[28] Clinton's police department called state troopers to help quell the disturbance, and Kasper was arrested again—this time for sedition and inciting a riot.[29] Taking precautionary measures to avoid widespread violence, Governor Frank Clement called in the Tennessee National Guard to police the town the next day, bringing about a temporary period of calm. On September 27, Kasper was arrested a third time and was charged with being linked to a bomb explosion in a nearby black community. Fortunately, no one was injured. Kasper was indicted by the local grand jury and faced possibly one year in jail.[30]

After being released on bond, Kasper and local segregationists confronted Principal Brittain and "told him to resign or get the Negroes out of the school."[31] Undaunted, Brittain informed Kasper that he was going to obey the law. On November 17, an all-white Anderson County jury acquitted Kasper and some of his followers of inciting a riot. Not long after Kasper's acquittal, the bullying of black students grew worse. Demonstrations started up again, and violence erupted. On November 27 and 28, the black students were forced to miss school due to the harassment and constant threat of violence. Seeking a possible solution, the Anderson County School Board offered the black parents the option to send their children to the all-black Austin High School in Knoxville, but "the students, parents, plaintiffs, and lawyers refused the offer." Perturbed by local resistance to desegregation efforts, on December 3, the school board castigated the federal government for its lack of assistance.[32]

In the midst of this turmoil, on December 4, the town held municipal elections. The White Citizens' Council backed an unsuccessful mayoral candidate who vowed to restore segregation. That same day, the Reverend Paul Turner, pastor of the First Baptist Church, along with Sidney Davis and Leo Burnett, decided to escort the students to class to ensure their safety. Later that day, Reverend Turner, while walking to his church office, was attacked and severely beaten by segregationists who had tried to enter the school that day. Sensing that the school environment was no longer safe, Principal Brittain decided to close the school for the academic year. However, student protests compelled him to change his mind. As Lovett noted, "That same day the local voters rejected the segregationist's candidate for mayor." The next day, Anderson County authorities arrested fifteen local white citizens, including W. H. Till (alleged leader of the Anderson County White Citizens Council), for violating court orders not to interfere with school desegregation. Because a possible federal sentence was hanging over John Kasper's head, protest demonstrations temporarily calmed down in Clinton. However, due to the resistance and hostility, by February 1957, only seven of the twelve black students were still enrolled at Clinton High School. The parents of the other students decided not to put them through the hardship.[33]

As the school year came to a close, Principal Brittain still faced some resistance from local white citizens who continued to oppose desegregation efforts. Lovett detailed, "As the school year ended, some students proclaimed that they had made it through the year 'in fellowship.' However, several teachers decided not to return the following year; the school superintendent said he would resign; and Brittain announced that he would accept a graduate fellowship at New York University." In May 1957, seventeen-year-old Cain became the first black to graduate from Clinton High School. On May 26, 1957, he was honored at the NAACP "Salute to Young Freedom Fighter" rally for his courage and bravery in desegregating Clinton High School. Speaking at the rally, Cain told of the ordeal he had faced at Clinton High School. He stressed how the school year had been both challenging and rewarding and contended that only through personal sacrifice were he and his peers able to integrate Clinton High School. He further noted that only through such personal sacrifices by youth would integration become a reality. For his heroism, baseball legend Jackie Robinson presented Cain with a NAACP freedom award at the ceremony.[34]

Upon graduation from Clinton High School, "Cain received private and institutional money to attend Tennessee A&I" (today known as Tennessee State University), where he graduated in 1961.[35] In July 1957, a federal district court jury convicted Kasper and six other protestors, sentencing them to one year in federal prison for having violated Judge Taylor's injunction. However, the judge's ruling was repealed, allowing for Kasper's release on bond.[36] Despite the violence and intimidation Cain and the other youth had suffered, their personal courage to desegregate Clinton High School revealed their determination to make the court-ordered school desegregation a reality for black youth.[37]

A year after the desegregation of Clinton High School, several other black youth were involved in an explosive school desegregation case that received more national attention. Under the leadership of Daisy Bates, president of the Little Rock, Arkansas, NAACP Branch, nine black youths (who would become known as the Little Rock Nine) desegregated Central High School.[38] However, the local citizens, students, and Governor Orval Faubus met the desegregation of the Central High School with much resistance.[39] On September 3, 1957, the Little Rock Nine attempted to enter Central High School. Resisting federal court orders, Faubus called out the National Guard, which proceeded to prevent the students from entering the school. Elizabeth Eckford, unaware that the meeting place had changed, arrived at the school alone and was confronted by an angry mob. Attempting to enter the school, she was turned away. Guided through the belligerent crowd by a white woman, Eckford managed to escape the mob that hurled racial epithets; she boarded public transportation and headed home.[40] The hostility the students faced revealed the extent to which Faubus and the local citizens would go to maintain segregation. For three weeks, the students tried to enter the school; however, the Arkansas National Guard prevented their entrance, and the local white citizens commenced acts of violence to deter desegregation of the school. The parents of the Little Rock Nine received death threats over the phone. Bates suffered similar harassment—and bullets riddled her home.[41]

On September 20, a federal district judge's ruling enjoined Faubus from preventing the students from entering the school.[42] Three days later, facing an angry mob, the students entered the school, only to be whisked away when the mob threatened to invade the building. The melee forced President Dwight Eisenhower to order federal troops into Little Rock to protect the students and to ensure school desegregation.[43] President Eisenhower stationed federal troops at the school to protect the students for that academic year. Despite their presence, federal troops could not successfully thwart all acts of violence committed against the students.

By November, members of the 101st Airborne Division were withdrawn from the school; however, the federalized Arkansas National Guard remained. Complaints from parents to restore some normalcy to the school environment led to the removal of the troops from inside the school.[44] According to Ernest Green, one of the Little Rock Nine, all hell broke loose. Recalling the events and the violent acts he and others had endured, Green asserted, "As they withdrew the troops from inside the corridors, you were subjected to all kinds of taunts, someone attempting to trip you, pour ink on you, in some way ruin your clothing, and at worst, someone physically attacking you. . . . I got hit with water guns. We got calls at all times of the night—people saying they were going to have acid in the water guns and they were going to squirt it in our faces."[45] He maintained that the young ladies bore the brunt of the harassment and acts of violence. Green contended, "The girls got it the most. . . . people took their femininity as a weakness and attempted to take advantage of that."[46] Minniejean Brown, one of the six girls, was expelled because she decided to protect herself from one of the school's bullies. One day, after being relentlessly taunted by a bully, Brown dumped a bowl of chili on his head.[47] Because it was looking for the black students to commit the slightest infraction to use against them, the administration used this isolated incident to expel Brown from the school.[48] After Brown's expulsion, Green recalled, some students had circulated small cards that read, "One down eight to go."[49]

In 1958, Ernest Green became the first black to graduate from Central High School. Green recalls, "It's the irony of my class that no matter what any of the others did that night, they were all going to be overshadowed by one event—my graduation. When they called my name, there were few claps in the audience, probably from my family. . . . At this point, I'm a high school graduate of sixteen. I've got a load off my shoulders."[50] That same year, at the forty-ninth annual convention of the NAACP, Ernest Green and other members of the Little Rock Nine were awarded the Spingarn Medal for their courage to desegregate Central High School. Their advisor, Mrs. L. C. Bates, NAACP president of the Arkansas State Conference, was also honored. Speaking courageously for the other black students who had helped to desegregate Central High, Green contended, "Negroes—especially the younger generation—in the South and in the rest of the United States will not be satisfied until everyone is granted full democracy."[51] The ordeal endured by these students revealed their determination to dismantle the racial barriers that had long relegated them to second-class citizenship. Green and the other black students knew that equal access to an education was a right, not a privilege.

Upon graduation, Ernest Green attended Michigan State University (MSU) on a full scholarship from an anonymous donor. He later discovered that the donor was John Hannah, president of Michigan State University. Hannah paid Green's tuition out of his personal finances.[42] Green maintains, "When I went back to MSU to receive an honorary doctorate, I learned that my anonymous benefactor 'twas [then MSU president] John Hannah, who paid for my scholarship out of his own pocket.[53] While at MSU, Green continued his activism as president of the Michigan State NAACP College Chapter, staging demonstrations around discriminatory practices on campus. When sit-in demonstrations commenced in the South, Green sponsored a massive rally on campus urging support for the black student cause.[54] Having learned that Hannah had financed his education, Green said, "I bet sometimes he looked out his window [when I was picketing], and wished he could get his money back."[55]

The NAACP did not overlook the personal sacrifices that these young men and women had made in the fight for freedom. In 1958, the NAACP awarded the coveted Spingarn medal to the Little Rock Nine and their advisor, Daisy Bates.[56] That same year, Faubus ordered all four high schools closed for the academic school year. Because Faubus resisted desegregation, like many southern governors, segregationists celebrated him as a defender of the southern way of life, which won him reelection six consecutive terms before his retirement in 1967.[57]

While the incidents at Clinton High School and Central High School were sparking national and international attention, NAACP youth staged other school desegregation efforts that did not receive widespread national coverage, but were equally important. On September 4, 1957, "wearing a prim brown dress with a stiff white collar," seventeen-year-old Josephine Boyd became the first black student admitted to Greensboro High School in Greensboro, North Carolina, which had a population of 1,950 students.[58] Serving as secretary of the Southeastern Regional NAACP Youth Conference, she was among the eleven black youths admitted to all-white schools in North Carolina. Unlike Central High School, the National Guard was not used to desegregate Greensboro High School; however, Boyd's ordeal was shocking in its own right. Describing her first day at Greensboro High School, Boyd maintained that she was frightened and terrified, as her mother, Cora Lee Boyd, could only accompany her to doorway of the school. "Neither of them was fully prepared for the hatred. 'Nigger go home!' screamed the students and rabble-rousers lining the sidewalk. 'We don't want you here! Go back to where you came from!'"[59]

During the nine-month school year, Boyd faced threats and violence from students and protestors alike. Protestors repeatedly threw eggs and snowballs at her. In the school cafeteria, boys spat in her food and squirted ketchup on her clothes. "Tacks were placed in her seat and ink was spilled on her books."[60] On one occasion, she maintained, a young man walked up to her and told her that his father told him to tell her that he had sexually abused her mother last night. She immediately shoved him against the locker—but before the incident got out of hand, one of the students ran and got a teacher. The teacher took the young man's side without even hearing the full story and warned Boyd that if she touched him again, she would be expelled. In addition to the hardships she endured at school, Boyd and her family were subjected to threats and actual violence at the hands of local white citizens. Boyd's family received harassing phone calls from the local KKK. The tires on the family car were slashed. Their two pet dogs were killed. Boyd's mother lost her job as a housekeeper, and her father's sandwich shop burned down under dubious circumstances.[61]

Despite the hostility she and her family suffered, Boyd persevered. In the midst of this hostile environment, she maintained a high scholastic average of 92.4 and honor roll status. In June 1958, Boyd became the first black to graduate from Greensboro High School.[62] Not until 1964 would another black student enroll at Greensboro High School. Upon graduation, Boyd attended Clark University in Worcester, Massachusetts, on a thirteen-hundred-dollar scholarship received from the Jessie Smith Noyes Foundation and a five-hundred-dollar supplementary grant from the North Carolina NAACP State

Conference.[63] Reflecting on her sacrifices years later, Boyd maintained that the experience was worth it for having provided access to educational opportunities. However, she lamented that schools were re-segregating themselves after all the sacrifices many in her generation had endured to make integration a reality.[64]

Protesting southern states' refusal to uphold the *Brown* decision, and calling upon the national government to enforce the ruling, youth councils and college chapters participated in the NAACP-sponsored "Youth March for Integrated Schools." The goal of the march was to "demonstrate the unity of American youth," and to show that black and white youth supported the *Brown* decision, handed down by the United States Supreme Court on May 17, 1954, to ban segregated public education.[65] The Youth March for Integrated Schools underscored the NAACP's educational campaign for immediate desegregation of public schools. In a letter urging youth chapters to support the march, the NAACP national youth director, Herbert Wright, maintained, "The purpose of the march is to enable American youth, both Negro and white, and from the South as well the North, to express their firm support for efforts aimed at securing compliance with the supreme court's rulings on desegregation in the public school."[66]

On October 25, a crowd of more than ten thousand, including fifteen hundred young people from NAACP youth chapters, descended on the nation's capital, protesting the South's resistance to the Supreme Court's ruling.[67] Lillie Jackson, president of the Baltimore NAACP branch, took more than two thousand young people to the march. W. Lester Banks, executive secretary of the Virginia State Conference and Roberta Robertson, state youth work chairperson, took more than one thousand youths to the march.[68] Prominent civil rights leaders and distinguished celebrities, such as A. Philip Randolph, founder of the Brotherhood of Sleeping Car Porters; Roy Wilkins, executive secretary of the NAACP; legendary baseball player Jackie Robinson; and renowned actor Harry Belafonte attended the rally. Martin L. King was scheduled to deliver a speech at the march; however, a month earlier at a book signing in New York, he was stabbed by Izola Curry. Because he was recovering from the stabbing, his wife, Coretta Scott King, delivered a speech on his behalf, encouraging the youth in their efforts.[69]

Although adults played a major role in organizing the march, youths were instrumental as well. Among the NAACP youths who played a prominent role in the demonstration was Minnijean Brown of the Little Rock Youth Council. Having participated in the desegregation of Central High School, she provided inspiration to youth across the United States who supported the march.[70] Not only did Brown participate in the march, but she was also one of the NAACP youth delegates invited to the White House. Other NAACP youth invited included Fred H. Moore of the Howard University NAACP Chapter,

Offie Wortham of the Peekskill, New York, Youth Council, and eleven-year-old Paula Martin, plaintiff in the Norfolk, Virginia school desegregation case. Led by Harry Belafonte, the youth delegates hoped to express to the president their concerns about the slow pace of school desegregation. However, the delegation was unable to meet with the president or his staff. Disappointed, they picketed for a half hour in protest and left a list of demands for the president. Although President Dwight Eisenhower had intervened in the Little Rock crisis, with the desegregation of Central High School, he did not push for the immediate integration of public schools. Politically motivated, he believed it was unwise to push too fast around such a polarizing issue. At the march, youth activists urged the president to take a firmer stance. Youth participants also passed a resolution encouraging young people to give full support to NAACP programs, including school desegregation, and to join NAACP youth chapters.[71]

In 1959, the "Youth March for Integrated Schools" was even grander. More than thirty thousand (of which thirteen thousand were members of youth councils and college chapters) black and white youths participated in the march, which was led by noted civil rights activists such as Martin Luther King Jr., A. Philip Randolph, and Roy Wilkins.[72] Protesting the slow pace of school desegregation, the youth circulated a petition that urged "the President and Congress of the United States to put into effect an executive and legislative program which will insure the orderly and speedy integration of schools throughout the United States."[73] Among the students participating in this march was NAACP student leader Josephine Boyd. Boyd and three other students met with different congressmen to discuss school desegregation.[74] Additionally, a delegation of youth again went to the White House to express concerns about school desegregation efforts. This time the students were met by the president's deputy assistant, Gerald D. Morgan, who reportedly told them that "the president is just as anxious as they are to see an America where discrimination does not exist, where equality of opportunity is available to all."[75]

Hoping to discredit the march, opponents wielded accusations of Communist infiltration. The day before the march, Randolph, Wilkins, and King issued a statement denying allegations of Communist involvement. The statement read, "The sponsors of the March have not invited Communists or Communist organizations. Nor have they invited members of the Ku Klux Klan or the White Citizen Council. We do not want participation of these groups, nor of individuals or organizations holding similar views."[76] Indeed, what was called the "Youth March for Integrated Schools" made the nation aware of the gross inequalities in education for black youth under the separate but equal system. Commenting on the significance of the march, Martin L. King Jr. told the youth, "In your great movement to organize a march for integrated schools, . . . you have awakened on hundreds of campuses throughout the land a spirit of social inquiry to the benefit of all Americans."[77] As King foretold, the march sparked support from other youth groups that endorsed the NAACP's efforts to end segregation in education, including the Young Adult Council (of the National Social Welfare Assembly) and the United States National Student Association (USNSA).[78] Supporting school desegregation efforts, the Young Adult Council (YAC) published a pamphlet entitled "Desegregation in Education, A Topic and Resource Guide for Discussion Leaders," which it distributed to all of its affiliate organizations. Both of these groups pledged their support to end segregation in education.

That same year, NAACP youth councils hosted workshops to educate young people and their parents about school desegregation. In 1959, for example, the Nashville NAACP Youth Council held a two-day workshop entitled "School Integration: Our Responsibility" to inform students and parents about school integration efforts in that city. The two-day workshop, which consisted of approximately fifty young people from Nashville, Knoxville, and Memphis, provoked concerns from local school board officials. William Henry Oliver, the city school superintendent, believed that the local NAACP chapter was pushing young people to integrate schools against their will. Marjorie Crump, one of the adult advisors for the workshop, asserted, "Some people, at least, have misinterpreted our purpose. We only want to show them [the parents] that if they decide to do so [participate in school desegregation], we are behind them 100 per cent."[79] Reiterating Crump's sentiments, Dr. Vivian W. Henderson, chairman of the Nashville NAACP Executive Committee, declared, "We have no plan to try to get parents to take advantage of the desegregated grades, but we hope all 200 Negro students eligible will assert themselves by going to these schools."

As school desegregation efforts got underway in Nashville, in September 1957, Kasper denounced such plans. Mayor Ben West opposed Kasper's tactics and denied him a permit to hold a rally at Centennial Park. Having been arrested for illegal parking and other infractions, Kasper posted bail and held a rally on September 8 against the mayor's wishes. At the rally, he encouraged local citizens to resist the school board's desegregation plan, claiming, "When they put the niggers in school with your kids in September, load your shotguns to defend your wife and home—be prepared for the worst: race riots, hanging, anything."[80] That year, as a result of a court order, Nashville's school board adopted the "grade-a-year plan," later known as the Nashville Plan.[81] The NAACP challenged the school board's decision, but the United States Court of Appeals in Cincinnati upheld a previous ruling by the district federal court that had backed the school board's measure.

Disappointed by the court's decision, attorney Avon Williams, counsel for the Nashville NAACP, saw the "grade-a-year plan" a step in the right direction but called for full integration.[82] Williams asserted, "The grade-a-

"With All Deliberate Speed"

year plan is not acceptable to the NAACP, but it is a step in the door."[83] On September 9, 1957, facing an angry white mob, nineteen black six-year-olds attempted to enroll in Nashville's all-white public elementary schools, including Reverend Kelly Smith's daughter, Joy. Smith, who was pastor of the First Colored Baptist Church, reflected on the decision to enroll his daughter in the all-white elementary school. He remarked, "'Before we allowed our daughter to be the first Negro child to enter a white school, my wife and I searched ourselves wondering if we had a right to submit her to such a task. The dangers of accepting the humiliation were worse than pioneering in a worthy cause."[84]

"Escorted by their parents and local civil rights activist," four of the nineteen students were denied admission into the all-white schools "for administrative reasons," explained historian Sonya Ramsey. That same day, according to Ramsey, local authorities "arrested three white women for throwing bottles at the black parents and students." Some parents were afraid to send their children to the all-white schools "after receiving bomb and death threats."[85] On September 10, shortly after midnight, Hattie Cotton Elementary School was bombed. Rumors surfaced that Kasper was responsible for the explosion, but authorities later charged five white men for the incident. The explosion, which forced the school to close for a week, amounted to $71,000 in damages. Furthermore, the only black student enrolled at the school did not return because of this violent episode.[86]

Although it was a setback, the bombing did convince the all-white Nashville City Teachers Association to support desegregation efforts. Denouncing the violence, the association members declared, "We join the Board of Education in calling on all people of goodwill to assist us in making the adjustments in our schools that may be demanded by this monumental change."[87] By the end of the school year, ten black students remained in Nashville all-white public schools. As a result of the grade-a-year plan, in 1958, thirteen black students were enrolled in the second grade, bringing the total number of black students enrolled in all-white public schools in Nashville to twenty-three. The city's black public schools remained segregated, as the fifty-three white children zoned to attend the black schools transferred.[88] The workshop hosted by the Nashville Youth Council represented the determination of many young people across the South to wage an ardent fight for school desegregation. In Nashville, like many southern cities, school desegregation moved at a slow pace. In 1966, as a result of the activism of the Nashville NAACP, "the Metropolitan Nashville-Davidson County Board of Education abandoned the 'grade-a-year' plan and began to integrate all grades"; however, not until several years later would schools become fully desegregated in Tennessee.[89]

While desegregation moved along slowly, members of the NAACP youth councils continued their fight against segregated public schools. In 1961, in Durham, North Carolina, Maxine Bledsoe and Claudette Brame became the first black students to graduate from Durham High School.[90] That same year, after much litigation, Martha Holmes, president of the Atlanta Youth Council, was among ten students who integrated Atlanta all-white public schools.[91] Although small steps of progress toward integration had been made prior to 1964, most southern states resisted school desegregation. And when integration did occur at state and local levels, only a small percentage of black students participated in the process. Certainly, this was the case when Atlanta's public schools desegregated.[92] Additionally, the state of Georgia provided school boards with options such as tuition grants and freedom-of-choice plans.[93] Although the association experienced a few victories with school desegregation, most schools in the South remained almost completely segregated for an entire decade after the *Brown* decision.[94] Although southern states operated "with all deliberate speed," full integration did not become a reality until decades later. Nonetheless, the personal sacrifices of these young people did not go unnoticed. Driven by personal courage, these young men and women braved the terror—the violence and death threats—to participate in school desegregation in the South. They defied the racial stereotypes and propaganda advanced by white segregationists and racists. In many instances, they were not even aware of the magnitude of their personal sacrifices in advancing civil rights for blacks, particularly where their selflessness concerned educational opportunities for black youth. Most did not consider themselves heroes for defying segregation, but rather saw their actions as law-abiding behavior and as fulfilling their social responsibility to the race.

During the 1950s, the NAACP chapters attacked not only segregation in education but also discrimination in public accommodations. In 1956, the Montgomery Bus Boycott received national attention. Sparked by the arrest of Rosa Parks on December 1, 1955, for refusing to give up her seat to a white man, a violation of the city's segregation law, the bus boycott became a link in the chain of direct action protest demonstrations that engulfed the southern region of the United States.[95] Before Parks's arrest, local citizens protested the discrimination and humiliation of black passengers on Montgomery's city buses. Organized in the early 1950s, under the leadership of Mary Fair Burks and Jo Ann Robinson, both professors at Alabama State College, the Women's Political Council (WPC), had raised concerns about the mistreatment of African Americans on the city buses. The WPC complained to the city commissioners about the discriminatory seating policy and the discourtesy that bus drivers displayed toward black passengers.

At a public meeting held by city commissioners to raise the bus fares, leaders of the WPC "pleaded for the city to make immediate change, but the only response they received was an agreement by the commission to take the WPC proposal under advisement."[96] That November and December of 1953, the WPC met directly with city commissioners and once again raised concerns about the mistreatment of black passengers on the city buses; however, the commissioners largely dismissed their concerns. Historian Troy Jackson maintains, "Despite a lack of early success, the WPC demonstrated a tireless commitment to challenge the racial status quo that would become more evident in the coming years."[97]

Similarly, before Parks's arrest, other instances of mistreatment of black passengers on the city buses had occurred. In March 1955, fifteen-year-old Claudette Colvin was arrested for refusing to obey the city's segregation law.[98] Colvin, a member of the Montgomery NAACP Youth Council and student at Booker T. Washington High School, insisted, "The busman kept saying, 'She won't get up, she won't get up.' He was turning red." Colvin told him, "This is my constitutional right . . . you have no right to do this!" But, she recalled, "The police knocked my books down. One took one wrist, the other grabbed the other, and they were pulling me off the bus."[99] Colvin was jailed for breaking the city's segregation laws. When Colvin's case was tried before the circuit court in Alabama that May, local authorities chose to try her on assault and battery. By dropping the charges made against her for violating the city's segregation laws, the local authorities prevented "the emergence of any constitutional challenge from the case." Colvin was convicted and placed on probation for a year.[100]

Montgomery's segregationist ordinance required blacks and whites to sit in different sections on the bus. Separated by a sign that identified white and black sections, whites usually sat at the front of the bus and blacks at the back. The bus driver determined how many seats would be allotted for each section. Oftentimes, there would be empty seats in the white section, but blacks could not sit in them—they would have to stand until a seat was available in their section. To make matters worse, if the bus reached capacity and no seats remained for whites, blacks had to stand up and give their seats to them. And, equally appalling, blacks had to enter at the rear of the bus after having paid their fare.[101] Parks's arrest served as a catalyst for local black citizens who decided that they had enough and had put up with the discriminatory practices for too long. After unsuccessful negotiations with city officials to end discriminatory practices on the city buses, the local black citizens decided to boycott.[102]

Coordinating their protest efforts, local black citizens organized the Montgomery Improvement Association (MIA) under the leadership of Martin Luther King Jr.[103] King, who was just a young adult himself, became a role model for many youth activists. Although historians have emphasized the role of adults in the bus boycott, they have placed little attention on youth participation. In fact, Colvin's ordeal was one of the catalysts for the boycott's initiation. Indeed, the Montgomery NAACP Youth Council supported the year-long boycott, which led to the desegregation of the Montgomery transit system. Organized in 1949 by Rosa Parks, who served as advisor, the Montgomery Youth Council had over two hundred members by 1956.[104] Under her leadership the youth council challenged Jim Crow practices in Montgomery. Before Parks's arrest she was preparing youth council members to boycott the city's library for refusing to allow black students to check out books. They had to order books through the mail, which took upwards of five to seven days.[105] While the boycott of the city's library was thwarted, participation in the bus boycott did allow youth council members to directly confront segregation practiced in the city. Assisting in the bus boycott efforts, many youths who attended Montgomery city schools chose to walk to school instead of riding the bus.[106] Joseph Lacey, one of the youths who participated in the bus boycott, maintained that he and many other youths walked to school. Lacey remembered, "As the buses passed me and my classmates, we said, 'Nobody's on the bus! Nobody's on the bus!' It was just a beautiful thing. . . . Everybody stuck together on the bus boycott. It lasted a year, and we walked and enjoyed walking. Everybody felt like a part of the struggle because everybody had a part."[107] Not only did the local youth council aid in the bus boycott efforts, but also youth councils and college chapters nationwide. In April 1956, NAACP youth groups contributed $1,100 to the bus boycott.[108] That same year, the youth councils and college chapters held "mass meetings, rallies, and other forms of protest to indicate support for the Montgomery bus protest" and raised $3,100 with the support of other student organizations.[109] Indeed, the support of NAACP youth chapters helped enable the success of the bus boycott.

After almost a yearlong struggle, on June 4, 1956, the United States district court ruled in *Browder v. Gayle* that segregation on Montgomery's city buses was unconstitutional. On November 13, 1956, the US Supreme Court upheld the district court's ruling. On December 20, the MIA suspended the boycott.[110] After a prolonged struggle, the bus boycott scored a victory against racial segregation for black residents in Montgomery, who had courageously fought to end discrimination on the city's buses. Furthermore, the *Brown* decision, Emmett Till's murder, and the Montgomery Bus Boycott became a catalyst for mass direct action protest to challenge Jim Crow practices and racial discrimination in the South. These events issued a clarion call to blacks and those who sympathized with their plight to spring to action and challenge the Jim Crow practices and racial discrimination that relegated them to second-class citizenship.

Chapter Five

"More Than a Hamburger and a Cup of Coffee": NAACP Youth and the 1960s Black Freedom Struggle

February 1, 2010, marked the fiftieth anniversary of the 1960 sit-in movement. The sit-in movement was initiated when four students from North Carolina A&T State University staged a sit-in on February 1, 1960, at the Woolworth's lunch counter in Greensboro, North Carolina. As a result of this demonstration, sit-ins spread across the South. These sit-in demonstrations facilitated the desegregation of public facilities and businesses; youth from across the United States, particularly southern black youth, initiated one of the largest protest movements of that decade. Although historians have written extensively about the role of the Student Nonviolent Coordinating Committee and the Congress of Racial Equality in 1960s student demonstrations, little research has attended to the activities of NAACP youth councils and college chapters and their role as early initiators and participants in the student demonstrations. This chapter examines the role of the NAACP youth councils and college chapters in the sit-in demonstrations of the 1950s and 1960s, and their efforts to end racial discrimination in the Jim Crow South.

Motivated by the legal victory of *Brown v. Board of Education* and the success of the Montgomery Bus Boycott during the late 1950s, NAACP youth chapters staged demonstrations that led to the desegregation of major department store chains and other local businesses. Unlike the national press coverage that the 1960s sit-ins received, many of the student protests during the late 1950s had not been covered by national and/or local press.[1] Certainly, this dearth of attention accounts for the lack of recognition in historical writings concerning these demonstrations. In 1956, the Louisville, Kentucky, Youth Council protested the discriminatory practices with sit-ins at the F. W. Woolworth and Kress department stores, which led to the desegregation of lunchrooms at those businesses.[2]

Two years later, in July 1958, the Wichita, Kansas, Youth Council conducted a sit-in demonstration at Dockum Drug Store. Ronald Walters, the twenty-eight-year-old council president and organizer of the protest, remembered, "We were motivated by the actions of other people in the struggle, especially by the pictures of people in Little Rock and King's Montgomery bus boycott."[3] Moved into action by both the civil rights efforts of other black activists and the grim reality of second-class citizenship that oppressed black people in Wichita, Walters maintained,

> Social and economic progress in those years were [*sic*] exceedingly difficult for Wichita's small, closely knit black community, a product of turn-of-the-century migration. We faced an implacably cold, dominant white culture. Blacks in the '50s attended segregated schools up to high school and were excluded from mixing with whites at movie theaters, restaurants, nightclubs, and other places of public accommodation. . . . Even though the signs "black" and "white" were not publicly visible as in the South, we lived in separate worlds, just as blacks and whites did in Southern states.[4]

Determined to eradicate the barriers that relegated blacks to second-class citizenship, Walters commenced the drugstore sit-in on Saturday, July 19, 1958. Although they were refused service, the young people were not deterred.

As the sit-in demonstrations gained momentum, Wichita youth council members occupied the lunch counters for longer periods. On August 2, 1958, Walters and youth council members occupied vacant seats at the lunch counters of Dockum from 12:00 p.m. to 10:00 p.m., closing time. Again, the young people departed without incident. On August 7, the youth resumed the sit-in demonstration. In a counter-protest, a group of whites entered the store and attempted to start a fight with the demonstrators, spitting on them and hurling racial slurs. The police were called, and the white youth dispersed. As momentum grew, the protest demonstration became popular among young people, and several white students from Wichita State University became involved.[5]

On Sunday, August 10, the Wichita branch held a mass meeting, and the youth informed the community of its efforts to desegregate Dockum Drug Store. After sustaining great financial loss from the demonstrations, Dockum decided to integrate. Walters remarked, "On a Saturday afternoon, into the fourth week of the protest, a man in his 30s came into the store, stopped, looked back at the manager in the rear, and said, 'Serve them. I'm losing too much money.' This was the conclusion of the sit-in—at once dramatic and anticlimactic."[6] Shortly thereafter, the vice president of the Dockum Drug Store chain met with Chester Lewis Jr., president of the Wichita NAACP Branch, and announced that the drug store would abolish all discriminatory practices.[7]

The Wichita Youth Council's protest of Dockum Drug Store's discriminatory practices symbolized black youth's determination to eradicate the barriers that relegated them to second-class citizenship and to enjoy the same rights and privileges that white youth enjoyed. Commenting on the sit-in demonstration, Lewis asserted, "This protest was planned solely by the youth group and was excellently perfected under the vigorous leadership of the youth council president, Ronald Walters."[8] The desegregation of the Dockum Drug Store chain paved the way for desegregation of other stores in Wichita, Kansas.

That same year, the Oklahoma City Youth Council, under the leadership of its advisor, Clara Luper, and youth council president Barbara Posey, organized sit-in demonstrations against five stores in Oklahoma City. Posey, a fifteen-year-old Douglass High School student, influenced by Luper, a local high school history teacher, mobilized students to challenge Jim Crow practices in the city.[9] According to Aldon Morris, the Wichita Youth Council's demonstration inspired the Oklahoma City protest.[10] Morris explained, "The adult leaders of these two groups knew each other; in addition to working for the same organization, several members were personal friends. Following the initial sit-ins in Wichita, members of the two groups made numerous phone calls, exchanged information, and discussed mutual support."[11] On August 19, 1958, Luper, Posey, and other youth council members commenced a sit-in demonstration at Katz Drug Store that lasted two days—until they were served. Desegregation occurred not only at Katz Drug Store in Oklahoma City, but also at thirty-eight other stores in Missouri, Oklahoma, Kansas, and Iowa.[12]

After the campaign against Katz, the youth council demonstrated against Kress Department Store, Veasey Drug Store, and the H. L. Green Company, which the youth council successfully desegregated.[13] Of the five stores targeted during the three-day demonstration, the John A. Brown Department Store was the only one to resist desegregation. When they attempted to sit down at the lunch counter, youth council members were met with resistance by local white youth who assaulted one of them. When the police arrived, one of the youth council members was arrested. In fact, the protest demonstrations had been without incident until the attempt to desegregate Brown Department Store, the largest department store in Oklahoma.[14] Although some business owners rebuffed the Oklahoma City Youth Council's sit-in demonstrations, the youth group managed to get thirty-nine businesses that year to put an end to their segregation policies.[15] By the time the Brown Department Store desegregated in 1961, 117 stores had discontinued their segregation practices. The protest demonstrations at Brown, which started on August 22, 1958 and lasted until June 23, 1961, marked the "longest single sit-in campaign in the nation."[16] The protest demonstrations led by the Oklahoma Youth Council received national and international attention. Newspapers including the *New York Times, Wall Street Journal, Times of London, Times of New Delhi, Times of Tokyo,* and *U.S. News and World Report* captured and publicized the activities of the youth council.[17]

Under the remarkable leadership of Luper and Posey, the Oklahoma City Youth Council garnered numerous accolades. For example, in 1960, *Parents Magazine* awarded the Youth Group Achievement Award to the Oklahoma

City Youth Council for its citywide sit-in demonstrations against local businesses that discriminated against blacks. Along with the Special Award medal, the youth council received $100.00 for its activism.[18] Honored for the success of the Oklahoma demonstrations, at the NAACP national convention in Minneapolis, Minnesota in 1960, Posey was invited to deliver a speech. Her speech expressed the sentiments of many black youth opposing racial discrimination and segregation. Posey stated, "The youth of America are not playing. We are young enough to have wisdom. With this wisdom, this courage, this knowledge, this faith in God, and all the dedicated NAACP leaders behind us, the youth are now ready to announce 'our plans for a democratic America.' Our first plan is to kill and bury the cancer of discrimination and segregation in order to make democracy work in America."[19]

In July 1963, at the Youth Freedom Fund Banquet, the NAACP Youth and College Division awarded the Oklahoma City Youth Council the Distinguished Service Award for "its continued excellence in the NAACP program, leadership, and dedication."[20] Although Clara Luper received hate calls and death threats from the white community—and was rebuffed by some African Americans for stirring up trouble—her devotion and service to the Oklahoma City Youth Council epitomize the prominent role that women played in advancing the association's aims and fight for civil rights.[21] Luper's activist work with the Oklahoma City Youth Council exemplifies women's commitment to the civil rights movement. As community organizers, women played a major role in breaking down the racial barriers that relegated blacks to second-class status.[22]

During the late 1950s, some NAACP college chapters also staged protest demonstrations against businesses that discriminated against blacks. On February 14, 1959, four student leaders of the Washington University NAACP college chapter in St. Louis, Missouri, staged a sit-in demonstration at Santoro Restaurant.[23] When the students entered the restaurant, the owner told them to leave because the restaurant did not serve blacks. Arguing that the establishment made most of its profits from student patronage, the students refused to leave. Because the students disregarded the owner's demand, the police were called and the four students were arrested. The police charged the students with illegal assembly and disturbing the peace.[24] Upon learning of the students' fiasco, the St. Louis NAACP Branch joined the students in protesting the restaurant's segregation policy and agreed to provide legal counsel. On February 25, a local judge convicted the students, fining them twenty dollars each. The two white students were fined an additional ten dollars each on illegal assembly charges. As a result of the incident, the Washington University chapter conducted a campus-wide protest, urging fellow students not to patronize the restaurant until it abolished its segregation policy. With the support of fellow students, the chapter was successful in getting the owner to serve all students regardless of race.[25]

That same year, students at the University of Chicago launched a successful "petition and picket" protest against discriminatory hiring practices at the Tropical Hut Restaurant. In early January, the Tropical Hut ran ads in the *Chicago Tribune* "for white waitresses only." Because the restaurant's largest clientele body was students, the chapter decided to confront the owner about the advertisement.[26] After unsuccessful negotiations with the owner over hiring practices, the chapter initiated a petition campaign urging students and faculty not to patronize the restaurant until the hiring practices were changed. Due to the overwhelming student response to the petition campaign, the owner met with the chapter leaders in early February, announcing that the discriminatory hiring practices at the restaurant would be eliminated and that future advertisement for employees would reflect the new policy.[27] Students at the university believed that all businesses within their community—especially those profiting greatly from their patronage—should treat all customers equally without respect to race.

Undoubtedly, the direct action protests of the late 1950s initiated by youth councils and college chapters set a precedent for youth activism in the 1960s. Aldon Morris asserts, "The Greensboro sit-ins represent a unique link in a long chain of sit-ins."[28] Ronald Walters, who led the sit-in demonstrations in Wichita, Kansas, echoed similar sentiments. Walters maintains, "The link between the Midwest actions and the Greensboro sit-in was more than mere sequence. Ezell Blair and Joseph McNeil, two of the four originators of the Greensboro protest, were officers in the Greensboro's NAACP Youth Council. It is highly unlikely they were unfamiliar with the sit-ins elsewhere in the country led by their organizational peers."[29] According to Morris, a militant wing of the NAACP favored direct action as a strategy to break down racial discrimination. He contended, "Following the Montgomery bus boycott, this group [militant wing] began to reorganize NAACP youth councils with the explicit purpose of initiating direct action projects. This group of activists (e.g., Floyd McKissick, Daisy Bates, Ronald Walters, Hosea Williams, Barbara Posey, Clara Luper, etc.) viewed themselves as a distinct group, because the national NAACP usually did not approve their direct-action approach or took a very ambivalent stance."[30]

By the 1960s, when protest demonstrations among youths became widespread, the NAACP national office became more receptive to the use of direct action measures to eradicate racial discrimination and segregation. One of the factors influencing the national office's decision was the direct action activity of the youth councils and college chapters, and the young people's dedication to this strategy to influence change. Partly convinced that this method could effectively create change when properly guided, and having seen the benefits of such undertakings in Kansas and Oklahoma, the national office did not discourage this kind of activism among its youth chapters. Although many older leaders of NAACP local branches were reluctant to embrace this tactic—preferring the route of litigation—they, too, saw the benefits of such activism.

In 1960, Ezell Blair, Joseph McNeil, Franklin McCain, and David Richmond, four students at North Carolina A&T in Greensboro, North Carolina, set into motion a chain of events that greatly changed the South. The sit-in demonstration at F. W. Woolworth was not the first sit-in demonstration to take place in North Carolina. In the late 1950s, Floyd McKissick, a young black attorney; Reverend Douglass Moore; and NAACP youth launched demonstrations to defeat racial discriminations in Durham. According to Christina Greene, during the 1950s, McKissick "revived NAACP youth councils in Durham," which had a strong female presence. And, by 1955, forty-five youth councils and college chapters were operating in North Carolina, making it the fifth largest NAACP youth membership base in the United States.[31] Under McKissick's leadership, NAACP youth and other local groups, staged direct action demonstrations at "local bus stations, waiting rooms, parks, hotels, and other places."[32] Blair and McNeil, former officers of the Greensboro Youth Council, were well aware of these early sit-in efforts in the state and with the Greensboro NAACP Branch's frustration with the local businesses' segregation practices.[33] Having also been subjected to these discriminatory practices, Blair and McNeil decided that something had to be done. Indeed, the sit-in demonstration at F. W. Woolworth Department Store was not happenstance—nor was it some impulsive plan on the part of the students, as historian Clayborne Carson claims: "The initial spark of the movement was a simple, impulsive act of defiance, one that required no special skills or resources. Planned the previous night, the "sit-in"—as it would be called—was not the product of radical intellectual ferment. Rather, it grew out of "bull sessions" involving college freshmen who were, in most respects, typical southern black students of the time, politically unsophisticated and socially conventional."[34] In fact, two nights before the protest demonstration, Blair had revealed his plans to his father (chairman of the Greensboro NAACP Branch executive board). His father assured him that he would support his actions.[35] Additionally, McNeil had had several conversations with Ralph Johns (a local white merchant and member of the Greensboro NAACP Branch executive committee) about their possible actions.[36] Johns assured McNeil that he would have his full support.[37] Understanding the importance of having students take the lead in the demonstration, the Greensboro NAACP Branch hid its connection. The Greensboro Branch leaders knew that if it were publicized that they backed the students' plan, merchants and the public would have written it off as a protest demonstration instigated by the NAACP—and not something that had originated with the students. Although it supported the students, the Greensboro Branch did not originate the plan for the sit-in demonstration at Woolworth.[38] According to the "Special Report on the Sit Downs": "Dr. [George] Simkins [president of the Greensboro NAACP] and Mr. Johns felt that the students should take the lead in the protest and that the NAACP should in no way be publicly identified with it. The branch, through Dr. Simkins, had made arrangements to secure bail bond for the students in the event any of them would be arrested. Arrangements had been made with a local attorney to handle all the legal problems which might develop as a result of the protest."[39]

On the afternoon of February 1, 1960, four students sat down at the lunch counter in Woolworth to be served; they were refused service. "We do not serve Negroes," one of the workers announced. In protest, the students remained seated until the store closed. After the sit-in demonstration, the students returned to campus and organized a plan of action to protest Woolworth's discriminatory policy. Blair, an accomplished and charismatic leader, rallied students on campus to support the effort. With Blair and McCain serving as spokesmen, the students organized the Student Executive Committee for Justice (SECJ). Gloria Brown of Bennett College served as cochair of SECJ along with Ernest Pitts from North Carolina A&T. This new organization coordinated student protest efforts by informing students of the demonstrations, recruiting new members, and coordinating carpools.[40]

The next day, approximately sixty to sixty-five students returned to Woolworth; they, too, were refused service. Later that afternoon, the manager closed the lunch counter to customers.[41] By Thursday, February 4, the students began occupying seats at Kress. The protest had grown into a mass movement. Students from the Woman's College of the University of North Carolina, Greensboro College, Guilford College, and Bennett College joined the protest efforts. On Saturday, February 6, a bomb scare caused the managers of Kress and Woolworth to close their stores; however, no bomb was found.[42] By the following week, the sit-in demonstrations had spread to every major city in North Carolina. NAACP college chapters at Winston-Salem Teachers College (Winston-Salem), Johnson C. Smith University (Charlotte), North Carolina College (Durham), Fayetteville State Teachers College (Fayetteville), Shaw University (Raleigh), St. Augustine College (Raleigh), Barber-Scotia College (Concord), and Elizabeth City State Teachers College (Elizabeth City) targeted chain stores such as Woolworth, Kress, Hudson-Belk, W. T. Grant, H. L. Green, and Walgreens. Additionally, twenty-six black students at William Penn High School in High Point, North Carolina staged a sit-in demonstration at Woolworth.[43] Protest demonstrations in these other cities were also influenced by the Greensboro sit-in and were spontaneous.

On February 13, the North Carolina State Conference called a meeting of all students and student leaders to discuss the sit-in demonstrations; however, a snowstorm forced the cancellation of the meeting. Three days later, CORE and SCLC called a meeting in Durham, offering advice and support to students and their leaders involved in the sit-ins. At the meeting, NAACP national youth director, Herbert Wright, conveyed that the students had the NAACP's full support as well. Following the meeting, Wright met informally with youth leaders of NAACP college chapters, assuring them that the NAACP would provide legal counsel and bail.[44] After they departed from the meeting, the students went back to their cities and tried to negotiate with store managers, to no avail. As a result, they resumed their protests. When the managers of these chain stores realized that the protest had crystallized into a mass movement, some stores temporarily closed or removed their seats; others kept their counters open but posted signs that read "For Employees and Their Guests."[45] On February 21, at the behest of the mayor, college officials, and local merchants, the students at North Carolina A&T called a truce so that city officials could work out a plan to end discrimination in the city.[46] However, negotiations fell through because local merchants refused to desegregate their lunch counters. As in Greensboro, students in other cities refused to accept an agreement that did not bring about complete desegregation.

As sit-in demonstrations accelerated, many southern governors ordered presidents of state colleges and universities to take action against students who participated in these events, which resulted in the expulsion of some students. In March 1960, North Carolina governor, Luther H. Hodges, issued an order to presidents of the state colleges and universities to prevent their students from participating in sit-ins because they threatened "peace and good order."[47] Because of pressure from governors and other state lawmakers—and the fear of losing state funds and their jobs—some presidents took action against students who participated in protest demonstrations. For example, the state board of education "warned all college presidents in Louisiana under its jurisdiction that they are expected to take stern disciplinary action against any student or students involved in incidents which would discredit the institution or the state educational system."[48]

Supporting the governor of Louisiana's mandate to stop the student sit-in demonstrations, Felton G. Clark, president of Southern University in Baton Rouge, expelled seventeen students for their involvement in sit-in demonstrations that had occurred at the Kress store lunch counter, Sitman's Drugstore, and the Greyhound Bus Terminal.[49] Additionally, Donald Moss, NAACP youth field secretary and student leader, was expelled from Southern University Law School because of his participation in sit-in demonstrations.[50] Protesting the expulsion, hundreds of students held a rally on campus and boycotted classes. Although the campus protest demonstrated student solidarity, their actions did not persuade President Clark to change his position on the sit-in demonstrations. Due to Clark's unwillingness to support the sit-in demonstrations, an estimated seven hundred to one thousand students left Southern University.[51]

Although many presidents of state colleges and universities maintained that concern for student safety had influenced their decision to expel students (noting their responsibility to protect students from the violence enacted by segregationists and local police who were adamant about preserving Jim Crow practices), fear of losing state funds and their jobs had most directly influenced their decision. Before the 1960 spring semester ended, thirty NAACP student leaders had been expelled from various schools in the South.[52] Commenting on the sit-in demonstrations, Roy Wilkins, NAACP executive secretary, remarked, "The students who sat on the stools of Woolworth's and other variety stores forced the nation, by this simple act, to take a new look at the old race problem. Basically, their protest is one against the long denial of civil and human rights, a denial that has been calculated and cynical on the political civil rights front."[53] The expulsion of Moss, and of countless other students from state colleges and universities across the South, revealed that black administrators were more concerned with preserving their jobs and funds for the universities than with protecting the rights of the youth protestors. Activism by these young people against white supremacy practices in the South helped to dramatize the socioeconomic inequalities and racial conditions from which blacks had long suffered.

Supporting the protest efforts of the students, the NAACP—with the assistance of the National Scholarship Service and the Fund for Negro Students (NSSFNS)—helped the expelled students enroll in other schools. Founded in 1948, the goal of NSSFNS was to increase opportunities for blacks to attend white schools. By the 1960s, it expanded services to include predominately black colleges and universities.[54] Through the NSSFNS, nine of the thirty student leaders who had been expelled from various colleges that spring semester were awarded scholarships totaling $5,450 Donald Moss, who had been expelled from Southern University Law School, was accepted into Howard University Law School and was awarded one thousand dollars toward his education.[55]

Whereas presidents at state colleges were threatened with the loss of state funding for allowing students to participate in sit-in demonstrations, presidents of private colleges and universities had more leeway to publicly support the sit-ins. The major source of funding for private colleges and universities did not come from the state government and state boards of education, and governors had less influence over these presidents' jobs. They did, however, face the possibility of sacrificing financial contributions from wealthy white donors because of their support of the sit-in demonstrations. When the sit-in demonstrations started in Nashville, Tennessee, the president of Fisk University, Stephen J. Wright, declared, "I approve the ends our students are seeking by these demonstrations. From all I have been able to learn they have broken no law by the means they have employed, and they have not only conducted themselves peaceably, but with poise and dignity."[56] Wright further maintained that their actions merely reflected their desire to enjoy the benefits of first-class citizenship. He contended, "[T]hey have been exposed all their lives to the teachings of the great American scriptures of democracy, freedom and equality, and no literate person should be surprised that they reflect these teachings in their conduct.[57]

Presidents of other private colleges and universities in the South shared Wright's sentiments. In October 1960, for example, the presidents of Atlanta University Center (which consisted of Morehouse College, Spelman College, Morris Brown College, Clark College, Atlanta University, and Interdenominational Theological Center) supported the student sit-in demonstrations at department stores in downtown Atlanta. James P. Brawley, president of Clark College, maintained, "We encouraged them, because we [the presidents] knew the best way to handle the situation of this kind was to assure the students that we were as much interested in what they were doing to bring about change as they were."[58] Harry V. Richardson, president of the Interdenominational Theological Center, expressed similar sentiments: "The general feeling among the presidents was that this was a justifiable cause, that the students were taking part in the push for civil rights to break down Southern segregation from which we all suffered."[59] Although student demonstrators from private colleges and universities had more support from their administrators, the combined efforts of students from private and public colleges and universities broke down the strictures of Jim Cow segregation in the South.

By April 1960, student protest demonstrations had spread to fifty-eight cities across the South, including fourteen states and the District of Columbia. At a student program at Fisk University in April 1960, Thurgood Marshall declared that the "whole force of the NAACP" supported the student efforts in the sit-in demonstrations that had spread across the South. He further maintained that the NAACP had raised as much as $150,000 in bond money for the student demonstrators. Marshall believed, "If we don't have enough lawyers or money we'll get more."[60] Praising the actions of the students, he further stated, "This is not just a protest to get a hamburger and a cup of coffee, both sides know it. It is a protest against the whole vicious system of segregation in the South."[61] Twenty nine of the sit-ins were staged by NAACP youth chapters. As result of the demonstrations, 1,306 students had been arrested, with fines totaling $103,400.[62] The NAACP state conferences provided legal counsel and bail for the vast majority of the students arrested.[63] Northern NAACP youth groups also supported southern sit-in demonstrations by raising funds to assist with legal defenses. For example, the Oberlin College NAACP Chapter raised $2,790 to assist the Southern Christian Leadership Conference (SCLC) with legal aid and bail for the Nashville students. The Washington University NAACP Chapter raised $410, which was divided between CORE and the NAACP.[64]

Throughout the South, protest demonstrations continued, slowing down only during examination periods and semester break; however, many high school students (belonging to youth councils) continued the demonstrations during their summer vacation. Such was the case in Greensboro and Durham.[65] By May 1960, many more department stores had ended their segregation policies. For example, in North Carolina, chain stores such as Woolworth and Kress ended segregated dining in Winston-Salem, Charlotte, Greensboro, High Point, and Durham.[66]

Sit-in demonstrations were not the only activities undertaken by NAACP youth councils and college chapters. The youth organizations launched selective buying campaigns and wade-ins at local beaches. During the summer of 1960, the Lincoln University NAACP Chapter in Jefferson City, Missouri, conducted a successful "Selective Buying Campaign" against Landwehr and Central dairies, companies that only employed blacks as janitors. After a ten-day protest, the dairies integrated their entire staff.[67] On August 28, the Kansas City, Missouri, Youth Council protest demonstrations were successful in getting the Kansas City Merchants Association to desegregate two hundred businesses. The youth council staged a "stand-in" at movie theaters in the downtown area that required blacks to be seated in the balcony. As a result of the "stand-in," thirteen major theaters desegregated, including Fox, Paramount, and Movietone in downtown Kansas City. The Kansas City Youth Council's "Don't Buy Where You Can't Work" campaign resulted in twenty-five blacks being employed at the Hallmark Greeting Card Company. Youth council members, in conjunction with the Kansas City NAACP branch, succeeded in getting the Kansas City Transit Authority to employ fourteen black bus drivers.[68]

Although the selective buying campaigns were successful, many wade-ins were not. That August, the Savannah, Georgia, Youth Council conducted a wade-in. Local police arrested ten council members and charged them with "disrobing in public, incitement to riot, and disturbing the public." After the local judge dropped two of the charges, the youths were fined fifty-four dollars for disorderly conduct.[69] NAACP youth groups from Charleston, Columbia, and Orangeburg, South Carolina attempted to conduct a wade-in at Atlantic Beach, South Carolina, but local authorities prohibited them from entering the beach. When students attempted to use facilities at Myrtle Beach, the local police also turned them away.[70]

By the end of 1960, sit-ins had been conducted in 156 cities and fifteen southern states. Most of these sit-in demonstrations were "organized, led, and directed by NAACP youth and college units."[71] Some 2,089 students had been arrested and fined a total of $128,400. Attorneys provided by NAACP local branches and state and regional conferences represented most of the students arrested. Additionally, "officers, members, and friends of the association have provided most of the bail money used to secure the release of those students who have been arrested."[72] Furthermore, administrators expelled six high school students and forty-three college students because of their participation in sit-in demonstrations. However, businesses in 116 cities throughout the United States were completely desegregated as a result of the students' efforts.[73] Certainly, young people within the youth councils and college chapters conducted most of these sit-in demonstrations. Membership in the NAACP Youth and College Division increased dramatically, from 27,430 during 1959 to roughly 46,789 in 1960.[74] Referring to the protest demonstrations, National Youth Director, Herbert Wright, commented, "1960 may well be called the 'Year of the Youth.' Without a doubt the most important event to take place in domestic affairs during the past year was the history-making revolt of thousands of southern Negro youths against discrimination and jim crow [sic]" in public accommodations and employment.[75] That year, the White House Conference on Children and Youth declared civil rights the number one issue facing the nation for the decade (1960–1970) and passed a resolution supporting the sit-in demonstrations.[76] Through mass action, NAACP youth chapters added an important and new dimension to the struggle for racial equality in the United States.

Although it was the "Year of the Youth," 1960 was overshadowed by malicious acts of violence. In March 1960, in Houston, Texas, twenty-seven-year-old Felton Turner was abducted at gunpoint from a street near his home and taken to "a desolate spot near an abandoned oil field," where he was brutally beaten.[77] He pleaded for his life, asking why he was being beaten. Turner's abductors told him that they had been paid to beat him up to show NAACP youth protestors what would happen to them if they did not stop the sit-in protests in the South. Dragged across a field and hung upside down by his feet from a tree, Turner saw his life flash before him. After the perpetrators left the scene, miraculously, he was able to free himself and "walk to a nearby shack where a night watchman called the police for him."[78] Though the incident was reported to local police, the perpetrators were never prosecuted. Turner's ordeal represented the violent resistance of white segregationists to blacks' demands for racial integration. As black youth began to challenge white supremacist practices in the South, many activists suffered violence at the hands of whites who were willing to resort to any measure to maintain the racial status quo. At the time of this malicious act against Turner, the NAACP national youth director, Herbert Wright, was at Texas Southern University in Houston meeting with protest leaders who organized sit-in demonstrations to confront the Jim Crow practices in that city. By attacking Felton Turner, white racists hoped to discourage the protest demonstrations orchestrated by NAACP youth.

That same month, students from South Carolina State and Claflin Colleges, headed by NAACP chapters, staged protest demonstrations against segregated facilities. The sit-in demonstrations initiated by college students during the 1960s in Orangeburg, South Carolina were influenced by a rich protest tradition among black South Carolinians that dated back to the 1950s. Black South Carolinians organized "Don't Buy Where You Can't Work" campaigns and consumer boycotts of businesses that reinforced Jim Crow practices of southern society and did not employ blacks. Historian Peter Lau maintains that in Orangeburg blacks boycotted businesses "owned by Citizens' Council members, but they also called for broader boycotts of national brand-name products sold by the leaders of massive resistance."[79] Blacks boycotted the local Coca-Cola bottling company, Palmetto Bakery, Orangeburg Fuel and Ice, and other brand names, such as Sunbeam Bread, Standard Oil, Ford Motor Company, the Lance Company (which makes "Nabs"), the Curtis Company (which makes "Baby Ruth" candy bars), and Lays. The boycott received national black press coverage and support from the NAACP. According to Lau, the consumer boycott in Orangeburg inspired leaders of the Montgomery Bus Boycott, as boycott leaders from Orangeburg traveled to Montgomery to discuss their experiences.[80]

During the winter of 1955–1956, the Orangeburg consumer boycott, backed by the NAACP, compelled students at South Carolina State to support the campaign. Students initiated a boycott of Palmetto Bakery and Coble Dairy because of their racially discriminatory practices and refused to eat the bread and drink the milk supplied to the school cafeteria by these businesses. As one of their demands, the students at South Carolina State asked university officials to stop patronizing Palmetto Bakery and Coble Dairy. When the administration resisted, students boycotted the cafeteria. State officials considered the students' activities subversive, and a probe was launched to investigate the matter. Faculty members backed the students and "endorsed resolutions defending their academic freedom and right to support the NAACP."[81] Lau noted, "In response to the increasingly aggressive state investigation into subversive activities, 1,500 students boycotted classes and demanded the removal of state law enforcement officials."[82] Although student expulsions followed, "the student and faculty actions pointed toward the increasing significance of the university in the battles ahead, as well as the emergence of a new cohort of activists enrolled in the region's black colleges."[83]

When they staged sit-in demonstrations against the segregated businesses in the city, the students at South Carolina State were operating from a rich protest tradition established in the black community in Orangeburg, South Carolina. Shortly after the Greensboro sit-in demonstrations, students at South Carolina State launched sit-ins at Kress. Among the student leaders of the protest was Julie Wright, secretary of the South Carolina Student Movement and South Carolina State NAACP Youth Conference, and Charles McDew (who would later become of the chairman of the SNCC).[84] Using high-pressured water hoses and tear gas, the local police attacked Wright and 487 students. During the melee, a seventeen-year-old blind girl from South Carolina State was knocked to the ground by the high-pressured water hoses. The police rounded up the protestors and placed them in stockades for two and a half hours before they were released on bail.[85] The following day, a mass rally was held in the auditorium at Claflin College. Speaking at the mass meeting, Herbert Wright proclaimed,

> I am deeply hurt and embarrassed that a group of grown men
> who profess to be intelligent, civilized, human beings, would
> use a high pressure fire hose to subdue and beat to the ground
> by force of the water, a blind, helpless, 17-year-old Negro coed.
> . . . I am ashamed that this display of brutality can take place in
> the United States today with apparent impunity under the guise
> of law enforcement, which is nothing more than a euphemism
> or local expression for "keep the Negroes in their place." . . .
> The handwriting is clearly on the wall. The winds of change are
> blowing not alone across the face of Asia and Africa, but also the
> South of the United States.[86]

From the protest demonstrations during the 1960s, the students at South Carolina State and Claflin College were not the only protestors to suffer extreme violence at the hands of the police. Indeed, the ordeals experienced by Felton Turner and by South Carolina State and Claflin College students exposed the pervasive violence used throughout the South against those seeking to secure first-class citizenship and end segregation.

As civil rights protest demonstrations accelerated in the South, in March 1961 more than one hundred students from Benedict College and Stark Theological Seminary participated in sit-in demonstrations in Columbia, South Carolina, to desegregate public facilities. Julie Wright, who headed up sit-in demonstrations in Orangeburg, South Carolina, assisted David Carter, president of the Benedict College NAACP Intercollegiate Chapter, with organizing and planning the demonstrations. Students staged demonstrations at several stores, including Eckard's Pharmacy, the only store to request that police arrest the protestors. Protesting the arrests of the demonstrators, students picketed at the jail. As a result, the police arrested an additional thirteen students for blocking the sidewalk in front of the jail. The Columbia, South Carolina, NAACP posted bail for the young people who were arrested.[87]

During those peaceful demonstrations in Columbia, twenty-four-year-old Lenny Glover, an NAACP student leader, was severely stabbed by a white assailant. Glover was rushed to the local hospital, and Dr. C. O. Spann performed an emergency operation on the pretheology student from Benedict College. Dr. Spann assessed that the student's condition was "grave and could have been fatal."[88] Not allowing this incident to discourage their efforts, and spearheaded by the Benedict College NAACP Intercollegiate Chapter, more than two hundred students protested the state's discriminatory policy in employment and public accommodations. Youth from eight cities in South Carolina descended upon the state capitol. Harry C. Walker, legal assistant to the governor, "told the students that they could walk around the capitol 'like anybody else' but that if larger groups marched, it would be considered a demonstration."[89] The local police told the student protestors that they had fifteen minutes to disperse. Disobeying the police orders, the students continued to march. As a result, mass arrests took place. Those arrested were taken to the courthouse in Columbia. Seventeen-year-old Frederick Hart, a white freshman from the University of South Carolina, reached over to shake the hand of one of the black protesters in the police car. When the police saw him, he was asked if he was a member of the NAACP. He responded, "I have just joined." Hart was immediately arrested. The NAACP posted $10,000 in bond for the release of the students, who spent the night in jail. Among other NAACP leaders who were arrested was Reverend I. DeQuincey Newman, field secretary for South Carolina. Protesting the arrests, Roy Wilkins, executive director of the NAACP, sent a message to Governor Ernest F. Hollings pointing out that the arrests were unwarranted. He reminded the governor that "the rights of free speech, peaceful assembly and petition of redress of grievances are all guaranteed by the Constitution."[90]

As the NAACP youth movement accelerated during the 1960s, the NAACP hired summer youth field secretaries (many of whom were student protest leaders) to organize new NAACP youth councils and college chapters in the South. As a result of the youth field secretaries' work, the association's youth work spread to small towns, where previous NAACP organizing efforts had been met with reservation. Among the student leaders chosen as field youth secretaries was Julie Wright. Having gained valuable organizing experience as a student leader of the South Carolina State NAACP chapter and the South Carolina Student Movement, she was well prepared to assist the association in breaking down the restrictions of Jim Crow segregation. During the summer of 1960, Wright organized youth councils in small towns throughout South Carolina, such as Bennettsville, Seneca, Sumter, and Manning.[91] Because her work impressed the association so much, she was offered permanent employment. Commenting on Wright's work in a memorandum to Wilkins, Gloster Current, director of branches, stated, "[S]he would make a worthwhile addition to our staff, since she has shown by her diligence and ability that she understands youth work and is able to carry it out effectively."[92]

In January 1961, Wright, who graduated summa cum laude from Claflin College, was appointed youth field secretary for the southeast region to work with Ruby Hurley in advancing the NAACP's youth work in that region. Having succeeded Lois Baldwin (three years later), she became the second woman appointed youth field secretary in the southeast region. Wright's position involved a great deal of travel and personal sacrifice. Serving until 1963, Wright organized one of the most dynamic youth movements in the southeast region.[93] Although Wright was assigned to organize NAACP youth groups throughout the southeast region and to coordinate direct action programs in these communities, her task was most challenging in rural areas. In many of these places, the work of the association was limited and black citizens feared reprisals from local authorities; however, not all black citizens in rural communities allowed threat and/or acts of intimidation to deter their protest against segregated facilities.

In June 1961, Wright traveled to her hometown of Summerville, South Carolina, to assist the youth with their direct action program. In Summerville, the NAACP branch was not very active, nor had it encouraged its members to stage direct action demonstration. Having a population of four thousand people (45 percent black and 55 percent white), Summerville had seen its share of racial violence. Under Sheriff H. H. Jessen's administration, whites had killed six blacks and the local authorities had done nothing. Julie Wright contended, "The town's authorities have been too content with killing Negroes without reason, mobbing some and beating others."[94] Local authorities intimidated black residents if they protested traditional practices; as a result, some black residents were afraid to protest against segregation practices in the town, and the parents did not want their children participating in protest activities.[95]

Although she grew up in Summerville, Julie Wright did not adopt the mentality of the local residents. Having been involved in protest demonstrations while at South Carolina State, she was not afraid to protest the town's discriminatory practices. Despite some reservations from the parents, in June 1960, a youth council was formed, and its membership grew to fifty youths. Gloria Livingston, a sophomore at Alston High School, served as the president of the Summerville Youth Council. Although it had been in existence for a year, the youth council had not carried on any direct action programs against racial segregation in the town. Since March 1961, when Julie Wright counseled youth council members about a direct action program at a South Carolina State Rally sponsored by the NAACP, parents of the youth and other adults had intimidated them. Parents had reservations about Wright's advice to the youth about how to carry out a direct action program to confront racial barriers that relegated them to second-class citizens. At that time, the young people agreed to plan a read-in at the municipal library, the only library in the small town—and it was for whites only. Wright moved ahead with plans to protest the white-only public library in spite of parents' reservations. She asserted, "The demonstration, at that time, was planned against the Municipal Library. There is only one library in this small town supported by tax funds, which is 'for whites only.' The adults frowned upon any such idea and refused to let it happen."[96]

Hoping to get support for another demonstration that June, Wright organized a plan to protest the discriminatory practices at Simmons Pharmacy. Supporting Wright's plan, Lucius High, a graduate of Claflin College and chemistry teacher at Alston High School, helped to organize the protest. High was eager to participate, because he and his wife bought all of their pharmaceutical supplies from the pharmacy. However, when parents learned about the possible sit-in demonstration, they refused to let their children participate. As before, parents interfered, and the plan was thwarted.[97]

On June 29, a special meeting was held to discuss the Red & White Grocery Store's discriminatory hiring policy. A survey conducted by two youth council members, Gloria Livingston and Melba Varner, revealed that 70 percent of the store's customers was black.[98] Wright believed that the youth council should boycott the store. At the meeting, one youth told her that their parents did not support the boycott against the grocery store. Wright asserted, "At Saturday's meeting everyone showed up. A damper had been placed on the Employment Program by parents who told their children that they were not hungry and could be supported, that they needed not to look for work."[99] A few parents sent their daughters to tell the NAACP youth field secretary Julie Wright that the "NAACP does not tell them where to shop and until [the] NAACP opens its own stores, they will shop where they wanted to."[100] Even after learning of the grocery store's discriminatory practices, local black patrons still would not boycott it.

At that same meeting, however, Summerville Youth Council members did renew their efforts to lead a sit-in demonstration at Simmons Pharmacy to protest its segregated lunch counter. The renewed spirit was provoked when several youth council members were discriminated against when they ordered soda pop at the lunch counter. One Sunday afternoon, Sandra Washington walked into Simmons Pharmacy and ordered a Coca-Cola and then sat down on one of the stools at the lunch counter. The waitress "snapped her fingers and said 'up-up-up;' you know you aren't suppose to sit there." Meanwhile, other youth council members entered and ordered sodas. Despite the discrimination, they all paid for their drinks. Having thought about the mistreatment, Washington decided to return her soda. After they all left, the waitress slammed the door behind them. When the youth informed Julie Wright of what happened, she told them that they should not have paid for their drinks, and that "the whole incident was nothing more than a demonstration." She also told the youth that a mass picketing of the business should have taken place to protest such humiliating treatment, and that the black community should initiate a mass program of "withholding of patronage."[101]

Heeding Wright's advice, youth council members planned to demonstrate on July 2 to protest the pharmacy's discriminatory practices. The day before the demonstration, the youth met to rehearse. According to the plan, only four students would sit at the lunch counter—Gloria Livingston, Donald Varner, the youth council's vice president, and Allen McClellan. The other six students would act as observers. Only the four students at the lunch counter would submit to arrest, if necessary. In the event of arrests, Charles Ross, president of the Summerville NAACP branch, would secure bondsmen. Picketing of the pharmacy would not stop until the store changed its segregation policy. Wright believed she had devised a solid plan to end the discriminatory practices at Simmons pharmacy.

That Sunday, July 2, the youths met at Wright's father's store around 3:30 p.m., thirty minutes before the demonstration was to take place, to organize themselves. "When everything was in order and just before the young people were on their way," Gloria Livingston yelled out that she could not participate. By that time, her father had walked in, along with Julie Wright's father. Wright contended that the men said nothing "but showed their superiority."[102] Pushed to the limits and disappointed that the demonstration did not happen, Wright decided to call a meeting with the parents and the Summerville Branch president at her father's store that same day. At the meeting, the parents claimed that they did not know anything about the planned demonstrations. Many of the youth claimed that their mothers knew, but their fathers did not, because their fathers would emphatically reject such actions. Protesting the parents' timidity and strictness, Wright told them that they could not keep their kids tied to "their apron string." She pointed out the numerous injustices that local blacks had endured and urged the parents to take a stand. For example, Wright noted how W. B. Etheridge, owner of the Etheridge Food Store, had made "many successful attempts to seduce and pet" teenage black girls. She also pointed out that Etheridge had slapped two blacks in his store, and that his son had killed a black person. However, no justice had been sought in either of these incidents.[103] In spite of all these horrible acts, blacks still patronized his business. Wright believed there was an urgent need for blacks in Summerville to throw off their timid and fearful mindsets.

After much discussion, the youth and the adults finally reached common ground, agreeing that the branch would organize a committee that would hold talks with the mayor (a die-hard segregationist) about ending segregation in all public places. If the mayor refused, then youth would hold demonstrations. Although local black residents and the Summerville NAACP Branch agreed to the plan, it was not carried out.[104] The struggle that NAACP youth field secretary Julie Wright experienced in Summerville to get parents to cooperate with the youth in direct action campaigns against racism in that town reflected the repression and fear of reprisals that blacks endured throughout the South. In many instances, blacks feared the loss of employment—and life. Although Wright's father owned a grocery store, many rural blacks were economically dependant and had little access to equal educational opportunities. To make matters worse, local authorities often disregarded many injustices that blacks suffered and were even, at times, responsible for supporting mob action against blacks who decided to challenge the status quo.

As civil rights activities spread across the South, blacks in Clarksdale, Mississippi, mobilized against Jim Crow and discriminatory hiring practices. The black organizing tradition against the white supremacy practices in Clarksdale dates back to 1940s, with the creation of Progressive Voters' League. After the Supreme Court had outlawed the all-white Democratic primary in *Smith v. Allwright,* blacks organized the League to initiate a voter registration campaign to register blacks. After serving in the military during WWII, Aaron Henry returned to Clarksdale in 1946 and began working with the League. Henry encouraged black residents to register and to vote. Henry wrote, "As soon as I got home I began trying to get Negroes to go down to the courthouse to register to vote."[105] Learning from white military veterans that veterans were exempted from paying the poll tax, he tried to register to vote. Each time Henry tried to register to vote, the clerk turned him away. He soon learned that he was being denied this right solely because of his race. The clerk allowed the white veteran men to register to vote and gave them a certificate showing that they were exempted from paying the poll tax. Having obtained the certificate from one of the veterans, he showed it to the clerk and was finally allowed to register to vote. Aaron Henry bragged that he was the first black in Coahoma County to vote in the Democratic primary. Not only did Henry vote, but also other black residents in Clarksdale.[106]

Although it experienced success in this area, the Progressive Voters' League lacked the financial resources to become a dominant civil rights organization in Clarksdale. The same was true for the Regional Council of Negro Leadership (RCNL), which set up voter registration drives and a voter education program to help blacks pass the literacy exam to vote. The League and the RCNL did not have the national influence or the financial resources that the NAACP could harness. In 1951, after the justice of peace court exonerated two white men who had raped two young black women at gunpoint, black residents in Clarksdale were outraged by the verdict. In response to the injustice, they organized a local NAACP branch. Henry said, "We were disappointed in the outcome of this case, but it had become clear that Negroes in Clarksdale needed broader legal protection. . . . we decided to organize an NAACP branch in Clarksdale."[107] Having returned to Clarksdale in 1950, after graduating from pharmacy school at Xavier University in New Orleans, Louisiana, Henry, now a licensed pharmacist, was determined to destroy the racial barriers in his city. He, like other black WWII veterans, was determined to make democracy work and would accept nothing less. Henry was elected president of the local branch, and Medgar Evers, who would later become a field secretary, was one of the branch's most dedicated members.[108]

Under Henry's leadership, black residents mobilized against the white supremacy practices in the city. One of the most tragic episodes in Clarksdale was the 1951 murder of Denzill Turner, an epileptic, by the local police. Turner and his father had gone to the bus station to pick up his brother. While at the bus station, Turner had a seizure, which caused him to "flounder around on the pavement outside the station."[109] Unaware that Turner was epileptic, local whites alerted the manager that a black man was drunk outside of the station. When the manager finally asked Turner why he was at the bus station, the seizure had passed, and Turner told the manager that it was none of his business, because he was not trying to purchase a ticket. Infuriated by Turner's remarks, the manager called the police and told them that an intoxicated black man at the bus station was grabbing white women. Turner's father tried to explain that his son was epileptic and was not in his right state of mind; however, the medical condition of Turner's son did not matter. When the police arrived, the father made further attempts to explain his son's health condition, but the police refused to listen. As the police attempted to arrest Turner, he resisted. The struggle ended with one of the officers shooting Turner in the head. Although the local black community was mortified and demanded justice, the local court exonerated the police officers because they claimed they had killed Turner in self-defense. In a meeting with the mayor and chief of police, Henry remarked that Turner had been killed because he was black. His outspokenness about the young man's death caused local authorities to label him as a rabble-rouser and a Communist. After an investigation, the Communist allegation was dropped.[110] This charge was commonly made against blacks who challenged the white power structure or spoke out against the racial injustices.

After the 1954 *Brown* decision, NAACP chapters in Mississippi filed petitions for school desegregation. Henry mobilized local black citizens in Clarksdale to sign a petition supporting school desegregation. More than four hundred black residents signed the petition, which was sent to the school. To Henry's surprise, the local newspaper published the names of those who had signed the petition. Through the Citizens Council, which was organized after the *Brown* ruling, whites retaliated against blacks who supported school desegregation. Black residents in Clarksdale experienced economic reprisals and physical intimidation. Many lost their jobs, and others fled the state.[111] Although the NAACP came under fierce attack and school desegregation efforts

"More Than a Hamburger and a Cup of Coffee"

dragged on until the 1960s, Henry continued to fight against Mississippi's repressive regime.

Adults in Clarksdale mobilized against the city's white supremacy practices, and so did the youth. On July 19, 1961, Helen Anderson participated in a protest demonstration in front of the Mississippi State Capitol in Jackson. NAACP youth council members decided to picket the legislative session. On July 22, Helen's mother and a few other workers were laid off from Superior Laundry for a period of two weeks because of a loss in business. However, when the employees did return to work, Mrs. Anderson was the only one not recalled. Anderson concluded that this reprisal was a direct result of her daughter's demonstration, and the Coahoma County NAACP Branch agreed. Supporting Mrs. Anderson's cause, the executive committee of the branch orchestrated a series of telephone calls to Gerald Commander, owner of Superior Laundry.[112] NAACP youth field secretary Julie Wright made the first call to Commander, expressing discontent about his actions toward Mrs. Anderson. During the telephone conversation, he expressed no regrets for firing Mrs. Anderson. Not knowing that he would be inundated with calls, the owner went to Aaron Henry, who was now president of the Mississippi State Conference and chairman of the Coahoma County Council of Federated Organizations, to find out what he could do to fix the situation, because 50 percent of his patrons was from the black community. Henry expressed Commander's concern to the executive committee. It was agreed that a conference would be held with Mrs. Anderson and the owner. In the interim, Commander asked Mrs. Anderson to work temporarily for an employee who was out due to illness. Anderson refused—so Commander decided not to attend the conference meeting. Supporting Mrs. Anderson's actions, the branch organized a boycott against the laundry and many blacks withdrew their patronage.[113]

Although the NAACP did not officially endorse the Freedom Rides, the NAACP's young people did challenge segregation practices in travel. In fact, several college students tested the Interstate Commerce Commission's ruling when they traveled home for the summer break by train or bus. For example, David Carter and Lennis Glover, student leaders of the Columbia NAACP Intercollegiate Chapter, were the first two blacks served at the Greyhound Restaurant in Charleston, South Carolina. Additionally, Amos Brown, who attended Morehouse College in Atlanta, Georgia, rode the train without incident from Atlanta to Jackson, Mississippi, until he reached Meridian, Mississippi.[114]

In August 1961, at the request of the Coahoma County NAACP Branch and Youth Council, Wright traveled to Clarksdale, Mississippi to assist the Clarksdale community with its direct action program against the segregated train station. On August 20, a meeting was held in the home of Vera Pigee, Coahoma Branch secretary and youth advisor, with youth council members and parents. At the meeting, they discussed that youth council members would stage a protest demonstration against the Illinois Central Railroad Company. That Wednesday, August 23, Mari June Pigee, Wilma Smith, and Adrian Beard attempted to purchase tickets from Clarksdale to Memphis, Tennessee in the "whites only" waiting room at the train station. They were refused service and later arrested by the local police. The youth council members were charged with "breach of the peace," and each was placed under a $500 bond. On Thursday, August 24, Aaron Henry called on black residents in Clarksdale to participate in a "Selective Buying" campaign so that the whites would know that the black community supported the youth demonstration against the Illinois Central Railroad Company.[115]

That same year, after blacks had been denied participation in the Christmas parade, the Coahoma County NAACP branch launched a boycott of all downtown stores in Clarksdale. Traditionally, "two black marching bands from the local high school and Coahoma Junior College had participated in the annual Clarksdale Christmas parade."[116] The mayor's decision crushed the holiday spirit of black youth and other black residents who participated in the parade every year. Henry maintained, "We were affronted by the mayor's edict. We had joined in the parade for years, and there seemed to be no reason for the decision. Apparently, he resented the progress that we were making all over the state." Angry and disappointed, the students wanted to demonstrate at city hall, but Aaron Henry dissuaded them, because he and other local black leaders did not have enough money to post bail if they were arrested.[117] Instead, the local NAACP organized a boycott of downtown stores under the banner "If we can't parade downtown, we won't trade downtown."[118] Young people, mostly connected with the youth council, were at the forefront of the demonstrations. Black residents wanted department stores to hire blacks for positions other than service jobs and to use courtesy titles when addressing black customers. After the boycott had commenced, Henry was asked by a local attorney Thomas H. Pearson to call off the demonstrations because they were illegal. Refusing to honor Pearson's request, he and seven other leaders of the boycott were arrested on trumped-up charges. After their release from jail, they resumed the boycott. As the boycott progressed, local white merchants began to feel the pressure. Using the selective buying campaign as a means to stop discrimination in public accommodations, Clarksdale residents boycotted businesses that did not offer blacks first-class treatment. The youth councils and the local branch's active stance against segregation and discriminatory practices signaled the importance of a community effort to create change.

As the boycott progressed, Henry was able to garner support from other black civil rights organizations, such as SNCC, CORE, SCLC, and other local black civil rights groups. Wanting the boycott to remain solely an NAACP endeavor, the national office chastised Henry for forming alliances with other civil rights organizations, because it did not want the other groups to get recognition for a campaign started by the Coahoma County NAACP Branch.[119] By spring of 1963, black residents in Clarksdale were demanding full integration of businesses and public facilities. Resisting their demands, whites orchestrated violence and physical intimidation against local black citizens. Henry's Pharmacy was vandalized, and his home was bombed. Youth council advisor Vera Pigee was severely beaten by a white service station attendant when she attempted to use a "white only" restroom and was later jailed for disturbing the peace.[120] Violence against the local black leaders of the boycott starkly revealed the unwillingness of the local white leaders to negotiate—and their brutal determination to break the will of black residents. On June 12, local authorities rejected the protestors' request to establish a biracial committee to reach a peaceful settlement. In response, blacks launched a series of sit-ins and other demonstrations against the downtown businesses. John Dittmer asserts, "Local blacks set up picket lines at city hall, the public library, the circuit clerk's office, and at the Southern Bell telephone office to protest unfair hiring practices." During August 1963, "nearly 100 protestors had been arrested" for violating a court-ordered injunction that prohibited demonstrations in the downtown area.[121] Despite violence, jail time, and physical intimidation, the protestors did not lose faith—but the courage and unity of the black community could not compel local white authorities to negotiate. Although it dragged on, the boycott was eventually called off after the passage of the 1964 Civil Rights Act, which outlawed discrimination in public accommodations. By that time, Henry maintained that blacks had begun to ignore the boycott, and the civil rights bill gave them a "dramatic way of ending it."[122]

The protest demonstrations carried out by the NAACP youth chapters showed how effective direct action tactics could be in helping break down racial barriers that relegated blacks to second-class citizens. Although it banned segregation in public accommodations, the Civil Rights Act of 1964 did not change the attitudes of many white southerners who were determined to maintain white supremacy in the South. In spite of meeting resistance to desegregation, NAACP youth launched rigorous campaigns across the South to dismantle the racial barriers that barred them from first-class citizenship.

Chapter Six

"And If Not Now, When?"
Securing Our Freedom

In 1962, after Herbert Wright had resigned to accept a position with higher pay with a newly formed foundation, the NAACP Youth and College Division named its new director. He had served ten years as national youth director.[1] Born in Cool Springs, Mississippi, in July 1934, Laplois Ashford was appointed in September 1962 to be the fifth national youth director of the NAACP Youth and College Division. His previous activism through the Rochester, New York, Youth Council as vice president and youth advisor made him well acquainted with the youth work of the NAACP.[2]

Committed to advancing the aims of the association, Ashford propelled the Youth and College Division into action. He began by restructuring the Youth and College Division to create its own distinct entity. Ashford stated, "[O]ne of the shortcomings of our youth program seems to be its complete submergence within the structures of the whole Association."[3] He also believed that firmer organization was needed throughout the Youth and College Division. He believed, "In too many youth units there are lackadaisical officers, unqualified and occasionally incompetent youth advisors, as well as apathetic branches."[4] Ashford organized NAACP youth chapters around civil rights problems, initiating direct action tactics when necessary. This chapter discusses the expansion of the NAACP youth movement under the leadership of Laplois Ashford, and the role of specialized NAACP youth task force groups in assisting youth chapters in advancing direct action campaigns to break down racial discrimination in the South. This chapter also examines the conflicts that surfaced between the national office and youth chapters, and the expansion of the NAACP youth work to urban slum areas through the Community Action Program launched by President Lyndon Johnson under the administration of Eugene Hampton.

Under Laplois Ashford's administration, and as a result of his urging, direct action demonstrations by youth councils and college chapters expanded. In November 1962, Ashford experienced firsthand the injustices of Jim Crow. On November 7, he entered the Greyhound Bus Station in Pascagoula, Mississippi. Ashford attempted to buy a ticket in the "whites only" waiting room and proceeded to the ticket counter; however, the clerk told him to go around to the other side. He asked her politely, "Is not this a Greyhound bus station?" Ashford informed the clerk that the Interstate Commerce Commission's ruling had abolished segregation in travel. Nevertheless, the clerk replied that things were done differently at this station. Because Ashford refused to adhere to the policy, the police were called. When the police arrived, they asked him to go around to the other side, but he refused. Ashford was arrested and charged with breach of peace.[5] While he was being booked, the chief of police harassed him extensively. Then, while he was in custody, the police struck him across the chest in an effort to get him to confess to public drunkenness. He was finally released on a $500 bond.[6] As a result of the incident, Ashford wrote to the Greyhound bus company; however, the Greyhound Corporation claimed that the Pascagoula terminal was independently owned. It only sold tickets there. The corporate office merely offered Ashford an apology.[7] Days after the incident, Ashford suffered an ulcerous condition, triggered by the violent trauma he had endured in police custody.[8] Despite this ordeal, Ashford moved the NAACP youth division forward with projects aimed at eliminating segregation in public accommodations.

As civil rights activities accelerated in the South and black youth remained determined to break down the tenets of Jim Crow segregation, the association intensified its organizing efforts through youth task forces. Laplois called for the organization of specialized youth task force groups that were highly trained in nonviolent direct action tactics and dedicated to the work of the NAACP. He maintained, "The Task Force is a team of NAACP youth members who travel to different areas and who are capable of executing every type of civil rights program, such as fund-raising drives, membership drives, direct action, negotiations, strategy conference, handl[ing] complaints of discrimination in all areas, and organiz[ing] an NAACP unit." Assisting the local branches, these youth council members organized mass demonstrations, new youth councils and college chapters, and held membership and fundraising campaigns. Dispatched throughout the South and labeling themselves Commandos, Matadors, and Bravados, each task force team consisted of ten youths and four alternates. Local NAACP branches financed their room and board.[9]

Under the leadership of attorney Floyd McKissick, North Carolina State Conference youth advisor, task force members in North Carolina called themselves the Commandos. That summer the NAACP hired nine NAACP students—including McKissick's son and daughter, Andree and Jocelyn—to served as task force members. They were paid twenty-five dollars a month. Seasoned NAACP activist Arthur Thomas was paid thirty-five dollars a month. These young men and women were chosen because they had distinguished themselves as outstanding leaders in their youth chapters. The youth Commandos launched direct action demonstrations throughout the state against segregated facilities. Commending the work of the task force members, National Youth Director Laplois Ashford wrote, "The work of these youth task forces has thus far been highly successful. The group, which is presently in

"And If Not Now, When?"

North Carolina, has named itself, NAACP Youth Commandos and has set about in a commando fashion." Although the Commandos had success in most cities throughout North Carolina, the group encountered opposition in Monroe, North Carolina. The main goal in Monroe was to organize protest demonstrations against segregated public facilities.[10]

As with many black southerners, black citizens in Monroe did not hesitate to advocate armed resistance to combat organized violence orchestrated by local white residents who were willing to use any tactic to maintain their superior status over them. To protect family and property, some black southerners armed themselves, ready to combat domestic terrorism by the KKK.[11] After WWII, returning black veterans, including Robert Williams, protested second-class citizenship, having risked life and limb fighting a war to preserve democracy abroad. These black veterans were determined to make democracy work in America. During the postwar years, many black veterans would become leaders and organizers of civil rights demonstrations that tackled Jim Crow practices and racial discrimination.

After the *Brown* decision, which outlawed segregation in public education, NAACP chapters across the South came under fierce attack by conservative white southerners and segregationists. The NAACP's demands for racial equality and integration angered many white southerners who tried to discredit it by labeling it a Communist organization. During the 1950s, when the NAACP was witch-hunted by conservative southern politicians and segregationists, membership declined drastically within the organization. Blacks associated with the NAACP suffered economic reprisal or physical intimidation. The Monroe NAACP almost disbanded as a result of these hardships. Nominated by former president Edward Belton to assume leadership of the defunct branch, Robert Williams resurrected and revamped the Monroe NAACP. Historian Marcellus Barksdale asserts, "In an effort to revitalize the Monroe NAACP, Williams went to the people: he recruited in the poolrooms, on the farms, on the street corners, in the cafes and in the private homes of black residents of the city."[12]

Born in Monroe, North Carolina, in 1925, Robert Williams attended public segregated schools. During the 1940s, he moved to Detroit, Michigan, and landed a job at the Ford Motor Company. Despite having a decent job, having grown up in the rural South, Williams did not like Detroit. According to Historian Timothy Tyson, "Williams found the city crowded, harsh, and impersonal."[13] In 1943, eager to leave Detroit, he took a job at the Mare Island Naval Yard in Port Chicago, California. Feeling unwelcome, witnessing racially charged fights in the dormitory where he stayed, and seeing how the police mistreated black workers, Williams decided he did not like California either. After three months in California, he returned to Monroe, North Carolina.[14]

In 1945, he enlisted in the army. He served eighteen months before he was discharged. For a short time, he returned again to Detroit for work. Williams worked for the Cadillac Motor Car Company. However, he did not stay long. In 1949, Williams was let go from Cadillac because of "excessive absenteeism" and insubordination to his supervisors. What really caused him to lose his job was his refusal to put up with the discriminatory treatment he had received from his supervisors. That same year, he and his family returned to Monroe.[15] During the early 1950s, he joined the Marine Corps. Williams's tenure in the Marine Corps was also short. Barksdale maintains, "When he was denied a position with the Information Division of the Marine Corp, for which aptitude tests showed he was well qualified, Williams filed a protest and threatened to take his complaint all the way to Washington. Because of his demand he was discharged from the Marine Corps." After being expelled from the Marine Corps, Williams returned to Monroe and assumed leadership of the Monroe NAACP branch.[16]

Under Williams's leadership, the Monroe branch began to directly challenge the racist practices of local white citizens that relegated blacks to second-class citizenship. Comprised largely of WWII veterans and working-class black residents, the Monroe NAACP did not bow to white supremacy practices in Union County, North Carolina. WWII veterans Woodrow Wilson, B. J. Winfield, John W. McDow, and Dr. Albert Perry and women such as Mabel Williams and Mae Mallory were the backbone of the Monroe NAACP branch. As dedicated supporters, these men and women aided the NAACP president in confronting white supremacy practices in the city. From organizing black youth to protest local segregated recreational facilities to petitioning the local school board to admit his two sons to the all-white East Elementary School and leading young people in sit-in demonstrations and boycotts of businesses that discriminated against black patrons, Williams and the NAACP branch stood at the forefront of change in Monroe.[17] Advocating armed resistance in the face of violence, Williams was viewed as a threat and a menace by whites who opposed racial equality. Because local authorities did not provide equal protection under the law, black citizens in Monroe were forced to take up arms to protect their families and homes from assaults by local white residents and the Ku Klux Klan.

Throughout the South, many blacks who confronted white supremacy suffered physical intimidation, economic reprisal, and death threats from whites who were committed to maintaining the racial status quo. When blacks raised concerns about violence and physical intimidation, which usually occurred after they challenged racially discriminatory practices, local authorities did little to address their problems. In Monroe, several incidents convinced Robert Williams and local black residents that there could be no justice for blacks down in Dixie.

In 1958, eight-year-old David Ezell Simpson and ten-year-old James Hanover Grissom Thompson, two young black boys, were charged with "molesting" three white girls. What was innocent child's play, a kissing game, during which the girls supposedly sat on the laps of black and white boys and kissed them, violated the acknowledged race rules in the South. Rumors surfaced that the black youth had trapped and forced the girls to kiss them in return for their release. One of the white girls, Sissy Sutton, became the face of the so-called "kissing case." Although allegations that the boys had threatened to restrain the girls was false, that the white girls had kissed the black boys at all was enough to enrage the local white community. The stereotypes of black men as hypersexual and rapists were projected onto the young boys accused of assaulting the white girls.[18] After the boys spent several days in jail, the local judge, without sufficient evidence, sentenced Ezell and Thompson to the Morrison Training School for Negroes in Hoffman, North Carolina, for an unspecified term, with the possibility of being released at the age of twenty-one for good behavior.[19]

Seeking legal justice for the young boys, the Monroe NAACP sprang into action. Williams turned to the NAACP national office for assistance, but he received no support. Tyson maintained, "The fact that this was a 'sex case' . . . carried a special set of political risks. The NAACP had consistently distanced itself from interracial sexuality, knowing that the deep-rooted taboo fueled white resistance to its goals."[20] After NAACP executive secretary Roy Wilkins refused to get involved, Williams moved forward to publicize this miscarriage of justice. According to Tyson, he "issued press releases, called television networks, hounded the national wire services, and sent yet another angry telegram to President [Dwight] Eisenhower."[21]

In spite of the lack of support from the national office and opposition from the local white community, Williams succeeded in bringing national and international attention to the young boys' situation. The big break came on December 15, 1958, when the *London News-Chronicle* published the story with a large photo of the two boys in the Morrison reformatory. The "kissing case" made headlines all over Europe and was finally featured in American newspapers. As a result of Williams's activism, the situation in Monroe was no longer a local matter, and the fate of the young boys was not left to local authorities. Although who ordered the young boys' release remains unclear, Williams's ability to bring international and national publicity to the case finally led to Thompson and Simpson's release from the reformatory on February 13, 1959. Although securing their freedom was a victory for the black community, the fight against white supremacist practices in the city had just begun to intensify.[22]

The "kissing case" not only signaled to Williams and black residents in Monroe that they could not depend on the local authorities for justice, but also exposed the appalling reality that assaults against black women by white perpetrators went unprosecuted. Historically, black women have not been afforded the same protection under the law as white women, especially when assaulted by white men. Because white racists perpetuated notions of black women and black men as hypersexual and promiscuous—in short, lustful beings—when any allegations of sexual misconduct surfaced, blacks had to be the perpetrators. In contrast, white women were viewed as pure, chaste, and virtuous. If a white woman accused a black man of rape, then he was guilty because of a supposedly innate sexual proclivity toward white women. In many ways, white men measured their masculinity and power by their ability to protect white womanhood and to control white women's sexuality. On the other hand, when black women suffered sexual assault at the hands of white men, local authorities largely ignored such atrocities. Timothy Tyson states,

> At the same time, a legal system controlled by white men winked at sexual assaults on black women by men both black and white, since these attacks posed no threat to—indeed, they expressed and strengthened—the racial and sexual caste system of which they were a part. "The rhetoric of protection—like the rape of black women," Jacquelyn Dowd Hall argues, "reflected a power struggle among men." Patriarchal control over women constituted an important part of the equation. "Absolutely inaccessible sexual property," states Hall, "white women became the most potent symbol of white supremacy."[23]

In Monroe, North Carolina, on more than one occasion, white men physically and/or sexually assaulted black women and were acquitted of all charges. For instance, Brodus F. Shaw, a white railroad engineer, physically assaulted Georgia Davis White, a black housekeeper at the Hotel Monroe, for disturbing his sleep. Apparently, White had spoken too loudly when calling to another maid to inquire whether the linen in another room had been changed. Shaw, awakened from his sleep, stormed out of his room in his underwear and asked her, "'Why the hell are you disturbing my sleep?'" Shaw "then struck White in the face with his fist and kicked her down a flight of stairs into the hotel lobby."[24] After Dr. Albert Perry, vice president of the Monroe NAACP, treated her at the local hospital, Williams went with her to the courthouse to file charges. Alleging that White had ignored the hotel's "Do Not Disturb" sign, Shaw was later released on a one hundred dollar bond. Ironically, the next day, White was jailed for failing to report wages earned from her temporary work at the Monroe Poultry Company back in 1957 when she filed for unemployment. Because she violated the implicit racial hierarchy by filing charges against a white man, White became the victim of white supremacist practices.

Other trumped-up charges also surfaced. Local black citizens were outraged, particularly the black women who wanted to lynch Shaw. However, Williams persuaded them not to resort to violence.[25]

On the day Shaw was brought to trial, Mary Ruth Reed, a twenty-five-year-old black woman, was in court seeking justice against Lewis Medlin, a white mechanic, who had tried to rape her in the presence of her five children. At the time of the assault, Reed was several months pregnant, but she managed to flee her assailant with one child in her arms; however, she was soon caught by Medlin and beaten mercilessly, until a white neighbor heard the screams and called the police. Medlin denied the charges but did admit to going to Reed's home. After Medlin had been arrested, one of his friends offered Reed a bribe of one hundred dollars to drop the charges. Having refused the bribe, Reed was harassed and received death threats over the phone. After learning of another assault against a black woman, the town's black women were persuaded that the only solution to the problem was to meet violence with violence—but, once more, Williams talked them out of it.[26]

On May 5, 1959, the doubts that Williams and local black residents had about blacks receiving justice in the local court were confirmed. That day, Judge Walter Johnson dropped the assault charges against Shaw, and an all-white jury acquitted Medlin of assault and attempted rape charges. Angry and disappointed, many of the black women scolded Williams for talking them out of using violence against the perpetrators. The women's anger made him realize that there was no justice for local black citizens in Monroe—and that the only viable alternative was armed resistance. After the trial, Williams told United Press International reporters, "It was time to meet violence with violence."[27]

Williams's advocacy of armed resistance created a firestorm and was greatly distorted by the media. A *New York Times* headline read, "N.A.A.C.P. Leader Urges Violence." Other newspapers had more provocative titles. The Jackson, Mississippi, *State-Times* announced, "Negro Calls for Lynch of Whiteness."[28] Robert Williams and the local black citizens in Monroe advocated self-defense; they did not advocate senseless violence against whites. Nor did Williams hate whites; some of his closest allies were white. Local black residents of Monroe were prepared to meet violence with violence, but the notion of armed resistance against whites, regardless of circumstances, was viewed as treasonous by the local authorities. The NAACP national office, seeking to distance itself from the explosive situation in order not to tarnish its reputation as an organization that promotes violence, called on Williams to set the record straight. NAACP executive secretary, Roy Wilkins, wanted Williams to make a public announcement that he was not speaking on behalf of the NAACP. Williams's position on armed resistance put him in disfavor with the national office; he was suspended as president of the Monroe NAACP Chapter.[29]

Not only was he suspended, but also black civil rights leaders, including Martin Luther King Jr., castigated him for advocating armed resistance. King championed nonviolent resistance as the most viable and safe strategy to confront white supremacy in the South. He believed that Mahatma Gandhi's strategy of civil disobedience and love for your enemies were potent weapons against white supremacy. But King and other civil rights leaders misunderstood the situation; the local NAACP leader did not reject nonviolent passive resistance—he just did not see it as an effective strategy to combat the terror and violence orchestrated by whites against blacks in the South. Williams believed that "nonviolence [was] a powerful weapon in the struggle against social evil," and that it was "the ultimate step in revolution against intolerable oppression, a type of struggle wherein man may make war without debasing himself." However, such a method could only work if the adversary had a conscience, and Williams believed that southern white racists did not have one.[30]

Although Roy Wilkins suspended Williams, members of the Monroe NAACP still embraced him as their leader. In fact, Williams's courage and willingness to stand up to white supremacists earned him respect among local black residents and blacks across the United States. During the 1960s, the FBI labeled Williams a threat because of his radicalism and his association with Communist leader Fidel Castro of Cuba. As civil rights activists learned of Williams's activism, some offered to lend the Monroe NAACP support. Upon Williams's invitation, during the summer of 1961, James Forman, executive director of SNCC, recruited some of the Freedom Riders (who had been released from Parchman State Penitentiary in Jackson, Mississippi) to aid Williams's campaign in Monroe.[31] These idealistic young people believed that nonviolence was the only viable strategy against white supremacy in the South. They wanted to show Williams that his strategy was counterproductive. Tyson contends, "Williams saw the arrival of the advocates of nonviolence 'as a challenge,' he said, 'but I also saw it as an opportunity to show that what King and them were preaching was bullshit.'"[32]

Under the leadership of a local black youth named Richard Crowder, local young people and adult civil rights activists established the Monroe Nonviolent Action Committee (MNAC). The Ten Point Program of MNAC, which was endorsed by the Monroe NAACP, called for the abolishment of discriminatory hiring practices in the local factories, equal treatment for blacks by the local welfare agency, the construction of a swimming pool in the black community, the removal of Jim Crow signs from the city, desegregation of public schools by 1962, and skilled or supervisory positions in city government for local black residents. Local black leaders presented these demands to the Monroe board of aldermen. MNAC also wanted all participants involved in demonstrations to take an oath vowing to be nonviolent. Although they did not consent to any oath, Williams and some of his supporters did promise the committee that demonstrations carried in downtown Monroe would be nonviolent.[33]

Not trusting that nonviolent passive resistance was a foolproof strategy against white supremacy, many local black residents did not disarm themselves. Shortly after nonviolent demonstrations against the white power structure were begun by MNAC in August 1961, many protestors recognized that their nonviolent tactics were ineffective. Even as violence against protestors escalated, local police often did not intervene. Demonstrations held by the MNAC provoked a wave of violence from local white residents in Monroe. Several protestors were severely injured by the white mob, and others were jailed. When a white mob threatened to descend on the black community of Newtown, Williams and members of the Monroe NAACP sprung into action, arming themselves to protect their property and family. When the dust settled, Williams and the Monroe NAACP were ultimately blamed for the melee.[34]

Wanted by local and federal authorities, Williams was faced with a decision: stay and fight, or leave Monroe. Tyson maintains, "If Williams had stayed and fought, [Julian] Mayfield believed, it likely would have led to a violent confrontation and the 'certain slaughter of large numbers of people. Even Williams recognized the limits of armed struggles under the circumstances that prevailed in the Jim Crow South."[35] With the aid of friends, Williams and his family (wife Mabel and two sons) escaped from Monroe to Cuba, where he lived in exile for several years. From Cuba, through his "Radio Free Dixie" broadcast, Williams continued to influence the black freedom fighters to mobilize against white supremacy in the South. Although exiled in Cuba, Williams's legacy remained strong among the local black residents of Monroe.[36] He advocated black pride and self-defense. His belief that violence must be met with violence resonated with many black southerners. However, his legacy also taught blacks valuable lessons about the limits of both nonviolence and armed resistance. One thing is for certain: nonviolent tactics never fully took root among black residents in Monroe, North Carolina. Two years later, the NAACP nonviolent direct action youth group, the Commandos, soon discovered that truth.

On Tuesday, June 2, 1963, two NAACP Commandos were dispatched to Monroe to appeal to black residents to lend their support to nonviolent protest demonstrations in the city. Having witnessed white resistance to nonviolent demonstrations organized by the Freedom Riders and local whites committing violent acts against the protestors, black residents were reluctant to embrace the Commandos's nonviolent demonstrations. The black residents of Monroe were not opposed to nonviolent protest; however, they understood firsthand the limits of this protest strategy in combating white supremacy. When the two Commandos arrived, NAACP leaders and the Monroe Action Committee (formerly headed by Robert Williams) assured their cooperation.

After preliminary organizational meetings were held that Tuesday, the Monroe Action Committee (MAC) and the NAACP Commandos agreed that nonviolent activities would commence on Saturday, June 8.[37]

On Wednesday evening of June 3, seven more Commandos arrived in Monroe. That Thursday, a rally was held and support from the local residents intensified. After the rally, that same day, the MAC decided that it should take over the operations, maintaining that as a local community group it should be solely in charge of the movement. MAC members also demanded that all the funds collected at the rally be turned over to them instead of sharing the funds with "the local NAACP units."[38] When the Commandos asked why they had changed their minds, the MAC members contended that "they did not agree with the non-violent approach; that the community of Monroe wanted stronger action; and they themselves were prepared to more strongly 'attack the white man.'"[39] The Commandos would later learn that the local black residents' support of nonviolent demonstrations was not, in fact, a commitment to be nonviolent. Black leaders and local black residents, who verbally supported the Commandos' plan, had no real intention of supporting a plan in which they had to commit to being nonviolent in the face of violence. To support their claims, MAC members revealed their stockpile of ammunition, guns, and other weapons. It was rumored that the machine guns were imported from Cuba.[40]

Having rejected MAC's position to support armed resistance, the Commandos experienced distrust and intimidation from local black residents. That Thursday night, the Commandos were harassed off and on by prowlers outside their windows. Sensing possible danger, they stayed in their rooms. On Friday, the Commandos were kicked out of the Stokes Hotel because MAC had pressured the owner to do so. Local black residents who had initially supported the Commandos' stance were now acting differently toward them. The young people left Monroe that Friday evening, declaring, "The situation looked too explosive."[41] They realized that MAC "was a very strong force in that community and that it would take too much time and effort to try and keep things going."[42] The Commandos experienced firsthand the influence MAC had on local black residents and believed that it would be very difficult to convince them to accept their nonviolence stance. Moreover, MAC had forced the Commandos out of town because it did not believe that change could occur through nonviolent efforts. The Commandos' failure to lead nonviolent demonstrations in Monroe, however, did not deter their work in other black communities in North Carolina.

While large-scale civil rights activities intensified in Fayetteville in 1963, small protest demonstrations had occurred before then. Influenced by the Greensboro sit-ins, students, mostly from Fayetteville State College (currently known as Fayetteville State University) and some affiliated with the local NAACP youth council, staged sit-in demonstrations in the downtown business district. On February 10, 1960, roughly forty students from Fayetteville State Teachers College conducted a sit-in at the F. W. Woolworth's lunch counter. That same day, students targeted McCrory's 5&10. Local college professor Henry M. Eldridge joined the protest. The demonstrations forced Woolworth's to close its lunch counter at 4:00 p.m. and McCrory's to close at 5:00 p.m., hours earlier than its normal operating time. In both cases, the students were denied service without incident.[43] On February 23, the students renewed their protest at Woolworth's and McCrory's 5&10; however, only twelve students participated. According to Brian Suttell, during the early 1960s, the protest demonstrations in Fayetteville "failed to maintain a steady momentum that could pressure local businessmen and city officials into action."[44]

When blacks showed trust in whites about race relations, as historian William Chafe notes, temporary declines in protest activities occurred. Likewise, when black activists perceived a loss of trust, they increased their protest activities. Declining momentum in the Fayetteville civil rights demonstrations was attributed to concessions that white city leaders had made with the black residents. For example, in 1962, the Fayetteville City Council and Mayor Robert L. Butler approved measures that would give black applicants equal consideration for city jobs, leading to a temporary reprieve in protest activities. Although such promises were made, de facto discrimination continued in hiring, and businesses did not end their practices of segregation. Failure by the Fayetteville's white city leaders to effectively end discriminatory practices by white businesses propelled the local black community into action once again.[45]

As blacks grew tired of broken promises from local white authorities and the second-class citizenship that stemmed from Jim Crow practices, civil rights activities increased across the South. The civil rights protest demonstrations that occurred in Birmingham, Alabama, in April 1963 greatly inspired protest demonstrations in other southern states, particularly in Fayetteville. Termed Project C (for confrontation), nonviolent demonstrations in Birmingham targeted racially discriminatory practices in that city. Led by Martin L. King Jr.'s Southern Christian Leadership Conference (SCLC), at the behest of Fred Shuttleworth, leader of the Alabama Christian Movement for Human Rights (ACMHR), the Birmingham movement to end racial discrimination and segregation attracted enormous resistance from city leaders, particularly Eugene "Bull" Connor, commissioner of public safety. Connor's infamous use of fire hoses and police dogs on peaceful protestors, including children, to stop the demonstrations revealed the magnitude of violence he was willing to unleash to maintain the racial status quo in the South.[46]

As the protest demonstrations escalated, Connor's staunch effort to enforce racial segregation and deny blacks equal rights would eventually lead to his political demise. Broadcast on national television, Connor's violent tactics backfired, as the spectacle of brutality used against peaceful demonstrators outraged many Americans and called into question America's commitment to democracy for all of its citizens. The Birmingham crisis created public outrage at home and abroad. The direct action of Birmingham demonstrations, which led to national and international attention, helped to facilitate negotiations with city leaders. On May 10, King and other black leaders brokered a deal with local authorities that outlawed racially discriminatory practices in the city. That July, the city council repealed all segregation ordinances, and businesses integrated; however, Birmingham, like most southern cities did not see substantial change in racial practices until after the passage of the Civil Rights Act of 1964.[47]

Influenced by the Birmingham victory and other civil rights activities in North Carolina, that May, students from Fayetteville State Teachers College revived the nonviolent sit-in demonstrations in downtown Fayetteville. Six students organized an informal committee called the "demonstration committee" to coordinate protest activities in downtown Fayetteville. The committee members posted signs across campus, alerting students of the demonstrations planned on May 18. When the demonstrations commenced, Willis McLeod (one of the founding members of the demonstration committee) would become the most influential student leader of the protest movement. On that day, 225 students from Fayetteville State picketed downtown businesses, including Sears Roebuck & Co., J. C. Penney Co., Capitol department store, Fleishman's Big Store, Belk-Hensdale Co., Colony Theater, Miracle Theater, and Broadway Theater. Suttell asserts, "The students sang and chanted from 1 P.M. to 5 P.M., carrying signs with phrases such as 'Integration Is Inevitable,' 'Hire Us Now,' and 'Let's Crush Segregation.'"[48] Having the support of the community, which included church leaders and the local NAACP, the students increased their protest activities.

As student demonstrations in the downtown business district escalated, Mayor Wilbur Clark established a coordinating committee to address the concerns of the protestors. At a city council meeting on May 27, Clark read a report (drafted by Thornton Rose, chairman of the mayor's coordinating committee) presenting the objectives of the student protestors. The report expressed the students' demands for desegregation of businesses and better job opportunities for black residents. City council members, including the mayor, expressed support for the students' resolutions; in return, the students agreed to cease protest demonstrations.[49]

Under the leadership of Arthur Thomas, that Monday night, June 10, fifty young people "were dispatched to the downtown area to test the facilities for their desegregation status." NAACP groups wanted "complete and immediate desegregation of all local establishments licensed for public service." However, the young people discovered that the businesses still adhered to segregation

"And If Not Now, When?"

practices.[50] On June 11, however, the protestors resumed their demonstrations because no real progress had been made in resolving segregation practices in the city. That Tuesday night, "there was a rally at Fayetteville State Teachers College from which there was a march to the downtown area." Some of the youth "were able to obtain tickets to theaters as well as gain entrance to restaurants."[51] However, most of the young people were arrested. That day, twenty-six demonstrators were arrested, marking the first large-scale arrest of the demonstrations. Also, a young female was severely beaten by two white men; as word of this incident spread, black soldiers stationed in the area expressed their resentment about the beating.[52] As tensions escalated, the protestors became more determined to attack racial discrimination in the city. The arrests outraged the students at Fayetteville State and provided the impetus for the protest movement. Additionally, Roosevelt J. Davis, chairman of the Fayetteville Freedom Council of the NAACP, along with Vice-Chairman Willis McLeod, issued a statement criticizing the city council for not taking measures to end segregation practices.[53]

The following day, a significant number of high school students joined the protest, especially students from E. E. Smith High School and Washington Drive Jr. High. As the movement expanded in participants, particularly the involvement of high school students, Fayetteville State student leadership became concerned, because the "high school students were more rambunctious, less disciplined, and more prone to retaliate against verbal or physical abuse." Concerns were validated when seventeen-year-old high school student Earl L. Freeman "was charged with assault and possession of a concealed weapon" at a demonstration in front of the Rainbo Restaurant.[54] Although Freeman typified the behavior of most high school protestors, the involvement of high school and junior high students was sporadic and never sustained large numbers as the protest demonstrations continued. And although educators supported the students, they did not openly demonstrate due to fear of losing their jobs.

On June 13, an NAACP press release read, "The NAACP Youth Councils have presently begun protest activities in two North Carolina cities, Fayetteville and Wilmington."[55] A major turning point of the protest demonstrations came on June 14. Earlier that day, more than a hundred demonstrators were arrested for violating the city's segregation ordinances, making it the largest number of arrests since the demonstrations started. However, the arrests did not deter the protestors. Around 7:00 p.m., approximately 150 demonstrators took part in a sit-in at the J. C. Penney Co. The situation escalated when William Martin, a white ROTC student from Western Kentucky State College, joined the demonstration. About 8:30 p.m., when the protestors left the store, white spectators followed and instigated a confrontation with them. At the 200 block of Hayes Street, insults were exchanged.[56]

As tensions grew between the protestors and the spectators, around 9:30 p.m., the police started throwing tear gas canisters at both groups in front of the Carolina Theater to prevent a possible melee. Irritated by the police method to disperse the crowd, Victor Lessard, a white solider threw one of the canisters back at the police. When the police retaliated, the two groups scattered. Lessard was later arrested, and the tension eventually faded. Narrowly averting a major riot, city officials and protest leaders knew a solution had to be reached. The presence of Brown, a white student, drew resentment from white observers, as they considered him an outside agitator who had incited the black students to demonstrate. Additionally, the situation with the soldier was an isolated one because servicemen had not become highly involved in the movement. After the incident, local NAACP president Sippio Burton and black clergymen denounced the violence and admonished the demonstrators to adhere to King's philosophy of nonviolence. Although individual acts of violence surfaced from time to time, the movement remained largely nonviolent.[57]

On June 16, twenty-five of Fayetteville's prominent residents, including the mayor, attended a meeting where William Crawley, president of the Restaurant Association, voiced his opposition to integration. He opposed any measure that called for all restaurants to desegregate. Not all prominent citizens opposed integration. Councilmen Ted Rhodes and Eugene Plummer favored a resolution introduced by business owner Monroe Evans, which called for immediate integration; however, the mayor was not too keen on immediate integration, as conservative business owners and local white residents pressured him not to support such a measure. Two days later, Governor Terry Sanford, responding to the civil rights protests in Raleigh, Greensboro, Fayetteville, and other cities across the state, called for a moratorium on demonstrations. He also planned a meeting with all black leaders the following week in Raleigh to address their concerns.[58] Sanford's appeal led to a temporary suspension of protest demonstrations in Fayetteville, as protestors hoped the governor could resolve the issue of segregation and racial discrimination across the state. NAACP field secretary Charles McLean used his influence to temporarily curb the demonstrations. Heeding the appeal of McLean, Willis McLeod and other protestors halted the demonstrations in Fayetteville. McLeod maintained, "'In response to an appeal made by state officers of the NAACP, we have discontinued demonstrations to force pending the outcome of the meeting of the governor with demonstration leaders next Tuesday [June 25].'"[59]

Although Sanford was not a staunch segregationist, as governor, he did not change the practices of segregation or produce tangible results for North Carolina's black residents during the cooling-off period. Moreover, his appeal to white business owners to end segregation practices produced few results. On June 19, a day after Governor Sanford's speech, Mayor Clark appointed a biracial committee (five whites and four blacks) to study the demonstrators'

"And If Not Now, When?"

objectives and to persuade business owners to change their segregation policy. However, no students were appointed to the committee, the group that was responsible for bringing attention to the racial inequalities in the city. With no substantial results during the cooling off period, on June 28, protestors resumed demonstrations after questioning the mayor's motives.[60]

On July 9, the demonstrations took on a different character, as black and white servicemen joined the protest. Their numbers increased as the week wore on, with fifty soldiers participating in the protests on July 12. Black soldiers understood that the fight for racial equality was more than the desegregation of a business; it was about the affirmation of human dignity and respect, which they had long been denied. If blacks could serve in the military, then they should be served at lunch counters or any public establishment. The soldiers carried signs with messages such as, "First Korea, now Fayetteville, we will win our freedom" and "GI's and students unite for civil rights." As the protest demonstrations intensified, conservative city leaders knew that they could no longer afford to ignore the demands of the demonstrators.[61]

On July 19, an agreement was reached between demonstrators and local authorities. The local NAACP Negotiating Committee agreed to the mayor's Bi-Racial Committee's five-point plan, which included increasing the employment of blacks in local department stores and desegregating businesses. Although there was some opposition to the five-point plan, desegregation efforts moved along without much resistance. By early October, all four downtown theaters and most of the restaurants, hotels, and motels had desegregated. At the close of the year, only a handful of businesses remained segregated. After the passage of the landmark 1964 civil rights legislation, which struck the death knell of segregated practices in public accommodation across the South, Fayetteville businesses that remained segregated were eventually integrated.[62]

In Jackson, Mississippi, local NAACP youth chapters fought against segregation practices in public facilities and local businesses. The Tougaloo Nine, student members of the Tougaloo College NAACP Chapter, carried out one of the earliest civil rights protest demonstrations against segregation in Jackson. On March 27, 1961, the Tougaloo Nine, under the leadership of Joseph Jackson, president, staged a "read-in" at the all-white public library in downtown Jackson. Violating the city's segregation ordinance, the nine students were arrested and charged with disturbing the peace. Outraged by the arrests, the following day, fifty students from Jackson State College "proceeded into town to sympathy picket the arrest of the nine demonstrators who were still in jail." The police dispersed the crowd of students by using clubs and dogs against them. Later that day, each of the nine students was released on a one-thousand-dollar bond.[63]

On March 29, the Tougaloo Nine was tried in court for violating the city's segregation law. NAACP field secretaries Julie Wright and Medgar Evers arrived at the courthouse to show support for the students. An officer told them that the courtroom was full, but that they could join the other spectators across the street from the courthouse. Outside the courthouse, around one hundred black men, women, and children, and a few whites, gathered to show their moral support for the students. When Reverend John D. Mangram, advisor to the Tougaloo NAACP Chapter, arrived with two of the defendants, the crowd applauded. Angered by the show of support for the students, police officers armed with dogs, night sticks, and guns violently attacked the spectators. Reverend S. Leon Whitney, pastor of the Farish Street Baptist Church, was bitten by one of the police dogs. An eighty-one-year-old news reporter for *Jet* magazine suffered a broken left wrist, and Medgar Evers was severely beaten by one of the police officers with a nightstick. Despite the brutality and violence inflicted on the innocent supporters of the Tougaloo Nine by the police outside of the courtroom on the day of the trial, the judge still convicted the students of disturbing the peace, and "each of them was fined $100 and given a 30-day suspended sentence."[64]

Protesting the police brutality, on March 30, local blacks held a mass meeting at a Masonic Temple. At that time, Julie Wright organized a "No Buying Campaign" of white businesses that discriminated against blacks in downtown Jackson. She urged blacks not to patronize the local white businesses. On April 1, assisting Wright, members of the local NAACP youth chapters passed out fliers to local Negro businesses, churches, and at Masonic Temple during the Easter sunrise services. The local radio station, WSIB, noted that the boycott affected white businesses by slowing down sales in the downtown district.[65] As a result of the selective buying drive, state chain stores lost $49,225 in sales tax revenues. Wright called upon black residents in "Jackson and throughout Mississippi to fight for first-class citizenship by continuing to refrain from buying in stores with discriminatory policies."[66]

Supporting local protest efforts and seeking to increase NAACP youth chapters in the state, on April 13, Wright organized the Jackson NAACP Intercollegiate Chapter. At this organizational meeting, plans were also made to protest segregated seating on the city buses in Jackson on April 18. Prior to the Jackson NAACP Intercollegiate Chapter's initiative to protest segregation on the city buses, the Interdenominational Ministerial Alliance had written a letter to the chamber of commerce asking for complete desegregation on the city buses. The chamber of commerce was given ten days to respond. After ten days had passed and no response, the group met with Mayor Allen Thompson concerning the issue. The mayor did not provide a satisfactory answer, so the Jackson NAACP Intercollegiate Chapter decided to move ahead with its plans to protest Jim Crow practices on the city buses. Medgar Evers and Dean Charles Jones, advisor to the Jackson NAACP Intercollegiate Chapter, supported the student protest plans.[67]

"And If Not Now, When?"

Information about the protest demonstration planned by the Jackson NAACP Intercollegiate Chapter spread quickly. On April 14, Evers telephoned Julie Wright about another group that wanted to participate in the demonstration. Eager to assist, a student group at Jackson State, led by Walter Williams, president of the student body, wanted to stage simultaneous demonstrations at Jackson's airport restaurant, the city bus system, and the Trailways Bus Company. Leery of Williams's intentions—and believing that the group was competing with the local NAACP youth chapters, Wright made it clear that the NAACP would provide leadership during the demonstration. NAACP youth were instructed to wave the NAACP banner during the demonstration to show that the Jackson NAACP Intercollegiate Chapter had orchestrated the protest. Wright also organized an NAACP Coordinating Committee, which was composed of the president and secretary of each of the NAACP youth chapters, to provide leadership during the demonstration.[68]

Believing that participation from other student groups would cause conflict, Julie Wright did not invite activists from CORE and SNCC to participate in the demonstration. At a meeting sponsored by the Tougaloo NAACP Chapter, she reiterated that all moves during the protest must be made under the direction of the NAACP and that the banner must be clearly displayed to make it known that the local NAACP youth chapters were responsible for staging the demonstration.[69] Although Wright believed this partisan activism would better serve their purpose, it only fueled conflict among the NAACP and CORE and SNCC, as each of these groups worked to organized blacks to protest racial discrimination in the state. As civil rights activities expanded in the South, many youth discovered that organizational affiliation was not as important, especially if it interfered with the larger effort of breaking down the racial barriers that relegated blacks to second-class citizenship.

Although a mass demonstration was thwarted, on April 19, four students from the Jackson NAACP Intercollegiate Chapter protested segregated seating on the city buses. Violating segregated seating practices, the students sat at the front of the bus. They were arrested and charged with disturbing the peace. The student demonstrators were later released after five hundred dollars for bail was posted for each. At the trial, they were fined one hundred dollars each and given a thirty-day suspended sentence in jail.[70] As civil rights activities increased in the state, NAACP youth were at the forefront of many of these protest demonstrations. On June 4, six members of the Jackson Youth Council were jailed for entering the Jackson municipal zoo. After the incident, Medgar Evers confronted Mayor Allen Thompson concerning his televised statement that the zoo was open to both blacks and whites. Reminded of his statement, the students were later released. Five days later, two NAACP youths, Amos Brown and John Hopkins, tested the "so-called desegregated" zoo, but they were also arrested and jailed for disturbing the peace. When they were tried, Brown and Hopkins were found guilty. Still determined, a few days after Brown and Hopkins' ordeal, six youth council members tested the zoo again; they were also jailed for disturbing the peace. Although there was resistance from the local authorities, NAACP youth was not discouraged, as it continued to stage demonstrations to fight against racism.[71]

By December 1962, under the leadership of youth council advisor John Salter, who was also a sociology professor at Tougaloo, and youth council president Bette Anne Poole, the Jackson NAACP Youth Council increased its civil rights activities. That year, the youth council initiated a boycott of the Woolworth's department store. The Jackson Youth Council was composed largely of local black high school students; however, students from Tougaloo also participated in the youth council. The young people planned the boycott to coincide with the Christmas holiday shopping spree in the downtown stores. On December 12, having alerted the media, Salter and youth council members picketed Woolworth's. After the picketing began, the demonstrators were arrested but later posted bail. Although Mayor Allen Thompson, in a televised broadcast, condemned the demonstration, the media coverage publicized the boycott to local residents in Jackson.[72]

To make sure that the black community supported the boycott, youth council members passed out leaflets, announced it in the local churches, and telephoned black residents. With support from Medgar Evers, the young people continued the demonstrations in the downtown area. Evers, who had been instrumental in organizing youth councils across Mississippi, was highly respected by the young people.[73] After Evers secured two property bonds, Tougaloo students Dorie Ladner and Charles Bracey picketed downtown several days before Christmas, and were jailed. That January, Evers communicated to the NAACP national office that the boycott was 60–65 percent effective. Having been reluctant to assist the young people, the national office came on board in May 1963. Historian John Dittmer maintains, "the national office changed course abruptly and made Jackson a priority, cranking out public relations releases, supplying bond money for picketers, and eventually flooding the city with top NAACP officials."[74] This change of heart was largely influenced by the success of the Southern Christian Conference (SCLC) demonstrations in Birmingham, Alabama. Because the situation in Jackson resembled that of Birmingham, the national office did not want the SCLC to move in on its turf. Dittmer notes, "In a revealing memorandum to the regional and field secretaries on May 13, [Gloster] Current called attention to the 'apparent success of the Birmingham protest,' speculating that 'Jackson, Mississippi will be the next scene of attack by the King forces. Such a move would 'make it harder for the NAACP to carry on its work effectively.'"[75]

Marking its turf, the national office committed resources to the local boycott movement that had been started by the young people. As a result of the national office's endorsement, conservative black leaders in Jackson, who had been hesitant to get involved, now supported the boycott. By mid-May, black businessmen and ministers formed the Citizens Committee for Human Rights, which included loyal members of the Jackson NAACP, such as I. S. Sanders, Sam Bailey, and R. L. T. Smith. The adult leadership of the NAACP began to hold regular meetings with the boycott planning committee. The older and conservative businessmen and clergy wanted to negotiate with local authorities, whereas the young activists wanted ongoing demonstrations to dramatize inequalities in the city. After reaching a compromise, committee members agreed that if the mayor did not support their grievances, they would continue picketing downtown stores. The committee wanted the mayor to hire black policemen and school crossing guards and to create a biracial committee to formulate plans to desegregate facilities and to guarantee fair employment practices.

Hoping to divide the black citizens, Mayor Thompson agreed to meet with some of the representatives from the committee. He also wanted Percy Greene and Jackson State president, Jacob Reddix, men on whose support he could count. Sensing the mayor's strategy, the boycott committee agreed to meet only after the mayor allowed more members of its delegation to attend the meeting. On May 27, after meeting with the boycott committee leaders, Mayor Thompson rejected their demands. The next day, Tougaloo students Pearlena Lewis, Memphis Norman, and Anne Moody staged a sit-in at the lunch counter in the Woolworth's department store. Evers alerted the local media. Around lunchtime, white students from the local Jackson Central High School and downtown workers poured into the store. At first, white residents heckled the demonstrators; however, former policeman Bennie Oliver initiated the violence by attacking Memphis Norman. Oliver dragged Norman off the stool and kicked him several times in the face. A detective finally intervened and arrested Oliver for assault and Norman for disturbing peace. As they sat at the lunch counter, the other protestors were doused with mustard and ketchup.[76]

When youth council advisor Salter showed up at the demonstration, he was attacked fiercely by the white mob, which called him a "nigger lover" and a Communist. Within a matter of minutes, someone from the mob started beating Salter ferociously. Others poured salt and pepper on his bleeding wounds. The demonstrators were assaulted by the mob for two hours before the manager closed the store, and the police calmed the mob. Having received national media attention, the incident at Woolworth's transformed the boycott into a mass movement. Mass demonstrations were carried out in the hope of forcing the city leaders to concede. Days later, over twenty picketers were arrested, and the police attacked hundreds of Lanier High School black students who were singing freedom songs on the school's lawn. On Friday, May 31, hundreds of black youths met at the Farish Street Baptist Church and organized a protest march. The young people marched from the church waving

American flags and chanting, "We want freedom." Confronted by local police and state troopers, the protestors were arrested and hauled off in "garbage trucks to a makeshift prison at the state fairgrounds."[77] In a letter to Laplois Ashford concerning the work of the Matadors task force and the restructuring of direct activities in Jackson, Theodore Henry, youth field secretary, contended, "The 'Matadors' have created quite a stir among the young people as well as the old."[78]

To show their support for the youth, the black community rallied together, and members of the NAACP national office showed up to support a mass march. The night before the march, Roy Wilkins delivered a stirring speech to a crowd of 1,500 demonstrators. The following day, Wilkins joined Evers in the downtown pickets. They were arrested. However, Evers soon learned that Wilkins had no grand stake in the boycott. The national office preferred negotiation to continuing the direct action demonstrations. On Sunday June 2, at a strategy meeting, officials of the national office introduced a proposal to add more conservative black leaders and to rotate the chairmanship of the committee. Seeking to reduce Salter's influence, the national office prevailed at a strategy meeting. Salter and the young militants wanted more mass demonstrations, but Gloster Current, director of NAACP branches, and Wilkins resisted the young activists' demands. Both men wanted to end the demonstrations and tone down the activism of the young NAACP militants. Although several small demonstrations were carried out that Tuesday, and twenty-eight protestors were arrested, things would soon change.[79]

With the support of conservative black leaders, the national office declared an end to demonstrations. By that Thursday, the city issued an injunction forbidding protest demonstrations in the downtown area. Several young people picketing downtown were arrested for defying the injunction. Word soon spread that the boycott was ending. The youth looked to Evers for answers. Placed in an awkward position, he was now torn between his friendship with officials in the national office and supporting the militant young people. Evers chose not to get directly involved with the internal strife between the youth council members and the national office over tactics. He had more pressing concerns. After the Woolworth sit-in demonstration, Evers had received several death threats and a bomb was thrown onto his carport. Personal safety was now his utmost concern.[80]

On June 11, Evers attended a NAACP rally at the New Jerusalem Baptist Church, which he found disappointing because it was mostly concerned with promoting NAACP T-shirts. The militancy that the boycott had generated had clearly given way to less important matters. After Evers left the rally, he pulled into his driveway around 12:20 a.m. White supremacist Byron De La Beckwith, who was later arrested and charged with murder, gunned him down in the front of his home. After the black community learned of Evers's

"And If Not Now, When?"

assassination, hundreds of angry people poured into the streets to protest his death. Over four thousand black people attended his funeral at the Masonic Temple, and around five thousand blacks joined the march from the Masonic Temple to Collins Funeral Home. His body was shipped by train to be laid to rest at Arlington National Cemetery. For a moment, it appeared that his death would revive the boycott; it did not. Influenced by the national office, conservative black leaders moved to negotiate with the local authority to end the demonstrations in the city. With support from John F. Kennedy's administration, the black leaders decided to focus their attention on voter registration. The black residents, particularly the young people, were disappointed with the conservative black leaders and the NAACP national office. Historian John Dittmer states, "Members of the north Jackson NAACP youth council, who started it all, felt betrayed as well."[81]

On the surface, the national office seemed not to support direct action demonstrations. All too often, scholars have interpreted the national office's hesitance to support direct action demonstrations as a sign that the NAACP preferred only to work through the courts. However, several reasons would explain the national office's preference for brokering peace with city officials. Posting bail for the demonstrators was costly. After bailing 640 protestors out of jail, the national office had spent approximately $64,000, and many officials believed that if the protests were to continue, that amount could double or triple. In many ways, the growing militancy of the youth under the leadership of John Salter, who had leftist leanings, did not sit well with officials in the national office. After the *Brown* decision, the NAACP national office began to distance itself from leftist radicals to avoid allegations of being a Communist organization. Lastly, the boycott showed the growing chasm between young militants and conservative NAACP leaders, who preferred litigation to direct action as a foolproof strategy to secure civil rights.[82] The young people believed that their nonviolent direct action strategy was the most viable option to break down racial barriers in the city. However, the Jackson movement revealed to the old and the young that repressive local governments in the South would resort to any measure to maintain the subordination of blacks.

The growing popularity of nonviolent direct action tactics among young people gradually made the conservative older leaders, both at the national and local levels, more receptive to the newer tactics. Dedicated young men and women who were members of task force groups like the Commandos, Matadors, and Bravados advanced the association's work greatly in the South. Understanding the growing militancy among young people, the NAACP national youth director Laplois Ashford had called for the creation of these specialized task forces. His reasoning was partly that the association was losing ground to other civil rights organizations, such as SNCC and CORE, which had stepped up their direct activities in the South.

During the 1960s, the national office realized that other youth organizations were attracting NAACP youth. This issue first surfaced with the Albany, Georgia Movement, a campaign launched in 1961 by Charles Sherrod and Cordell Reagon, which centered on voter registration and the desegregation of public facilities in that city.[83] That September, before Sherrod's arrival, youth council members discussed plans to organize direct action demonstrations in Albany with Vernon Jordan, Georgia field secretary. Youth Field Secretary Julie Wright suggested that projects be organized, but made sure that the youth understood that direct action was more than sit-ins, read-ins, or kneel-ins. She maintained that direct action could also be a "voter registration campaign, a program of withholding patronage, mass meetings or working toward the desegregation of public schools."[84] However, that October, Sherrod arrived in town and started soliciting support from the local youth of the community for SNCC's direct action project.

After Sherrod solicited the support of the Albany Youth Council, the council's secretary requested advice from the southeast regional office about cooperating with SNCC in carrying out the direct action operations. Sherrod wanted the youth council members to assist him in testing the recent ruling of the Interstate Commerce Commission, which outlawed segregated travel.[85] A local citizen telephoned the southeast regional office expressing concern about the demonstrations that SNCC and the Albany Youth Council had planned. As a result, on October 30, 1961, Ruby Hurley, Wright, and John Patton (NAACP voter registration chairman) met with the youth council and cautioned them about their activities with SNCC. At the meeting, the youth voted to follow the NAACP's program and policy concerning its participation in the demonstration.[86] Sherrod and Reagon could not attend the meeting because they had to go back to McComb, Mississippi, for the trial.[87] Having missed the meeting, they were unaware that Hurley had cautioned the youth concerning cooperating with the project. But when the demonstrations began, events did not turn out the way Hurley expected.

Several hundred youths were arrested as a result of the protest demonstrations in Albany.[88] And, to make matters worse, SNCC did not have adequate resources to provide for their bail.[89] The national office of the NAACP chided SNCC for being impulsive and irresponsible with the demonstrations. In November, when a meeting took place between SNCC and the NAACP, allegations surfaced that SNCC was "raiding' their youth chapters."[90] James Bevel, chairman of the Nashville Student Movement, countered by saying that if SNCC's program appealed to NAACP youth, then it was more of an indictment of the association than of SNCC.[91] The fact of the matter was that SNCC was not "raiding" NAACP youth councils for members. Bevel's observation concerning the association's youth program resonated with young people in the NAACP youth councils and college chapters, many of whom had grown dissatisfied with the association's unwillingness to give youth more latitude over their own programs. Although some youth did defect to SNCC, the NAACP did not suffer a significant loss in Albany. In February 1962, Julie Wright noted that the NAACP's presence was still strong in the city. She maintained that the thirteen-day membership campaign conducted by the Albany Youth Council was very successful.[92] Although it was unsuccessful in immediately breaking down discrimination in the city, the Albany movement revealed the significance of youth and its ability to influence the direction of the civil rights struggle.

Like the Albany Movement, which revealed NAACP youth's dissatisfaction with the association's bureaucracy, events in North Carolina reflected this discontentment. In October 1962, Gloster Current, in a letter to NAACP Youth Field Secretary Julie Wright, commented that CORE was attracting youth in North Carolina. That year, attorney Floyd McKissick, the state youth advisor, assumed a paid position with CORE as legal counsel. Current stated, "It is true that CORE is making a bid for their allegiance. Moreover, this bid is sanctioned by the peculiar relationship which now exists between CORE and Attorney McKissick who has assumed a paid position with CORE."[93] That November, in a letter to the national youth director, Laplois Ashford, North Carolina youth field secretaries John Bradley and Robert Blow wrote, "There are efforts made to establish chapters of other civil rights organizations in this area. We have seen many of those that worked this summer for the NAACP change organizations."[94] Various allegations suggested that McKissick may have had something to do with youths abandoning the youth councils for CORE.

In May 1963, Ashford maintained that action must be taken to prevent youth council members from leaving the association and joining other civil rights organizations. The problem was particularly great in North Carolina. He maintained that the measly salary that the North Carolina State Conference paid the youth field workers was probably one reason for their joining other groups. Ashford contended, "From what I ascertain, many of these youth are basically loyal NAACPers and would jump at the opportunity to participate more extensively in NAACP programs."[95] The issue with youth joining other civil rights organizations in North Carolina had less to do with McKissick and more to do with the senior branches' lack of support for youth programs. The senior branches wanted to have more control over the direct action projects that the youths were staging. That year, the association took steps to strengthen the relationship between the senior branch and the youth units.

In 1963, at the NAACP Annual Convention, the board of directors revised the constitutions of the youth council and college chapters with the hope of creating a better relationship between the seniors and the youths. Because it interpreted the word "subordinate" in the youth council constitution to mean that it had absolute control over the types of programs that the youth initiated, the senior branch eliminated and replaced "subordinate" with the word "co-ordinate." Because the word subordinate was ambiguous and created hostility between the youth councils and senior branches, the association hoped that the revision to the constitution would create a mutual relationship between the youth council and the senior branch. Additionally, the national office created the Young Adult Council to address the problem of age difference in the youth council (which ranged from ages sixteen to twenty-five). The Young Adult Council consisted of young people from ages twenty-one to twenty-five. The national office created this council largely because many young adults complained of feeling out of place in the youth council due to the age differential, and the association did not want to lose this group to CORE and SNCC.[96] The Medgar Evers murder in 1963 brought short-lived solidarity between the senior branches and the youth units.[97] Evers's death not only brought about temporary unity, but it also became an inspiration for many protest demonstrations staged throughout the South, especially in Jackson, Mississippi.[98]

In 1964, civil rights activities in Mississippi caused some youth to defect to CORE and SNCC. Under the auspices of the Council of Federated Organizations (COFO), civil rights groups organized mass voter registration drives throughout Mississippi.[99] Like other civil rights organizations, the NAACP youth groups' voter registration projects targeted rural communities in Mississippi. Although it was affiliated with COFO, the NAACP cautioned youth groups to maintain their distinct identity as youth councils and college chapters of the association. Before NAACP youths could collaborate with SNCC and CORE on voter registration projects, they had to get permission from the national office. That summer, many NAACP youth resisted the association's position that they should remain a distinct group. Commenting on the organizing efforts in Mississippi, Ashford asserted, "Nowhere in the state, except with the possibility of Clarksdale under the strong advisorship of Vera Pigee, are NAACP youth units firmly organized and undertaking their individual programs; the rest are losing or have lost their identity in cooperative efforts with COFO."[100] Taking issue with the association's bureaucratic position, the former president of the Moss Point Youth Council flat out rejected the idea of reactivating the youth council, maintaining that COFO and the Mississippi Student Union "do the same thing and we don't have to get approval from nobody."[101] Indeed, this former youth council member voiced the sentiments of many NAACP youth workers in Mississippi that summer, especially those who worked on a voluntary basis. The NAACP youth criticized the association for not fully cooperating with the other civil rights organizations in Mississippi, and this bureaucracy caused many youth to join CORE and SNCC that summer.[102]

Hoping to save the association's youth units in Mississippi, Ashford appealed to John Morsell, assistant executive secretary, to hire more youth field workers to revamp the association's youth work. He pleaded, "We desperately need help with our youth units in Mississippi."[103] That summer, the association hired Johnny Frazier, a former Mississippi youth field secretary, to assist Charles Evers, Mississippi field secretary, with reorganizing the NAACP youth units in Mississippi.[104] Charles Evers had graduated from Alcorn College in 1951 and moved to Philadelphia, Mississippi, where he worked "a series of jobs as a teacher, mortician, cab driver, and disc jockey."[105] However, his civil rights work angered the local whites, and he was forced to flee the state. Returning to Mississippi after Medgar Evers's death, Charles unofficially appointed himself the new field director, taking on his brother's role. Seeking to avoid public confrontation with the "slain martyr's brother," Wilkins reluctantly backed the decision, something he would later regret.[106] Hoping to salvage the youth groups, Evers audaciously told NAACP youth members in Mississippi not to work with SNCC. Unlike Medgar, who had developed a mutual relationship with SNCC and CORE, Evers chose not cooperate with them.[107] Donald White, NAACP youth field worker, wrote Wilkins protesting the position taken by Evers, which foiled a protest demonstration that Jackson State University's NAACP chapter had planned with SNCC.[108] The protest was against the Jackson police for not taking action against a man who had run over a young lady and broken her leg. Disappointed with the association's unwillingness to work with other civil rights organizations, White severed his relationship with the NAACP. He further stated that young people were losing confidence in the NAACP.[109] Similarly, R. Hunter Morey, a Jackson State student, dropped his membership with the association. He maintained, "What your agent, Mr. Charles Evers did last night in Jackson, Mississippi [is] in utter contradiction to everything that the civil rights movement stands for."[110] Young people within the association were not infected with the partisan politics that festered among older members of the NAACP. Grassroots organizing in Jackson revealed that NAACP youth did not support the turf warfare waged by the national office against SNCC and CORE. They were willing to work with other young people to mount a formidable effort against entrenched racism in Mississippi.

With the passage of the Civil Rights Act of the 1964, which outlawed discrimination in education and public accommodations, the NAACP Youth and College division organized a program called "Action Education."[111] Through Action Education, which consisted of workshops, NAACP youth groups educated blacks on the significance of the Act and how it could be implemented in their communities. This program had the greatest impact in the southeast region.[112] The following year, the Voting Rights Act outlawed discriminatory practices, including the literacy test that was used to prevent blacks from voting. These two pieces of legislation signaled victory for the civil rights movement—a long, hard battle to end racial discrimination and segregation. As a result of the 1964 Civil Rights Act and the Voting Rights Act of 1965, youth activism among NAACP groups declined. Sherrill Marcus, youth field director, maintained, "Through the region, there has been found generally a relaxed attitude toward the fight for freedom. This attitude in many instances can be traced to the many programs of the federal government, and the few successes in local communities that have come about since the passage of the 1964 Civil Rights Bill and the 1965 Voting Rights Act."[113] Apart from voter registration drives (which the association launched throughout the southeast), youth activism slowed in momentum and membership declined in the youth chapters.

Although they were landmark pieces of legislation, the Civil Rights of 1964 and the Voting Rights of 1965 acts did not immediately change the hearts and minds of southerners who wanted to maintain the status quo in race relations. In April 1965, NAACP National Youth Director Laplois Ashford resigned to become the Deputy Public Safety Commissioner for Rochester, New York. By 1965, the NAACP youth membership had dropped to 65,000 from 75,000 in 1963. Hoping to reenergize the youth work of the association, the national office appointed Eugene Hampton on July 19, 1965, as the seventh national youth director of the NAACP Youth and College Division. Born March 29, 1939, in Chicago, Illinois, Hampton had attended public schools in Chicago and Pike County, Mississippi. In 1961, he graduated as class valedictorian, receiving an engineering degree from Tennessee State University. By 1965, "married and the father of two young daughters," he completed work toward his master's degree at the universities of Iowa and Washington.[114]

Before joining the NAACP staff, Hampton served as an engineer at the Rock Island Arsenal in Davenport, Iowa. While in Iowa, Hampton helped to reorganize the Davenport branch and youth council. He also served as a member of the Davenport branch's executive committee, and he chaired the housing committee. Hampton was also active in other religious and civic organizations. He was a member of the Iowa United Church of Christ Task Force for Racial Justice Now, and he was the chairman of Iowa's Quad-Cities Council on Human Rights (QCCHR). His work with QCCHR led to the establishment of human rights agencies in Davenport. Hampton's broad background in civil rights work had prepared him well to become the NAACP's national youth director. Commenting on Hampton's appointment, Wilkins asserted, "With Mr. Hampton's youth and experience we expect the youth program of the NAACP to move forward at an accelerated pace."[115]

Like Ashford, the former youth director, Hampton was a student leader in the NAACP. He served as one of the student coordinators for the 1960 sit-in movement in Nashville, Tennessee. Because of his participation in the Nashville sit-ins, Hampton was "arrested and threatened by the National Association for the Advancement of White People (NAAWP)."[116] As a former Nashville sit-in leader and a community organizer, he was a capable leader and possessed the talent to revive the youth work of the NAACP. Hampton was a great administrator and organizer. He stressed the importance of fully understanding the operations of the association to the youth members and leaders. Hampton stated, "Every member of any unit of the Youth and College Division of the National Association of the Advancement of Colored People *should know* the purpose and history and philosophy of the National Association. . . . Without the foundation of knowledge of and pride in belonging to the association, it is doubtful whether any worthwhile and meaningful building can be accomplished."[117] He knew that to revive the youth program, this understanding had to be promoted.

Noting the challenges that lay ahead for the NAACP youth councils and college chapters, Hampton proclaimed, "A great deal of responsibility, we must assume, will be in our hands. A number of challenges will confront us. Whether we want to or would like to experience leadership and assume responsibility is not a question. The fact is—we will have to do this."[118] During the early 1960s, protest demonstrations in the South influenced the scope of the NAACP's youth work. Although northern NAACP youth groups were engaged in breaking down discrimination in the inner city during the 1940s and 1950s, during this period the national office endorsed a program geared specifically at improving the quality of life for those in the inner city. In fact, by the mid-1960s, the work of the association's youth focused greatly on the problems that plagued residents in blighted urban or slum areas throughout the United States. The antipoverty programs initiated by President Lyndon B. Johnson greatly influenced this shift in activism. Under Hampton's leadership, the NAACP youth groups' participation in the Community Action Project (CAP) flourished. CAP, one of Johnson's antipoverty programs, was established to show "residents of ghettoes" how to organize and make effective use of the resources at their disposal to solve their community problems.[119]

CAP offices were established in impoverished communities, and the programs were set up to address the particular needs of the community. Most programs focused on housing, education, employment, and voter education and registration.[120] For example, the Brooklyn, New York, CAP (run by members of the Frederick Douglass Young Adult Council, an NAACP youth organization) tackled housing code violations in Brooklyn and reported them to the City Building Department for investigation. As a result of CAP's activism, the landlord provided rent reduction to tenants and made repairs to several buildings. With the assistance of the Brooklyn Sanitation Department, the Brooklyn Youth Council cleaned up many vacant lots.[121] Additionally, the Chicago CAP and NAACP youth helped local residents with employment referrals and building code complaints. Assisted by the Chicago Urban League, Chicago CAP and NAACP youth launched a back-to-school campaign to combat the high dropout rate in the Lawndale community.[122] In Wilmington, Delaware,

NAACP young people and CAP launched a tutorial project for elementary school students (grades one to six). Tutorials were held each morning Monday through Friday. CAP also distributed a petition calling for the passage of a fair housing law.[123]

The CAP program increased the association's presence in the inner city, providing underprivileged youth with viable options for a better life. A common criticism leveled against the association was that its programs were not relevant to the needs of the community. In many ways, CAP was an answer to that criticism. CAP was not a program that the organization participated in to compete with other civil rights groups. The program represented a legitimate effort by the association to improve life for the underprivileged and poor. Whereas antipoverty programs had largely influenced its origin, CAP—from its inception—took on a life of its own, as young men and women's activism in the NAACP spread to urban slums.

At the close of 1965, the activism of the NAACP youth councils and college chapters had come full circle—from staging sit-in demonstrations and organizing "Buy Where You Can Work" campaigns to leveraging CAP to confront social ills plaguing blacks in the urban slums. Indeed, NAACP youths' efforts to secure first-class citizenship were fraught with many complications, but they persevered. Although membership in the youth chapters did not reach the level of success it had experienced in 1963, the youth chapters' hard-won civil rights victories against white supremacy practices helped to establish a more egalitarian and democratic American society.

Epilogue

In Howell Raines's *My Soul Is Rested: The Story of the Civil Rights Movement in the Deep South*, Ruby Hurley elaborates on her role as the NAACP southeast regional director and her involvement in the freedom movement. Looking back years later, Hurley bemoans that many young people did not fully understand and appreciate the struggles and sacrifices that her generation of blacks had made to advance civil rights. She asserts, "And I listen to young people nowadays talking about old folks 'taking it.' They don't know how we didn't take it. There were those who died rather than take it, and there were those who suffered much more than I did who didn't take it."[1] In further discussion with Raines, Hurley's lament doesn't stop there. She states, "I think young people need to know, and some older people need to know, that it didn't all begin in 1960."[2]

Commencing their activism during the height of the Great Depression, NAACP youth councils and college chapters drew upon a vibrant American youth movement that swept the nation. The youth groups throughout the nation protested the socioeconomic injustices that they faced. They also denounced the fascist governments that were spreading across Europe. Indeed, the nation's fight against racial bigotry abroad (which led to a second world war) heightened sensibilities toward racial injustice at home. Amid this vibrant youth activism, the NAACP youth movement developed. Although white youth groups protested racial injustices, these issues did not always take center stage in their protest demonstrations. Sensing the need for black youths to mobilize and take concerted action to improve their plight, Juanita Jackson motivated the association to revamp its youth movement. Reorganized in 1936 under her leadership, the NAACP youth groups played a significant role in advancing the fight for civil rights in the United States. Through her fiery activism, the youth councils and college chapters tackled socioeconomic inequalities that held blacks as second-class citizens. Jackson urged the NAACP youth to fight for rights that had been guaranteed under the United States Constitution—entitlements that every citizen should enjoy. The denial of equal access to the nation's resources was an infringement on their citizenship. Understanding this significance, the youth councils and college chapters sprang into action. The NAACP youth movement tackled the most fundamental issues that concerned blacks throughout the United States. Adopting a four-pronged agenda, which reflected the initiatives of the NAACP national office, the youth councils and college chapters advocated equal education, employment opportunities, civil liberties, and antilynching legislation. Of these initiatives advocated by the

NAACP youth groups, procuring antilynching legislation and equal education opportunities took center stage. The campaigns launched by the NAACP youth groups to stop lynchings and inequalities in education raised awareness among Americans concerning these injustices.

The NAACP youth movement's campaign against lynching was one of the most significant contributions to the fight for civil rights. NAACP youth councils and college chapters demonstrated against lynching because it was one of the most inhumane and malicious injustices from which blacks suffered. These demonstrations dramatized the precarious state that lynching created for blacks regardless of their socioeconomic status. They showed that lynching was an American problem and not a black problem. These protest demonstrations were staged annually on Abraham Lincoln's birthday—a president who had become synonymous with freedom and justice. Additionally, mourning those who had died at the hands of lynchers, youth wore black arms bands during these demonstrations. NAACP youth also wrote letters to their congressmen, calling for federal legislation to outlaw lynching. Indeed, the protest activities of NAACP youth groups raised awareness concerning the inhumanity of these insufferable acts.

Understanding the importance of a quality education, the NAACP youth councils and college chapters staged demonstrations protesting educational inequalities. Jim Crow segregation denied black youth access to equal educational opportunities. Under the dual education system, black schools lacked significant resources and their facilities were dilapidated. Mobilizing against these injustices, NAACP youth conducted protest marches during Annual Educational Week. Exemplifying the determination of black youth to break down inequalities in education was the protest march led by four hundred members/supporters of the Lumberton Youth Council. Although the aim of the association during the 1930s and 1940s was not integration, gross inequalities revealed that integration was the only viable solution. By highlighting the glaring education inequalities through protest demonstrations, NAACP youth groups revealed that under Jim Crow, education opportunities could never be equal. Indeed, segregation itself was discriminatory, which led the association to push for integrated educational facilities; however, not until the 1950s, with the *Brown* decision, were segregated facilities outlawed. During this period, the NAACP youth played a major role in helping to facilitate the Supreme Court's ruling. Black young men and women across the South braved violence and racial slurs from segregationists. Their personal sacrifices and courage became catalysts that propelled black youth across United States to protest against racial segregation.

As the protest activities of NAACP youth groups accelerated during the 1940s and 1950s and the movement expanded, direct action campaigns became a common feature. The expansion of direct action campaigns can be attributed in large part to the work of Ruby Hurley. Like Jackson, Hurley believed, via direct action projects, that the association's youth work could be greatly advanced. Working within the scope of the national office directives, youth councils and college chapters launched direct action projects against public accommodations. These demonstrations were waged outside the South. During this period, the association was reluctant to endorse any direct action project in the South outside of voter registration. Certainly, one of the NAACP youth groups' greatest contributions was the success with voter registration projects. And the association's willingness to endorse such programs was intensified after the Supreme Court outlawed the all-white primary in the South. However, during the late 1940s and 1950s, NAACP youth groups wanted to expand the scope of their work. In many ways, by not consenting, the national office stifled youth activism. Youths wanted to have more control over their programs and how they would be carried out. The association initiated several operational changes; however, the bureaucratic hand of the association still controlled the types of youth programs that were initiated. In fact, this bureaucracy was largely responsible for the friction that arose among NAACP youth groups, senior branches, and the national office—friction that became increasingly apparent during the 1960s. Moreover, NAACP youth councils and college chapters constantly insisted on more direct action campaigns and control over their programs; however, during this period, the association resisted such requests.

Although they were staged outside of the South, these early direct action projects did advance the fight for civil rights. They proved vital to breaking down de facto segregation that existed in urban communities of the North and the Midwest. Staged mostly in states that had civil rights laws that were not being enforced, these demonstrations against public facilities provided a model for the youth activism that would engulf the South during the 1960s. These early sit-in demonstrations and boycotts were well known by student activists. In fact, student demonstrators during the 1960s drew upon early direct action campaigns that had successfully broken down discrimination in public accommodations. While the association resisted efforts to stage direct action projects outside the South, not all youth groups followed that directive, as was evident with the direct action project launched by the Dallas Youth Council to eliminate discrimination at the Texas State Fair. Additionally, the successes of the sit-in demonstrations and the selective buying campaigns of the Wichita and Oklahoma City youth councils revealed that these direct action strategies could be effective in the South. Moreover, these successful sit-in demonstrations—and the withholding patronage campaigns staged by NAACP youth groups—provided the basis for youth activism in other civil rights groups, such as CORE and SNCC.

Even though the NAACP endorsed these programs in the South during the 1960s, its bureaucratic hand dictated the procedures for operation. The

NAACP frowned upon the helter-skelter direct action projects of SNCC and CORE. Condemning the actions of SNCC in Albany, Georgia, the association maintained that the project was poorly planned. When youth councils and college chapters decided to stage direct action projects, the events had to be cleared first through the national office. However, some NAACP youth groups rebuffed such directives, as made evident in the direct action projects coordinated by COFO in Mississippi. The association mandated that NAACP projects could not be distinguished as programs carried out by SNCC and CORE. The association did not want its youth groups' identity to be submerged within COFO, an arrogance that put the association at odds with other civil rights organizations. Criticism of the NAACP and its youth groups resulted not from the type of programs carried out, but from the bureaucratic hand that guided them. As a result of the association's autocratic leadership, some youth defected to the less bureaucratic civil rights organizations, such as CORE and SNCC. Although it criticized other civil rights organizations for helter-skelter projects, the association failed to recognize its own shortcomings. The youth movement within the association could have been far more successful if the national office would have loosened its tight hold over programs initiated by the youth councils and college chapters. Having to call the national office to get permission before staging mass demonstrations proved cumbersome, especially in crisis situations that demanded immediate attention.

During the mid-1960s, the association focused its direct action projects on urban slums throughout the United States. The association made a bold attempt to provide programs that were more relevant to the needs of inner-city residents. Participating in President Lyndon Johnson's Community Action Project programs, NAACP youth groups created significant change in urban areas. Through CAP programs, NAACP youth councils and college chapters provided underprivileged youth living in crime- and drug-infested environments viable alternatives for better lives. Indeed, CAP brought about change to alleviate problems for many underprivileged residents in urban slums throughout the United States.

Hence, this work on the NAACP youth movement provides valuable insight into the complex early history of black youth's fight for civil rights long before the decade of the 1960s. Black youth activism did not begin with the activism of CORE and SNCC student activists. Having traced a vibrant youth movement within the NAACP, although fraught with internal and external problems, this research revealed that youth councils and college chapters greatly advanced the fight for civil rights across the United States. Although heavily manned by the national office, NAACP youth group programs created a model for youth activism that other groups could embrace. Much has been written about the general history of the association; however, little has been written about the activism of its youth groups. *NAACP Youth and the Fight for*

Black Freedom captures the history of the NAACP youth movement, focusing largely on the direct action campaigns staged by youth councils and college chapters. The common narrative of the NAACP as a legalistic organization, working only through the courts to achieve civil rights, dies hard. This version of the story has largely shaped our understanding of NAACP activism. Deeper research into the youth councils and college chapters, however, paints a very different picture of the work of the association. By insisting on having more direct action campaigns, youth councils and college chapters forced the national office to expand the scope of its programs. The direct action strategies employed by the youth councils and college chapters secured many civil rights victories at the state and local levels. The nonviolent direct action protest takes center stage within this study, catapulting the work of the NAACP beyond the narrow legalistic framework embedded in historical narratives of the organization. In many ways, this research disproves the received opinion that NAACP civil rights victories came largely through the courts. Although the association's bureaucratic hand controlled the scope of the youth's program, the youth councils and college chapters' contributions to the advancement of civil rights reached beyond the organization's bureaucratic hand. Indeed, the activism of the NAACP youth movement must now be incorporated into the annals of civil rights history.

Notes

Introduction

1. Rebecca de Schweinitz, *If We Could Change the World: Young People and America's Long Struggle for Racial Equality* (Chapel Hill: Univ. of North Carolina Press, 2009), 170.

2. Ibid.

3. Ibid., 5.

4. These demonstration campaigns against public facilities succeeded in the North, Midwest, West, and parts of the Upper South. See *Papers of the National Association for the Advancement of Colored People,* ed. John Bracey, Sharon Harley, and August Meier, Manuscripts Division, Library of Congress, Washington, D.C. (Washington, D.C.: Univ. Publications of America, 1995), microfilm, pt. 19, ser. B, reel 14 (hereafter cited as *NAACP Papers*).

5. See 1944 Annual Report of the Youth Secretary, in *NAACP Papers,* pt. 19, ser. B, reel 5.

6. Patricia Sullivan, *Lift Every Voice: The NAACP and the Making of the Civil Rights Movement* (New York: New Press, 2009), xviii.

7. See Flora Bryant, "NAACP Sponsored Sit-ins by Howard University Students in Washington, D.C., 1943–1944," *Journal of Negro History* (Sept. 2000): 275–83.

8. See *NAACP Youth News Letter* [*sic*], Mar. 1949, in *NAACP Papers,* pt. 19, ser. C, reel 27.

9. See 1949 Annual Youth Report, in *NAACP Papers,* pt. 19, ser. B, reel 1.

10. Mary Dudziak, *Cold War Civil Rights: Race and the Image of American Democracy* (Princeton, NJ: Princeton Univ. Press, 2000), 27.

11. See press release, "Negro Girl Becomes First Grad of Integrated School in North Carolina," in *NAACP Papers,* pt. 19, ser. D, reel 16.

12. For a personal account of the desegregation of Central High School, see Daisy Bates, *The Long Shadow of Little Rock* (Little Rock: Univ. of Arkansas Press, 1987). See also Melba Patillo Beals, *Warriors Don't Cry* (New York: Washington Square Press, 1994).

13. See "Special Report on Sit Downs: NAACP Staff Activity in the Sit Downs," in *NAACP Papers,* pt. 19, ser. D, reel 19. Note: Ezell and Joseph McNeil were officers in the Greensboro Youth Council.

14. Blacks were mostly hired in janitorial positions in many department stores.

15. See monthly report by Julie Wright, Sept. 6, 1961, in *NAACP Papers,* pt. 19, ser. D, reel 20.

16. See monthly report of Julie Wright, Oct. 5–Nov. 8, 1961, in *NAACP Papers,* pt. 19, ser. D, reel 20.

17. See 1961 Annual Report on Youth Work, in *NAACP Papers,* pt. 19, ser. D, reel 6.

18. Clayborne Carson, *In Struggle: SNCC and the Black Awakening of the 1960s* (Cambridge, MA: Harvard Univ. Press, 1981), 19–20.

19. Barbara Ransby, *Ella Baker and the Black Freedom Movement: A Radical Democratic Vision* (Chapel Hill: Univ. of North Carolina Press, 2003), 245.

20. See Report of Youth Secretary, July 25–Aug. 2, 1964, in *NAACP Papers,* pt. 19, ser. D, reel 17.

21. See the Community Action Project, in *NAACP Papers,* pt. 19, ser. D, reel 8.

1. "Ours Is an Immediate Task"

1. Robert Cohen, *When the Old Left Was Young* (New York: Oxford Univ. Press, 1993), 209.

2. Ibid., xiv.

3. See Miss Campbell, memorandum to Mr. Morrow, Dec. 21, 1938, in *NAACP Papers,* pt. 19, ser. A, reel 1; and 1938 Annual Report on Youth Councils and College Chapters, in *NAACP Papers,* pt. 19, ser. A, reel 1.

4. Walter White to the NAACP's National Board of Directors, Feb. 2, 1933, in *NAACP Papers,* pt. 19, ser. A, reel 1. This restructuring of the youth program came at a time when leaders within the association were debating the organization's traditional commitment to legalism, as opposed to using direct action as a viable way to achieve civil rights. The old guard wanted to hold fast to the tradition of legalism, whereas the new guard believed that direct action could be combined with legalism to achieve civil rights. This debate of legalism versus direct action influenced Walter White's and Juanita Jackson's positions on youth activism. See Kenneth Mack, "Law and Mass Politics in the Making of the Civil Rights Lawyer, 1931–1941," *Journal of American History* 93 (June 2006): 1–24; and Beth Tompkins Bates, "A New Crowd Challenges the Agenda of the Old Guard in the NAACP, 1933–1941," *American Historical Review* 102 (Apr. 1997): 340–77.

5. Juanita Jackson to the national board of directors, June 25, 1938, in *NAACP Papers,* pt. 19 ser. A, reel 3.

6. Jackson started her education at Morgan College (now Morgan State University), but when her mother, Lillie Jackson, learned that the college was unaccredited, she withdrew her from the school. Lillie believed that Juanita should receive a first-class education. Believing that a quality education was of utmost importance, Lillie brought Juanita to Philadelphia, where she was able to get her into the University of Pennsylvania. See "Law in the Lives of People" by Juanita Jackson Mitchell, available at http://www.upenn.edu/almanac/v28pdf/n10/111081-insert.pdf (accessed Nov. 17, 2006).

7. *The Reflector,* Sept. 9, 1935, 1. See also the Maryland Women's Hall of Fame, "Juanita Jackson Mitchell," available at http://www.mdarchives.state.md.us/msa/educ/exhibits/womenshall/html/mitchell.html (accessed Nov. 17, 2006).

8. John Hope Franklin and Genna Rae McNeil, eds., *African Americans and the Living Constitution* (Washington, D.C.: Smithsonian, 1995), 60.

9. Juanita Jackson Mitchell, "Law in the Lives of People," available at http://www.upenn.edu/almanac/v28pdf/n10/111081-insert.pdf (accessed Nov. 17, 2006).

10. Ibid.

11. Katherine Kenny and Eleanor Randrup, *Juanita Jackson Mitchell: Freedom Fighter* (Baltimore, MD: PublishAmerica, 2005), 26–27.

12. Juanita Jackson Mitchell, "Law in the Lives of People," available at http://www.upenn.edu/almanac/v28pdf/n10/111081-insert.pdf (accessed Nov. 17, 2006).

13. Kenny and Randrup, *Juanita Jackson Mitchell*, 27.

14. Juanita Jackson Mitchell, "Law in the Lives of People," available at http://www.upenn.edu/almanac/v28pdf/n10/111081-insert.pdf (accessed Nov. 17, 2006).

15. For more information about Lillie Jackson's life and activism, see "Dr. Lillie M. Carroll Jackson: 'Mother of Freedom' (1889–1975)," available at http://www.naacpbaltimore.org/bio-jackson.html (accessed Nov. 17, 2006). See also Tom Chalkley, "Mother Figure," *Baltimore City Paper,* available at http://www.citypaper.com/printStory.asp?id=2483 (accessed Nov. 17, 2006); and Barbara Ransby, *Ella Baker and the Black Freedom Movement: A Radical Democratic Vision* (Chapel Hill: Univ. of North Carolina Press, 2003), 122–23.

16. Sonya Ramsey, *Reading, Writing, and Segregation: A Century of Black Women Teachers in Nashville* (Urbana: Univ. of Illinois Press, 2008), 47.

17. Juanita Jackson Mitchell, "Law in the Lives of People," available at http://www.upenn.edu/almanac/v28pdf/n10/111081-insert.pdf (accessed Nov. 17, 2006).

18. *The Crisis* 43 (Aug. 1936): 248–49. See also *The Crisis* 43 (Sept. 1936): 281–82.

19. General Session for Youth Section NAACP Conference, in *NAACP Papers,* pt. 19, ser. A, reel 1. See also *NAACP Papers,* Youth File, Box I E1, Folder 15.

20. *NAACP Papers,* Youth File, Box I E1, Folder 15.

21. This was not the initial policy. An early draft of the NAACP Youth Division constitution set the ages from eighteen to thirty. In the 1938 Annual Youth Report, Jackson noted that after the junior branches were scrapped, the junior youth council's age range was set from twelve to fifteen, and the youth council's age range was set from sixteen to twenty-five. The age change resulted from growing concerns about incorporating younger youth into the association's youth work. See *NAACP Papers,* pt. 19, ser. A, reel 1.

22. The membership fee for youth under twenty-one years old was fifty cents, and for youth twenty-one years old and older, the fee was one dollar. For youth who wanted a subscription to *The Crisis,* an additional fee was added. See constitutions for youth council and college chapter, in *NAACP Papers,* pt. 19 ser. A, reel 1. In 1953, the fees were increased for the first time due to the increased cost of operating the youth division. See also the *News and Action Letter,* Mar. 2, 1953, in *NAACP Papers,* pt. 19 ser. C, reel 27.

23. See document titled "Relationship between Branches, Youth Councils, College Chapters with National Office," in *NAACP Papers,* pt. 19 ser. B, reel 7.

24. This information was taken from a document that outlined the objectives of the youth councils and the officers and their duties. See *NAACP Papers,* pt. 19, ser. A, reel 1.

25. This information can be found in many reports outlining the youth work of the NAACP. However, this information was taken from the 1938–1939 National Youth Program. See *NAACP Papers,* pt. 19, ser. A, reel 1.

26. See document titled "The Youth Council of the N.A.A.C.P.," in *NAACP Papers,* pt. 19, ser. A, reel 1.

27. Notably, holding meetings in the home only worked for small groups. Large youth groups held their meetings at local churches, community centers, or sometimes at the YMCA or YWCA.

28. Juanita Jackson, letter to college and university administrators, Mar. 4, 1936, in *NAACP Papers,* pt. 19, ser. A, reel.

29. Juanita Jackson, letter to the youth members of the NAACP, Aug. 5, 1936, in *NAACP Papers,* pt. 19, ser. A, reel 1. See also *NAACP Papers,* Youth File, Box E1, Folder 7.

30. Robert Zangrando, "The NAACP and a Federal Anti-lynching Bill, 1934–1940," *Journal of Negro History* 50 (Apr. 1965): 106; and *The NAACP Crusade Against Lynching, 1909–1950* (Philadelphia, PA: Temple Univ. Press, 1980), 10–11.

31. Zangrando, "The NAACP and a Federal Anti-Lynching Bill," 108.

32. Ibid., 107–8.

33. Ibid., 109–11.

34. Juanita Jackson, outline of the "Nationwide Anti-Lynching Demonstrations," in *NAACP Papers,* pt. 19, ser. A, reel 1.

35. Ibid. See also *The Crisis* 44 (Jan. 1937): 26.

36. See Juanita Jackson, letter to Youth Council and College Chapter Officers, Jan. 22, 1937, in *NAACP Papers,* pt. 19, ser. A, reel 1.

37. In 1937, the NAACP youth chapters raised $2,696.70. Most of this money was used to cover the operational expenses of the youth department (which $1,860.00 covered the salary of the national youth director, Juanita Jackson). See itemized financial Report of Youth Work, Jan.–Dec. 1937, and Report of Youth Work, June 25, 1938, in *NAACP Papers,* Youth File, Box II E3, Folder 1. See also Juanita Jackson, letter to the youth members of the NAACP, Aug. 5, 1936, in *NAACP Papers,* pt. 19, ser. A, reel 1.

38. This information was taken from the written version of a speech given by Senator Robert Wagner over the radio on February 12, 1937, to garner support for the Costigan-Wagner Bill. To reference the entire speech, see *NAACP Papers,* Youth File, Box I E1, Folder 2. See also *NAACP Papers,* pt. 19, ser. A, reel 1; and *The Crisis* 44 (Feb. 1937): 56.

39. Report of youth councils and college chapters, Sept. 1937, in *NAACP Papers,* pt. 19, ser. A, reel 1. By November 16, 1937, the Boston Youth Council was holding weekly radio broadcasts on WORL each Tuesday under the leadership of Reynold Costa. See *The Crisis* 45 (Jan. 1938): 24.

40. By 1938, southern congressman filibustered the Costigan-Wagner bill, but the NAACP did not end its fight against lynching.

41. See Molly Yard, letter to Juanita Jackson, June 16, 1937, in *NAACP Papers*, Youth File, Box I E2, Folder 2.

42. Cohen, *When the Old Left was Young*, 141, 212.

43. C. Alvin Hughes, "We Demand Our Rights: The Southern Negro Youth Congress, 1937–1949," *Phylon* 48 (First Quarter 1987): 43. See also the *Norfolk Journal and Guide*, Feb. 5, 1938; and *The Crisis* 43 (Aug. 1936): 238.

44. Robin G. Kelley, *Hammer and Hoe: Alabama Communists During the Great Depression* (Chapel Hill: Univ. of North Carolina Press, 1990), 195–226. See also Hughes, "We Demand Our Rights," 38–50.

45. Dorothy and Louis Burnham were both active members of the ASU. As an ASU organizer, Louis Burnham made little leeway in the South organizing black youth. This failure was in part due to the ASU's lack of financial resources. As a predominately white youth organization, ASU was unable to gain the mass following of blacks necessary to combat the strictures of segregation in the south. Many black youths were suspicious of white organizations and civil rights activists who worked for them. However, Burnham experienced a different reaction when he attempted to organize black youth through the SNYC. Because it was a black-led organization and was specifically set up to address the needs of southern black youth, SNYC proved effective in mobilizing youth in the fight against Jim Crow and racism in the south. That SNYC was a spin-off from NNC perhaps quelled many suspicions that blacks had concerning the organization's legitimacy and sincerity in the fight for civil rights. SNYC mobilized many blacks in the South and had great success in mobilizing industrial workers, but this organization's ardent campaigns for civil rights came to an end when it disintegrated in 1949 as a result of racist and anticommunist repression. This information was obtained from Dorothy Burnham's presentation on July 17, 2006, at the NEH Summer Institute on Civil Rights hosted by the W. E. B. Du Bois Center, Harvard University. She provided valuable insight into the role of the SNYC and the NAACP youth councils in their fight for civil rights. See also Cohen, *When the Old Left Was Young*, 221.

46. This information was taken from Inequalities in the Education Report, Oct. 15, 1937, in *NAACP Papers*, pt. 19, ser. A, reel 1.

47. Kriste Lindenmeyer, *The Greatest Generation Grows Up* (Chicago: Ivan R. Dee, 2005), 135–39. See also *The Crisis* 43 (July 1936): 200–201.

48. Lindenmeyer, *The Greatest Generation*, 135–39.

49. Ibid. See also Tanika White, "Marshall Led Way to Ruling," *The Baltimore Sun*, May 16, 2004, available at http://www.baltimoresun.com/news/opinion/oped/bal-pe.md.marshall16may16,0,3262197.story?page=2 (accessed Feb. 10, 2012).

50. In the late 1930s, eleven southern states had higher public education expenditures for white students than for black students. In the 1930–31 school year, the average expenditure for white students was $44.31, compared to $12.57 for black students. For example, in South Carolina, the figures were $56.06 for

whites and $7.84 for blacks. In Mississippi, the average amount spent for white students was $45.50 and $5.45 for black students. *Report of the Commission on Interracial Cooperation,* quoted in the fourth edition of *Recent Trends in Race Relations,* in *NAACP Papers,* pt. 19, ser. A, reel 1.

51. This information was taken from the Sept. 1937 Report on Youth Councils and College Chapters, in *NAACP Papers,* pt. 19, ser. A, reel 1.

52. *Nation's Progress* was published in 1931, and the *History of the American People* was published in 1927. These history textbooks were widely used in public schools across the United States. The latter textbook was used in New York public schools well into the 1940s. Dr. Stephen F. Bayne, associated superintendent and chairman of the curriculum department of the board of education in New York pledged to Councilman Benjamin J. Davis Jr. that he would get rid of or correct all textbooks that were undemocratic and "anti-Negro." See press release, June 15, 1944, from Councilman Benjamin J. Davis Jr., in *NAACP Papers,* General Office File, Box II A147, Folder 2.

53. This information was taken from a report on Textbook Survey for Youth Councils. See *NAACP Papers,* pt. 19, ser. A, reel 1. On June 22, at the 31st annual conference of the NAACP, the youth put forth a resolution condemning racist notions about African Americans in textbooks. The resolution stated, "We [NAACP youth] deplore the textbooks furnished in our public schools which either ignore the valuable contributions made by Negroes or else contain vicious and perverted statements about them. We urge that this glaring injustice be speedily remedied by effective legislation or statue so that children of America may know the truth concerning ten per cent of its population." See also *The Crisis* 47 (Sept. 1940): 298; and *NAACP Papers,* Youth File, Box I E1, Folder 9.

54. *NAACP Papers,* Youth File, Box I E3, Folder 4.

55. This information was taken from a document entitled "The Negro—A Short Bibliography." See *NAACP Papers,* pt. 19, ser. A, reel 1.

56. Ibid.

57. See Walter White's comments on the Edward Lawrence's article, in *NAACP Papers,* pt. 19, ser. A, reel 1.

58. Genna Rae McNeil, *Groundwork: Charles Hamilton Houston and the Struggle for Civil Rights* (Philadelphia: Univ. of Pennsylvania Press, 1985), 138–39. See also *The Crisis* 42 (Aug. 1935): 239; and *The Crisis* 42 (Dec. 1935): 364, 370, 372.

59. See Edward Lawrence, letter to "Youth Council Officers," Nov. 2, 1936, and Juanita Jackson, letter to "Officers of Youth Councils and College Chapters," Nov. 23, 1936, in *NAACP Papers,* pt. 19, ser. A, reel 1; and *The Crisis* (Aug. 1938): 275

60. See Joel Spingarn, address delivered at the NAACP annual conference in Detroit, Michigan on July 1, 1937, in *NAACP Papers,* Youth File, Box I E2, Folder 4.

61. Oliver C. Cox, "Provisions for Graduate Education among Negroes, and the Prospects of a New System," *Journal of Negro Education* 9 (Jan. 1940): 22–31; Jayne R. Beilke, "The Politics of Opportunity: Philanthropic Fellowship Programs, Out-of-State Aid, and Black Higher Education in the South," *History*

of Higher Education Annual 17 (1997): 53–96. Oklahoma was the only state to provide support for out-of-state living expenses.

62. Daniel T. Kelleher, "The Case of Lloyd Lionel Gaines: The Demise of the Separate but Equal Doctrine," *Journal of Negro History* 56 (Oct. 1971): 262–71.

63. Juanita Jackson Mitchell, "Law in the Lives of People," available from http://www.upenn.edu/almanac/v28pdf/n10/111081-insert.pdf.

64. See youth councils and college chapters' financial reports in *NAACP Papers,* Youth File, Box I E2, Folder 10.

65. Richard A. Reiman, *The New Deal and American Youth: Ideas and Ideals in a Depression Decade* (Athens: Univ. of Georgia, 1992), 4.

66. Cohen, *When the Old Left Was Young,* 191. For further discussion on the NYA's educational and work relief programs for both black and white youth, see Kriste Lindenmeyer, *The Greatest Generation Grows Up,* 206–40. See also Cohen, *When the Old Left Was Young,* 191.

67. Cohen, *When the Old Left Was Young,* 191.

68. Ibid., 189.

69. Ibid., 191.

70. Ibid., 192.

71. Juanita Jackson to youth members of the NAACP, Aug. 5, 1936, in *NAACP Papers,* pt. 19, ser. A, reel 1. See also *NAACP Papers,* Youth File, Box E1, Folder 7.

72. Audrey Thomas McCluskey and Elaine M. Smith, *Mary McLeod Bethune: Building a Better World* (Bloomington: Indiana Univ. Press, 1999), 6; B. Joyce Ross, "Mary McLeod Bethune and the National Youth Administration: A Case Study of Power Relationships in the Black Cabinet of Franklin D. Roosevelt," *Journal of Negro History* 60 (Jan. 1975): 7. See also Walter G. Daniel and Carroll L. Miller, "The Participation of the Negro in National Youth Administration Program," *Journal of Negro Education* 9 (July 1938): 359; and Marian Thompson Wright, "Negro Youth and the Federal Emergency Programs: CCC and NYA," *Journal of Negro Education* 9 (July 1940): 397.

73. Walter G. Daniel and Carroll L. Miller, "The Participation of the Negro in National Youth Administration Program," *Journal of Negro Education* 9 (July 1938): 359.

74. B. Joyce Ross, "Mary McLeod Bethune and the National Youth Administration: A Case Study of Power Relationships in the Black Cabinet of Franklin D. Roosevelt," *Journal of Negro History* 60 (Jan. 1975): 7. See also Daniel and Miller, "The Participation of the Negro in National Youth Administration Program," 359.

75. Cohen, *When the Old Left Was Young,* 191.

76. Ross, "Mary McLeod Bethune and the National Youth Administration," 7.

77. Ibid., 13.

78. McCluskey, *Mary McLeod Bethune,* 216–26.

79. Manfred Berg, *"The Ticket to Freedom:" The NAACP and the Struggle for Black Political Integration* (Gainesville: Univ. Press of Florida, 2005), 62.

80. Andrew M. Fearnley, "'Your Work Is the Most Important, but without Branches There Can Be No National Work': Cleveland's Branch of the NAACP, 1929-1968," in *Long Is the Way and Hard: One Hundred Years of the NAACP,* ed. Kevern Verney and Lee Sartain, 209 (Fayetteville: Univ. of Arkansas Press, 2009).

81. Ardelia Bradley, letter to Juanita Jackson, Mar. 7, 1938, in *NAACP Papers,* pt. 19, ser. A, reel 3. See also *NAACP Papers,* Youth File, Box I E4, Folder 14.

82. Ibid.

83. Barbara Ransby, *Ella Baker,* 37. See also *The Crisis* 43 (Aug. 1936): 247–49, *The Crisis* 48 (Mar. 1941): 86; and *The Crisis* 108 (July–Aug. 2001): 38–41, which note Baker's role in the consumer cooperative movement.

84. See Ella Baker, address to youth in "General Session: Youth Council N.A.A.C.P., Baltimore, Maryland, June 30, 1936," in *NAACP Papers,* Youth File, Box I E1, Folder 15.

85. *The Crisis* 47 (Sept. 1940): 282.

86. In a report entitled "The Youth Movement in the NAACP," Juanita Jackson outlines the accomplishments of the association's youth movement. See *NAACP Papers,* pt. 19, ser. A, reel 1. See also *The Crisis* 44 (Feb. 1937): 57, and *The Crisis* 46 (May 1939): 153.

87. This information was taken from the Annual Youth Report, Sept. 1937, in *NAACP Papers,* pt. 19, ser. A, reel 1. See also *The Crisis* 44 (Jan. 1937): 27.

88. This information was taken from a document entitled "Objectives of Youth Council." See *NAACP Papers,* pt. 19, ser. A, reel 1.

89. Manfred Berg, *"Ticket to Freedom,"* 69–93, examines black voting rights campaigns in the 1930s, but makes no mention of the activities of the NAACP youth organizations.

90. de Schweinitz, *If We Could Change the World,* 7.

91. Ibid., 8.

92. Sullivan, *Lift Every Voice,* 146.

93. *The Crisis* 86 (Nov. 1979): 400.

94. de Schweinitz, *If We Could Change the World,* 9.

95. *The Crisis* 44 (Feb. 1937): 58.

96. Juanita Jackson, letter to youth leaders, July 19, 1937, in *NAACP Papers,* pt. 19, ser. A, reel 1. See also *The Crisis* 44 (Jan. 1937): 26–27; and *The Crisis* 44 (Oct. 1937): 314.

97. The 1938 Annual Youth Report in *NAACP Papers,* pt. 19, ser. A, reel 1. See also *The Crisis* 45 (Aug. 1938): 273–74; and *NAACP Papers,* Youth File, Box I E3, Folder 4.

98. *NAACP Papers,* Youth File, Box I E3, Folder 4; and *The Crisis* 45 (Aug. 1938): 273–75.

99. For more information on the life and activism of Juanita Jackson, see "Mrs. Juanita Jackson Mitchell, Esq.: Avowed Freedom Fighter," available at http://www.naacpbaltimore.org/bio-mitchell.html (accessed Nov. 17, 2006).

100. Kenny and Randrup, *Juanita Jackson Mitchell*, 33; Ransby, *Ella Baker*, 122.

101. Kenny and Randrup, *Juanita Jackson Mitchell*, 33.

102. Ransby, *Ella Baker*, 122.

103. Eben Miller, *Born along the Color Line: The 1933 Amenia Conference and the Rise of a National Civil Rights Movement* (New York: Oxford Univ. Press, 2012), 213.

104. Juanita Jackson, letter to the National Board, June 25, 1938, in *NAACP Papers*, pt. 19, ser. A, reel 3.

105. NAACP youth councils in the late 1950s organized sit-in demonstrations at restaurants and lunch counters in midwestern cities after launching the Montgomery bus boycott in 1955–56. See Aldon Morris, *Origins of the Civil Rights Movement: Black Communities Organizing for Change* (New York: The Free Press, 1984), 124–25.

2. To "Keep Our Vision Unclouded"

1. The First World Youth Congress was held in 1936 in Geneva, Switzerland, under the auspices of the International Federation of the League of Nations Societies. This information was taken from the keynote address delivered by Walter White at the first annual NAACP student conference on March 29, 1940. See proceedings of the first annual student conference, in *NAACP Papers*, pt. 19, ser. B, reel 2. See also *The Crisis* 47 (May 1940): 154.

2. See the pamphlet for the Second World Youth Congress, in *NAACP Papers*, Youth File, Box I E2, Folder 9.

3. The News Service of the National Catholic Welfare Conference condemned the Second World Youth Congress conference as "irreligious and communistic." It was believed that the conference served as a communist front to further communistic activities within the United States. The NAACP had some concerns about allegations of communist domination. Juanita Jackson noted in a letter to William Hinkley, an official of the Second World Congress, that the NAACP delegate Virginia Anderson would only serve as an "observer," and made clear that the NAACP was not affiliated with the organization. The World Youth Congress, like other American youth organizations, would come under close scrutiny and surveillance by the Dies Committee, headed by Martin Dies. See Ted Morgan, *Reds: McCarthyism in Twentieth Century America* (New York: Random House, 2004) and *NAACP Papers*, Youth File, Box I E2, Folder 9.

4. See Betty Shield-Collins, "Statement on Religious Aspects of the World Youth Congress," in the *NAACP Papers*, pt. 19, ser. A, reel 2.

5. See Virginia Anderson, report on the Second World Youth Congress, in *NAACP Papers*, pt. 19, ser. A, reel 2.

6. Cohen, *When the Old Left Was Young*, 193–94.

7. Ibid., 82–83.

8. Because the Oxford Pledge called for isolationism and opposed all wars, the Vassar Pact allowed Communist students within the American Youth Congress and the American Student Union to denounce the Oxford Pledge and embrace

the Comintern's policy of collective security against the spread of Fascism. YCAW argued that the Comintern, not its commitment to the youth movement, influenced the Communist students' political position. The YCAW assertion was valid because the Communist students' position on collective security changed in 1939 when the Soviet Union signed a nonaggression pact with Germany, dissolving the Popular Front. The YCAW did not denounce the Soviet Union's alliance with Nazi Germany.

9. Cohen, *When the Old Left Was Young,* 184–86. See also Virginia Anderson's report on the Second World Youth Congress, in *NAACP Papers,* Youth File, Box I E2, Folder 9.

10. Cohen, *When the Old Left Was Young,* 184–85.

11. Virginia Anderson specifically notes that she talked with delegates from Czechoslovakia and India. See her report on the Second World Youth Congress, in *NAACP Papers,* Youth File, Box I E2, Folder 9.

12. Jackson asserted, "I resigned to marry my prince." Although Jackson was unconventional in social activism, she embraced the traditional practice of delaying her career goals to become a wife and mother. See Kenny and Randrup, *Juanita Jackson Mitchell,* 33. For information on James Robinson's appointment, see *NAACP Papers,* Youth File, Box E3, Folder 3.

13. See the biographical sketch of James H. Robinson, in *NAACP Papers,* pt. 19, ser. B, reel 2. See also Robinson's autobiography, *Road Without Turning: The Story of Reverend James H. Robinson* (New York: Farrar, Straus and Company, 1950), 140–55; and James Robinson's biographical sketch, in *NAACP Papers,* Youth File, Box II E49, Folder 6.

14. This endeavor was a community project sponsored by students and faculty of Union Theological Seminary and Barnard College. See biographical sketch of Robinson, in *NAACP Papers,* Youth File, Box II E49, Folder 6. See also Robinson, *Road Without Turning,* 205.

15. The original name of the church was the Morningside Presbyterian Church, and it had been closed prior to Robinson's appointment in May 1938. Upon his appointment, Robinson renamed the church the Church of the Master and considered himself the founder of the new church. See Robinson, *Road Without Turning,* 227.

16. See James Robinson, memorandum to Walter White, Apr. 17, 1941, in *NAACP Papers,* pt. 19, ser. B, reel 2. In this memorandum, Robinson inquires of White whether the national board of directors has found someone to replace him because he cannot continue to serve as acting youth director beyond June. He tells White that he is disappointed that no youth director has been named yet and that he took this position at great sacrifice to himself and the church and did not want to see his work come to nothing. Although Robinson would no longer serve as youth director, he maintained that he would remain dedicated to advancing the association's youth work.

17. Peter Lau, *Democracy Rising: South Carolina and the Fight for Black Equality since 1865* (Lexington: Univ. Press of Kentucky, 2006), 99.

18. Ibid., 99–101.

19. Ibid., 101.

20. Ibid., 102.

21. Ibid.

22. Ibid.

23. See *The Crisis* 46 (Oct. 1939): 312.

24. See *NAACP Papers,* Youth File, Box I E3, Folder 3.

25. Information concerning the horrific ordeal that William Anderson underwent with local authorities in Greenville, South Carolina, can be found in many correspondences. For a full account of the incident, see the 1940 Annual Youth Report, in the *NAACP Papers,* pt. 19, ser. B, reel 2. See also *The Crisis* 46 (Oct. 1939): 312; and *NAACP Papers,* Youth File, Box I E3, Folder 3.

26. See the 1940 Annual Youth Report, in the *NAACP Papers,* pt. 19, ser. B, reel 2. According to the Youth Councils and College Chapter Financial Report for 1939, the Boston Youth Council contributed $108.65, the largest amount contributed to the William Anderson Fund. See *NAACP Papers,* Youth File, Box I E2, Folder 10. Under the leadership of Marie Benton, president, and Dr. Josephine Jett Davis, youth advisor and vice president of Rockford Branch, the Rockford, Illinois, Youth Council contributed twenty-five dollars to the William Anderson Fund, which was the second largest single donation from the youth chapters. See *The Crisis* 46 (Oct. 1939): 312; and *NAACP Papers,* Youth File, Box I E3, Folder 16.

27. *The Crisis* 47 (Apr. 1940): 120.

28. For his heroic stance, William Anderson was invited to be one of the speakers at the first annual youth conference, which convened on March 29–31, 1940, at Virginia Union University in Richmond, Virginia. At the chapel service, Anderson told of his ordeal. He maintained that by stressing the brotherhood of Christianity and its principles he was able to win over the cooperation of many whites in this fight. See Anderson's letter to Robinson, the First Annual Student Conference Proceedings, and the 1940 Annual Youth Report, in *NAACP Papers,* pt. 19, ser. B, reel 2.

29. Lau, *Democracy Rising,* 105.

30. The first annual student conference was instituted on a trial basis. Before consenting to future conferences, the association wanted to make sure that this conference would be successful. The conference was more than a success. Although the first student conference was held during the spring semester, the other student conferences were held annually during the fall semester. See the programs outlining the first student conference, in the *NAACP Papers,* pt. 19, ser. B, reel 2.

31. See the proceedings at the first annual student conference, in *NAACP Papers,* pt. 19, ser. B, reel 2.

32. Ibid.

33. Based upon the proceedings of the first annual student conference, these youth do not appear to have been pacifists. They were only opposed to war because

they were reluctant to fight for a country that had not granted them full democracy.

34. Desmond King, "The Racial Bureaucracy: African Americans and the Federal Government in the Era of Segregated Race Relations," *Governance* 12 (Oct. 1999): 345–77.

35. Ibid.

36. Ibid.

37. Ibid.

38. Beth Tompkins Bates, "A New Crowd Challenges the Agenda of the Old Guard in the NAACP, 1939–1941," *American Historical Review* 102 (Apr. 1997): 340–77. See also the extensive labor files on labor conditions and workplace discrimination, in *NAACP Papers,* pt. 13, ser. A and B.

39. Patricia Sullivan, *Days of Hope: Race and Democracy in the New Deal Era* (Chapel Hill: Univ. of North Carolina Press, 1996), 135–36.

40. See Walter White, closing address at the third annual student conference, Nov. 1, 1941, Hampton Univ., Richmond, VA, in *NAACP Papers,* pt. 19, ser. B, reel 3.

41. *The Crisis* 49 (July 1942): 231.

42. See Walter White, closing address, Nov. 1, 1941.

43. See the Youth Proceedings of the Thirty-Second Annual NAACP Convention, June 24–27, 1941, Houston, Texas, in *NAACP Papers,* pt. 19, ser. B, reel 3.

44. Ibid.

45. See the 1941 Annual Youth Report, in *NAACP Papers,* pt. 19, ser. B, reel 1.

46. Ibid.

47. See the 1942 Annual Youth Report, in *NAACP Papers,* pt. 19, ser. B, reel 1.

48. Ibid.

49. Ibid.

50. Madison Jones, who replaced acting youth director James Robinson, served as national youth director from November 1940 to February 1943. While serving as youth director, Jones displayed great talent for conducting membership campaigns. Toward the end of his tenure, he divided his time between youth work and assistant field secretary for membership. See Mar. 1943 *NAACP Youth News Letter,* in *NAACP Papers,* pt. 19, ser. C, reel 27.

51. Jessie Carney Smith, *Notable Black American Women* (Detroit: Gale Research, 1992), 540–43.

52. Ransby, *Ella Baker,* 106.

53. *NAACP Youth News Letter,* Aug. 1943, in *NAACP Papers,* pt. 19, ser. C, reel 27.

54. Several letters reveal that many of the youths thought of Hurley as their friend. Albert Henderson's letters capture the essence of this sentiment. See Albert Henderson, letter to Ruby Hurley, June 19, 1949, in *NAACP Papers,* pt. 19, ser. C, reel 2.

55. See 1943 Annual Youth Report, in *NAACP Papers,* pt. 19, ser. B, reel 1. See also Annual Report to Gloster Current on May 13, 1953, in *NAACP Papers,* pt.

19, ser. B, reel 1; and "Memorandum to the Youth Work Committee from the Youth Secretary," in *NAACP Papers*, pt. 19, ser. C, reel 27.

56. Howell Raines, *My Soul Is Rested* (New York: Penguin Books, 1977), 131.

57. Ibid., 132.

58. Ibid., 133.

59. Langston Hughes, *Fight For Freedom: The Story of the NAACP* (New York: W. W. Norton and Co., 1962), 183.

60. For a more detailed account of Ruby Hurley's work with the NAACP, see the personal interview with Hurley in Raines, *My Soul Is Rested*, 131–37.

61. Raines, *My Soul Is Rested*, 137.

62. Hurley's activism within one year was incredible, which was only surpassed by the chartering of thirty-four youth councils and seven college chapters the previous year. See the 1943 Annual Youth Report, in *NAACP Papers*, pt. 19, ser. B, reel 1.

63. Ike Smalls, former president of the Des Moines, Iowa, and the executive director of the Ike Smalls Medical Aid Fund, donated this award to inspire enthusiasm for the association's youth work. See the July 1944 *NAACP Youth News Letter*, in *NAACP Papers*, pt. 19, ser. C, reel 27.

64. See the resolutions of the fifth annual student conference, in *NAACP Papers*, pt. 19, ser. B, reel 4.

65. This policy of the college chapters meeting separately from the youth councils was abandoned by 1944. The sixth annual student conference, which was renamed the annual youth conference, brought together college chapters and youth councils. This change resulted largely from the growth of the association's youth work and the national office's belief that the youth division could benefit greatly by having its own annual youth conference.

66. See the Annual Youth Report dated March 14, 1940, in *NAACP Papers*, pt. 19, ser. B, reel 1.

67. Notably, numerous youth councils were composed of college students and high school students. Normally, when they returned home for summer break, college students would continue their youth work through their local youth councils. However, there are recorded instances where the high school students and the college students could not work together and the college students left the council. For example, the Louisville, Kentucky, Youth Council experienced a conflict between the high school and the college youth. The report noted that the college youth dropped off gradually from the youth council. See report of the NAACP Thirty-Second Annual Conference, June 25, 1941, Houston, Texas, in *NAACP Papers*, pt. 19, ser. B, reel 3. These incidents were less common than the run-ins with the senior branch over youth activities.

68. This arrangement was not the initial policy. The policy was developed because some colleges existed in communities where there were no senior branches. Additionally, some college administrators did not want their chapters subjected to the authority of the local branch. See document titled "Relationship between

Branches, Youth Councils, College Chapters with National Office," in *NAACP Papers,* pt. 19, ser. B, reel 7.

69. Notably, during the 1940s, NAACP college chapters were largely found on the campuses of northern and Midwest white colleges and universities.

70. This niche segregation was a problem faced by NAACP college chapters in northern and midwestern states. Although institutions in these states admitted black students, college officials resisted efforts to desegregate dormitories, clubs, and Greek-letter organizations. Efforts to eradicate these discriminatory practices were waged by students at Cornell, Columbia, Bucknell, and Penn State, to name a few. In 1947, the first chapter of the NAACP was organized at the University of Texas. Subsequently, other chapters would be organized on college campuses in the south. At southern institutions, chapters consisted mainly of white youth because black students had not gained admission to these institutions. In 1948, the NAACP had four all-white college chapters, and they were on the campuses of the University of Texas (Austin), Phillips University, Cornell College, and Skidmore College. There were thirteen interracial groups on white college and/or university campuses: University of Chicago, Indiana University (Bloomington), Wayne State University, Aquinas College, Brooklyn College, Columbia University, New York University, Queens College, Long Island University, Cornell University, Sampson College, Syracuse University, and Pennsylvania State College. As the youth movement grew, chapters would be established on most college/university campuses.

71. The sit-in launched by Howard University's NAACP chapter shows that NAACP youth activists were using sit-ins as tactics long before SNCC members employed them. See Flora Bryant Brown, "NAACP Sponsored Sit-ins by Howard University Students in Washington, D.C., 1943–1944," *Journal of Negro History* 85 (Autumn 2000): 274–86.

72. Ibid. Pauli Murray must be noted for her determination and zeal. After being denied entrance into the University of North Carolina Law School, she later received her law degree from Howard University and played a vital role in advancing the youth work of the association. See also Pauli Murray, *Proud Shoes: The Story of An American Family* (Boston: Beacon Press, 1984).

73. Brown, "NAACP Sponsored Sit-ins," 279.

74. Ibid., 281.

75. Ibid.

76. Bryant questioned Johnson's lack of knowledge about the demonstration against Little Cafeteria, given that it was highly publicized around the school through flyers and student meetings.

77. Bryant, "NAACP Sponsored Sit-ins," 281–82.

78. Ibid.

79. See the resolutions adopted at the Wartime Conference and the resolutions adopted at the sixth annual youth conference, in *NAACP Papers,* pt. 19, ser. B, reel 5.

80. Ibid.

81. See Adam Clayton Powell, keynote address, in *NAACP Papers*, pt. 19, ser. B, reel 5.

82. See the resolutions adopted at the sixth annual youth conference, in *NAACP Papers*, pt. 19, ser. B, reel 5.

83. See the proceedings of the sixth annual youth conference, in *NAACP Papers*, pt. 19, ser. B, reel 5.

84. See 1944 Annual Report of the Youth Secretary, in *NAACP Papers*, pt. 19, ser. B, reel 5.

85. Ibid.

86. Although NAACP youth did not get Congress to pass Executive Order 9463, two decades later, the poll tax was outlawed with the passage of the Twenty-Fourth Amendment to the Constitution.

87. See Hurley, memorandum to Walter White, Nov. 28, 1944, concerning the sixth annual youth conference, in *NAACP Papers*, pt. 19, ser. B, reel 5.

88. See memorandum and full report of the World Youth Conference from Gloster B. Current, delegate to the Fourth World Youth Congress, in *NAACP Papers*, pt. 19, ser. B, reel 5.

89. See Charles Wesley, keynote address, in *NAACP Papers*, pt. 19, ser. B, reel 5.

90. See document entitled "Reports from the Various Youth Groups," which highlights the work that youth councils and college chapters performed in 1945, in *NAACP Papers*, pt. 19, ser. B, reel 5.

3. To Finish the Fight

The title of the chapter was inspired partly by Ruby Hurley's use of the phrase "To Finish the Fight" in many of her communications to the youth councils and college chapters, and by the provocative keynote address "Freedom From Fear," given by Judge Hubert Delany in 1946 at the eighth annual youth conference at Dillard University in New Orleans, Louisiana.

1. Hubert Delany was a judge of the New York Circuit Court of Domestic Relations and chairman of the NAACP National Board of Directors.

2. This information was taken from the keynote address "Freedom from Fear," delivered by Judge Hubert Delany in 1946 at the eighth annual youth conference at Dillard University. See *NAACP Papers*, pt. 19, ser. B, reel 6.

3. Many historians, like Jacquelyn Dowd Hall, argue that the beginning of the modern civil rights movement in America has a far more robust and long history than that proclaimed in many narratives on the movement. See Jacquelyn Dowd Hall, "The Long Civil Rights Movement and the Political Uses of the Past," *Journal of American History* 91 (Mar. 2005): 1233–63; and Vincent Harding, *There Is a River: The Black Struggle for Freedom in America* (New York: Harcourt Brace Jovanovich, Publishers, 1981). I contend, like Hall and Harding, that the civil rights movement was born long before the landmark Supreme Court decision in *Brown v. Board of Education* and the Montgomery Bus Boycott. Indeed, the movement was about more than the fight to transform

a legally segregated South or charismatic leaders calling for interracialism or sociopolitical self-determination. The movement that I capture is far more complex and inclusive; it transcends the South and national leaders, capturing the essence of ordinary black Americans and their day-to-day struggles against racial injustices, regional particulars, community and organizational challenges, and the will to keep fighting for equality. Although periodizing any social movement is always difficult and controversial, this work situates the fight for civil rights beginning in the late 1930s and accelerating shortly after the Second World War to show that the mass mobilization efforts of black Americans did not appear out of nowhere in the mid-1950s.

4. Isaac Woodard allegedly had been drinking with other servicemen and acting disorderly; however, these were trumped-up charges that the authorities used to justify actions taken against Woodard. Far more outrageous is that Shull claimed that Woodard was armed, so the action he took against him was in self-defense. Woodard's beating caused permanent damage to his eyes and left him blind. For a discussion on this incident and how it influenced Harry S. Truman's position on civil rights legislation, see Michael Gardner, *Harry Truman and Civil Rights: Moral Courage and Political Risks* (Carbondale: Southern Illinois Univ. Press, 2002). See also *The Crisis* 53 (Sept. 1946): 276.

5. See press release, Nov. 27, 1946, for the eighth annual youth conference, in *NAACP Paper*, pt. 19, ser. B, reel 6.

6. See Gardner, *Harry Truman and Civil Rights*, 18.

7. Sullivan, *Days of Hope*, 245. See also Gardner, *Harry Truman and Civil Rights*, 20–23.

8. See "Born of Controversy: The G.I. Bill of Rights," available at http://www.gibill.va.gov/GI_Bill_info/history.htm (accessed May 21, 2007).

9. See *The Crisis* 52 (Nov. 1945): 309; and *The Crisis* 52 (Dec. 1945): 340.

10. See "Youth Secretary's Speech to Delegates," an address by Ruby Hurley at the ninth annual youth conference, Houston, TX, in *NAACP Papers*, pt. 19, ser. B, reel 7.

11. See proceedings of the eighth annual youth conference, in *NAACP Papers*, pt. 19, ser. B, reel 6.

12. See *NAACP Youth News Letter*, Apr. 1948, in *NAACP Papers*, pt. 19, ser. C, reel 27.

13. See *NAACP Youth News Letter*, Oct. 1950, in *NAACP Papers*, pt. 19, ser. C, reel 27.

14. A. Philip Randolph and Grant Reynolds called upon black men to resist the draft until segregation was ended in the military. See *NAACP Youth News Letter*, Oct. 1950, in *NAACP Papers*, pt. 19, ser. C, reel 27.

15. See *News and Action Letter*, Jan.–Mar. 1951, in *NAACP Papers*, pt. 19 ser. C, reel 27. Thurgood Marshall maintained that the thirty-two black soldiers who were court-martialed for violating the 75th Article (misbehaving before the enemy) in the 25th Division received sentences ranging from death and life imprisonment to five years in prison. The two white soldiers accused of the same crime received only five- and three-year sentences each. As a result of the NAACP's

activism, twenty of the sentences were reduced. Thurgood Marshall blamed Jim Crow practices for the discrimination.

16. During the Korean Conflict, the federal government implemented the directive to phase out segregation in the military. The directive was met with resistance. The Korean Conflict was the first military engagement in which some blacks and whites fought in integrated units.

17. See press release, "End Armed Forces Segregation," in *NAACP Papers,* pt. 19, ser. B, reel 8.

18. Ibid.

19. See the *NAACP Youth News Letter,* Apr. 1948, in *NAACP Papers,* pt. 19, ser. C, reel 27. The NAACP held its last annual legislative youth conference in 1949, largely due to the fact that the association channeled all resources to support the 1950 Civil Rights Mobilization Conference and to declining youth membership. Notably, 80 percent of the NAACP's funding came from membership, so a decrease in membership would affect the association's ability to carry on certain programs. In 1954, the annual youth legislative conference reconstituted itself as the national annual youth legislative conference. Most youth were under twenty-five years of age but not younger than fifteen years old.

20. Although the conference was open to most youth organizations, the association during the 1950s denied attendance to youths who were affiliated with communist organizations. At the 1954 national annual youth conference, delegates Leon Wofsy and Roosevelt Ward (both members of the Labor Youth League) were turned away because of their organization's communist ties.

21. In the monthly newsletters sent out to the youth councils and college chapters, the association provided a detailed outline of each bill's provisions and its authors. Indeed, this information provided the youth with great knowledge about each bill so that they could speak intelligently about each bill in their meetings and communities, and when they visited their congressmen's offices. Additionally, this knowledge was beneficial in aiding the youth in writing letters to their respective congressmen to urge their support for certain bills.

22. See *NAACP Youth News Letter,* Apr. 1947, in *NAACP Papers,* pt. 19, ser. C, reel 27.

23. Ibid.

24. Ibid.

25. Ibid.

26. See the *NAACP Youth News Letter,* Apr. 1949, in *NAACP Papers,* pt. 19, ser. C, reel 27.

27. Ibid.

28. See "NAACP Youth Urged To Use Excursion Steamers," in *NAACP Papers,* pt. 19, ser. B, reel 9.

29. Ibid.

30. See proceedings of the eighth annual youth conference, in *NAACP Papers,* pt. 19, ser. B, reel 6.

31. See *News and Action Letter,* Oct. 1950, in *NAACP Papers,* pt. 19, ser. C, reel 27. Notably, there are numerous references to increasing the membership base throughout almost all of the newsletters and other memorandum sent to the youth councils and college chapters.

32. See Jacqueline Rouse's "'We Seek to Know . . . in Order to Speak the Truth': Nurturing the Seeds of Discontent—Septima P. Clark and Participatory Leadership," in *Sisters in the Struggle: African American Women in the Civil Rights–Black Power Movement,* ed. Bettye Collier-Thomas and V. P. Franklin (New York: New York Univ. Press, 2001), 107.

33. Ibid.

34. See Walter White, letter to youth officer, Sept. 26, 1950, in *NAACP Papers,* pt. 19, ser. B, reel 14.

35. See Herbert Wright, memorandum to youth councils, college chapters, and state youth conference officers, in *NAACP Papers,* pt. 19 ser. B, reel 13. See also biographical sketch of Herbert Wright, in *NAACP Papers,* pt. 19, ser. B, reel 8.

36. See the many memorandum referencing the Fighting for Freedom Fund, in *NAACP Papers,* pt. 19, ser. B, reel 13.

37. Before the March on Washington, wealthy whites under the guise of the Council on the United Civil Rights Leadership donated $800,000 for civil rights campaigns in the South. CORE and the NAACP received the largest allotment of the funds. See James Foreman, *The Making of Black Revolutionaries* (New York: Macmillan, 1972), 364–65.

38. See a more detailed discussion on the problems that surfaced between NAACP youth groups and the national office in chapter four.

39. In a document labeled "Projects which are especially suitable for Youth Councils which are located in Eastern, MidWestern and Far Western States," youth council members were advised on what strategies to take to combat discrimination in states that had civil rights laws. The association believed that many people accepted the limited use of facilities because they were not informed about the civil rights laws in their states. See *NAACP Papers,* pt. 19, ser. B, reel 14.

40. See *NAACP Youth News Letter,* Mar. 1949, in *NAACP Papers,* pt. 19, ser. C, reel 27.

41. Ibid. The entire dialogue was included to capture the essence of the conversation with the manager. The document did not state which councilor conversed with the manager, nor did it give the name of the manager. I could not locate this information in other documents. Likewise, the document provided limited information about the legal redress chairman; his full name is not given.

42. See *NAACP Youth News Letter,* March 1949, in *NAACP Papers,* pt. 19, ser. C, reel 27.

43. Ibid.

44. Robin Hoecker, "The Black and White Behind the Blue and White: A History of Black Protest at Penn State" (BA thesis, Pennsylvania State University, 2001), 21.

45. See "NAACP on the College Campus," in *NAACP Papers,* pt. 19, ser. C, reel 27.

46. See "The NAACP to Boycott Local Barbershops," *Daily Collegian,* Dec. 10 1948, available at http://digitalnewspapers.libraries.psu.edu/Default/Scripting/Article

Win.asp?From=Archive&Source=Page&Skin=collegian&BaseHref=DCG/ 1948/12/10&PageLabel=1&EntityId=Ar00101&ViewMode=HTML (accessed May 20, 2007).

47. Hoecker, "The Black and White," 21.

48. See "The NAACP to Boycott Local Barbershops," *Daily Collegian,* Dec. 10 1948, available at http://digitalnewspapers.libraries.psu.edu/Default/Scripting/Article Win.asp?From=Archive&Source=Page&Skin=collegian&BaseHref=DCG/ 1948/12/10&PageLabel=1&EntityId=Ar00101&ViewMode=HTML (accessed 20 May 20, 2007).

49. See "Picket Line to Continue in Barber-NAACP Fight," *Daily Collegian,* Dec. 14, 1948, available at http://digitalnewspapers.libraries.psu.edu/Default/Skins/ collegian/Client.asp?Skin=collegian&AppName= (accessed May 20, 2007).

50. Hoecker, "The Black and White," 22. Notably, the date given in the thesis is incorrect. After reading about the story in the "NAACP on the College Campus" and Hoecker's thesis, I discovered that the two sources presented different dates for the start of the boycott. After checking the *Daily Collegian,* the Penn State student paper (which is online), I was able to get the correct date and more information about the boycott; available at http://digitalnewspapers.libraries. psu.edu/Default/Scripting/ArticleWin.asp?From=Archive&Source=Page&Skin =collegian&BaseHref=DCG/1948/12/14&PageLabel=1&EntityId=Ar00103& ViewMode=HTML (accessed May 20, 2007).

51. See "NAACP to Hold Rally against Discrimination," *Daily Collegian,* Dec. 11, 1948, available at http://digitalnewspapers.libraries.psu.edu/Default/Scripting/ ArticleWin.asp?From=Archive&Source=Page&Skin=collegian&BaseHref=DC G/1948/12/11&PageLabel=1&EntityId=Ar00103&ViewMode=HTML (accessed May 20, 2007).

52. See "Barbers Refuse to Comment on Pickets' Effect," *Daily Collegian,* Dec. 15, 1948, available at http://digitalnewspapers.libraries.psu.edu/Default/Scripting/ ArticleWin.asp?From=Archive&Source=Page&Skin=collegian&BaseHref=DC G/1948/12/15&PageLabel=1&EntityId=Ar00100&ViewMode=HTML(accessed May 20, 2007).

53. Hoecker, "The Black and White," 23.

54. See the "NAACP on the College Campus," in *NAACP Papers,* pt. 19, ser. C, reel 27.

55. Black students composed less than 1 percent of the student population at white colleges and universities. Several factors must be taken into consideration to understand why they constituted such a small percent. First, black students preferred to attend their own institutions because of discriminatory practices at white schools. Second, many white colleges and universities had quotas, which restricted the number of black students. Lastly, many black students lacked money for a college education. See "School Aid for Negroes: Scholarship Service Finds 67,900 to Help 160 Students," *New York Tribune,* undated clipping, in *NAACP Papers,* pt. 19, ser. C, reel 3.

56. See memorandum to NAACP Youth Councils from the University of Rochester NAACP Chapter, in *NAACP Papers* pt. 19, ser. B, reel 14.

57. See Herbert L. Wright, memorandum to Mr. Current, Nov. 2, 1951, in *NAACP Papers,* pt. 19, ser. C, reel 3. The NSSFN was a social welfare agency whose endowments came from grants from foundations, college chests, and individual patrons. The NSSFN provided scholarship support to qualified black students to attend white colleges and universities. Wright, in conjunction with his visit to the South on official NAACP youth business, would collect data for the NSSFN on the admissions practices and racial attitudes toward blacks on white college and university campuses. In return for his services, the NSSFN agreed to assume half of his expenses.

58. See "School Aid for Negroes," *New York Tribune,* in *NAACP Papers,* pt. 19, ser. C, reel 3.

59. See the 1949 Annual Youth Report, in *NAACP Papers* pt. 19, ser. B, reel 1.

60. See May 1953 *News and Action Letter,* in *NAACP Papers,* pt. 19 ser. C, reel 27.

61. See "Report of the Student Board Committee against Discrimination," in *NAACP Papers,* pt. 19, ser. B, reel 11.

62. Ibid.

63. See Commission on Social Law and Action of the American Jewish Congress report, "Expanding Educational Opportunity, The Report of the President's Commission on Higher Education," in *NAACP Papers,* pt. 19, ser. B, reel 11.

64. See 1948 *NAACP Youth News Letter,* in *NAACP Papers,* pt. 19, ser. C, reel 27.

65. See previous discussion, in chapter two, on the NAACP youth affiliations with the World Youth Congress, which brought together young people from all backgrounds to mobilize against injustices that youth faced.

66. See June 1950 *News and Action Letter,* in *NAACP Papers,* pt. 19 ser. C, reel 27. For more information on the McLaurin case, see also "School Desegregation and Civil Rights Stories: University of Oklahoma" on the National Archives Mid Atlantic Region's website, available at http://www.archives.gov/midatlantic/education/desegregation/oklahoma.html (accessed May 20, 2007).

67. See "R. O'Hara to Jester, April 14, 1949" on the Texas State Library and Archives Commission, available at http://www.tsl.state.tx.us/governors/personality/jester-lanier.html (accessed May 20, 2007).

68. See *NAACP Youth News Letter,* Apr. 1947, in *NAACP Papers,* pt. 19, ser. C, reel 27.

69. See "NAACP Pickets Defy Segregation" and the numerous newspaper articles on the pickets at the Texas State University, in *NAACP Papers,* pt. 19, ser. B, reel 7.

70. See undated newspaper clipping "NAACP Official Asks UT Help," in *NAACP Papers,* pt. 19, ser. B, reel 7.

71. Thurgood Marshall expressed optimism about ending segregation. The Ada Sipuel, Herman Sweat, and George McLaurin cases set a precedent for the *Brown* decision (1954). See *News and Action Letter,* Sept. 1950, in *NAACP Papers,* pt. 19, ser. C, reel 27.

72. See *NAACP Youth News Letter,* Sept. 1947, in *NAACP Papers,* pt. 19, ser. C, reel 27.

73. See press release for the tenth annual youth conference held in 1948 in St. Louis, Missouri, in *NAACP Papers,* pt. 19, ser. B, reel 8.

74. See the 1946 Annual Youth Report, in *NAACP Papers,* pt. 19, ser. B, reel 1. See also the *NAACP Youth News Letter,* Jan. 1947, in *NAACP Papers,* pt. 19, ser. C, reel 27.

75. See "A Guide to Juanita Jewel Shank Craft Collection, 1939–1983," available at http://www. Lib.utexas.edu/taro/utcah/00086/cah-00086.html (accessed May 21, 2007).

76. See resolution adopted by delegates to the first annual state conference on youth and human rights, in *NAACP Papers,* pt. 19, ser. B, reel 14.

77. See the 1955 Annual Youth Report, in *NAACP Papers,* pt. 19 ser. B, reel 1. See also the *Youth and College,* in *NAACP Papers,* pt. 19, ser. C, reel 27.

78. See the many memorandums regarding this incident, in *NAACP Papers,* pt. 19 ser. B, reel 9.

79. Ruby Hurley, letter to Eleanor Cunningham, Nov. 23, 1948, in *NAACP Papers,* pt. 19, ser. B, reel 9.

80. Ibid.

81. See 1952 Annual Youth Report, in *NAACP Papers,* pt. 19, ser. B, reel 1.

82. Ibid.

83. de Schweinitz, *If We Could Change the World,* 174.

84. See anticommunist resolution passed at the 42nd Annual NAACP National Convention, in *NAACP Papers,* pt. 19, ser. B, reel 14.

85. See newspaper clipping "Racial Stand by New Group under Inquiry," in *NAACP Papers,* pt. 19, ser. B, reel 14. Because part of the newspaper clipping was cut off, it did not show where the article originated.

86. Ruby Hurley, letter to Dr. Milton Konvitz, Jan. 23, 1947, in *NAACP Papers,* Youth File, Box II E14, Folder 1. Hurley writes to Dr. Konvitz to see if he knew anything about the communist allegations, because she claimed that she did not know who was faculty advisor of the Cornell chapter.

87. See Ruby Hurley, letter to F. L. Marcuse, Feb. 13, 1947, in *NAACP Papers,* pt. 19, ser. B, reel 10.

88. Ruby Hurley, letter to Dr. Milton Konvitz, Feb. 3, 1947, and memorandum to Mr. Jones from Mrs. Hurley, Feb. 7, 1947, in *NAACP Papers,* Youth File, Box II E14, Folder 1.

89. Walter Lewis, letter to Ruby Hurley, Feb. 5, 1947, in *NAACP Papers,* pt. 19, ser. B, reel 10.

90. See F. L. Marcuse, letter to Ruby Hurley, Feb. 10, 1947, in *NAACP Papers,* pt. 19, ser. B, reel 10 and *NAACP Papers,* Youth File, Box II E14, Folder 1.

91. Ibid.

92. Ruby Hurley, letter to Walter Lewis, Feb. 19, 1947, in *NAACP Papers,* Youth File, Box II E14, Folder 1.

93. Ruby Hurley, letter to Albert Henderson, July 28, 1949, in *NAACP Papers,* pt. 19, ser. C, reel 2. See also the 1953 fall program for youth councils and college chapter, in *NAACP Papers,* pt. 19, ser. B, reel 14.

94. When the plan was initially introduced at the tenth annual youth conference in 1948, the youth division was divided into four regions. Region two was divided to provide greater means for member participation. The regional division was modeled after the NAACP annual national conference division.

95. See Albert Henderson, letter to Ruby Hurley, June 19, 1949, in *NAACP Papers,* pt. 19, ser. C, reel 2.

96. After 1955, the association reduced its human rights legislative agenda to a narrower civil rights plank to suit the political machinations of congressmen who felt that measures were too socialistic and un-American, especially southerners Theodore Bilbo and John Rankin, both from Mississippi. See further discussion on this subject in chapter four. See also Carol Anderson, *Eyes Off the Prize: The United Nations and the African American Struggle for Human Rights, 1944–1955* (Cambridge, UK: Cambridge Univ. Press, 2003).

97. See minutes from the emergency National NAACP Youth Leaders Conference held in 1950 at Howard University in Washington, D.C., in *NAACP Papers,* pt. 19, ser. C, reel 2.

98. See Report of the National Youth Work Committee to the 44th National Convention of the association, in *NAACP Papers,* pt. 19, ser. C, reel 7.

99. See press release, "Assistant Named to the NAACP Youth Office," in *NAACP Papers,* pt. 19, ser. B, reel 14.

100. See report of Muriel C. Gregg, youth field secretary, Pennsylvania Tour, July 5–31, 1955, in *NAACP Papers,* pt. 19, ser. B, reel 14. The last two problems were largely endemic to Pittsburgh and Philadelphia.

101. Ibid.

102. Muriel Gregg, letter to Herbert Wright, Oct. 2, 1955, in *NAACP Papers,* pt. 19, ser. B, reel 14.

103. Muriel Gregg, letter to Roy Wilkins, Oct. 12, 1955, in *NAACP Papers,* pt. 19, ser. B, reel 14.

104. Herbert Wright, memorandum to Gloster B. Current, Dec. 9, 1955, in *NAACP Papers,* pt. 19, ser. B, reel 12.

4. "With All Deliberate Speed"

1. Charles J. Ogletree Jr., *All Deliberate Speed: Reflections on the First Half Century of Brown v. Board of Education* (New York: W. W. Norton and Co., 2004), 127.

2. Ibid.

3. See *Youth and College Reporter,* Aug. 2, 1954, in *NAACP Papers,* pt. 19, ser. B, reel 14.

4. See "An Appeal to Youth of America," in *NAACP Papers,* pt. 19, ser. B, reel 14.

5. See "NAACP Youth Conference Urged to Help Implement School Rule," in *NAACP Papers*, pt. 19, ser. B, reel 14.

6. See "The Murder of Emmett Till" on the PBS website, available at http://www.pbs.org/wgbh/amex/till/peopleevents/e_trial.html (accessed May 21, 2007).

7. Ibid.

8. Ibid.

9. Raines, *My Soul Is Rested*, 133.

10. See 1955 *Youth and College Reporter*, in *NAACP Papers*, pt. 19, ser. C, reel.

11. See monthly reports of the youth and college division for February and June 1956, in *NAACP Papers*, pt. 19, ser. D, reel 17.

12. James T. Patterson, *Brown v. Board of Education: A Civil Rights Milestone and Its Troubled Legacy* (New York: Oxford Univ. Press, 2001), 105. See also Diane McWhorter, "The Day Autherine Lucy Dared to Integrate the University of Alabama," *Journal of Blacks in Higher Education* 32 (Summer 2001): 100–101. Note: Polly Myers also applied to the university and was accepted, but the school administration rescinded her admission on the grounds of "conduct and marital status." Because she was pregnant and unmarried when she applied for admission, Polly Myers had her application rescinded by the university. See McWhorter, "The Day Autherine Lucy Dared to Integrate the University of Alabama," 101.

13. See monthly report of the youth and college division for January 1956, in *NAACP Papers*, pt. 19, ser. D, reel 17. See also the 1956 annual report of the youth and college division, in *NAACP Papers*, pt. 19, ser. D, reel 16.

14. Patterson, *Brown v. Board of Education*, 105.

15. McWhorter, "The Day Autherine Lucy Dared to Integrate the University of Alabama," 101.

16. Ibid.

17. See the 1956 annual report of the youth and college division, in *NAACP Papers*, pt. 19, ser. D, reel 16. The annual report does not mention the names of the youth groups or student organizations at the university that supported Lucy's cause.

18. Ibid.

19. See the monthly report of the youth and college division, Apr. 1–May 31, 1956, in *NAACP Papers*, pt. 19, ser. D, reel 17.

20. Bobby L. Lovett, *The Civil Rights Movement in Tennessee: A Narrative History* (Knoxville: Univ. of Tennessee Press, 2005), 43–55. See also Clinton Beauchamp and Amanda Turner's "The Desegregation of Clinton Senior High School: Trial and Triumph," available at http://www.jimcrowhistory.org/resources/pdf/hs_es_clintonhs_deseg.pdf (accessed July 21, 2007).

21. Lovett, *Civil Rights Movement in Tennessee*, 44.

22. de Schweinitz, *If We Could Change the World*, 125.

23. See George McMillan, "'The Ordeal of Bobby Cain': Racial Confrontation at a Newly Integrated Southern High School," available at http://historymatters.gmu.edu/d/6254/ (accessed July 2, 2007).

24. Qtd. in Lovett, *Civil Rights Movement in Tennessee*, 44.

25. Lovett, *Civil Rights Movement in Tennessee*, 44–45. See also Clinton Beauchamp and Amanda Turner's "The Desegregation of Clinton Senior High School: Trial and Triumph," available at http://www.jimcrowhistory.org/resources/pdf/hs_es_clintonhs_deseg.pdf (accessed July 1, 2007).

26. Lovett, *Civil Rights Movement in Tennessee*, 45. See also Patterson, *Brown v. Board of Education*, 102.

27. Lovett, *Civil Rights Movement in Tennessee*, 45–46.

28. Ibid.

29. Ibid., 46.

30. Ibid., 46–47. See also George McMillan, "'The Ordeal of Bobby Cain.'" For a month, the National Guard maintained peace and order in the small town.

31. Lovett, *Civil Rights Movement in Tennessee*, 47.

32. Ibid., 47.

33. Ibid., 47–50.

34. See monthly report of youth and college division for May 1957, in *NAACP Papers*, pt. 19, ser. D, reel 17. See also "Youth Tell of Their Fight For Freedom in South," in *NAACP Papers*, pt. 19, ser. D, reel 17. Lovett, *Civil Rights Movement in Tennessee*, 53. The rally was to honor the personal sacrifices the youth made to advance the fight for desegregation and first-class citizenship. Other students honored at the rally were Jolee Fritz, who was dismissed from her position as "director of the Wesley Foundation, Women's College, the University of North Carolina, because of her affiliation with the NAACP"; Fred Moore, "former president of the student body at South Carolina State, who was expelled from the college because of the students' counter-boycott against the White Citizen Council"; and Ernest McEwen, who was the former student body president of Alcorn College, was "expelled because of his leadership in the student protest against anti-NAACP articles published by Alcorn professor, Clennon King." See *NAACP Papers*, Youth File, Box III E51, Folder 4.

35. Lovett, *Civil Rights Movement in Tennessee*, 53. See also the brief biography on Robert "Bobby" Cain Jr. in *Tennessee Encyclopedia of History and Culture*, available at http://tennesseeencyclopedia.net/imagegallery.php?EntryID=C002 (accessed July 2, 2007).

36. Lovett, *Civil Rights Movement in Tennessee*, 53. See also Patterson, *Brown v. Board of Education*, 105.

37. On October 5, 1958, Clinton High School was bombed and the school was destroyed. In November two men were jailed for their connections to the school bombing. Kasper called the bombing "'a great victory for the white people of Tennessee." See Lovett, *Civil Rights Movement in Tennessee*, 58.

38. Ellen Levine, *Freedom's Children: Young Civil Rights Activists Tell Their Own Stories* (New York: Puffin Books, 1993), 40–41. See Patterson, *Brown v. Board of Education*, 110. For a more personal account of the desegregation of Central High School, see Melba Patillo Beals, *Warriors Don't Cry*. Beals was one of the nine students who desegregated Central High School in 1957.

39. Notably, Governor Faubus entered politics as a moderate on race issues; however, he realized that political success meant vehemently opposing integration. See Ogletree, *All Deliberate Speed,* 128.

40. Patterson, *Brown v. Board of Education,* 110.

41. Ibid., 112. See also Bates, *The Long Shadow of Little Rock.*

42. Patterson, *Brown v. Board of Education,* 110–11.

43. Ibid.

44. Levine, *Freedom's Children,* 45.

45. Ibid.

46. Ibid., 46.

47. Ibid.

48. Ibid., 47.

49. Ibid.

50. Ibid., 48.

51. See *The Crisis* 65 (Aug.–Sept. 1958): 445–49.

52. See Jake Weber, "'There's a Lot to Fight For': 'Little Rock Nine' Member Ernest Green Highlights Civil Rights Movement" in the *Albion View,* available at http://www.albion.edu/ac_news/AlbionViews2005-06/ernestgreen.asp (accessed July 2, 2007).

53. Ibid.

54. See press release, "Michigan State NAACP Plans Mammoth Right Rally," in *NAACP Papers,* pt. 19, ser. D, reel 16. See also Daniel Neusom, Annual Report to the Michigan Conference of NAACP Branches on May 20, 1960, in *NAACP Papers,* pt. 19, ser. D, reel 4.

55. See Jake Weber, "'There's a Lot to Fight For.'"

56. See *Newsletter: NAACP Youth and College Reporter,* Aug. 1958, in *NAACP Papers,* pt. 19, ser. D, reel 20. See also *The Crisis* 65 (Aug.–Sept. 1958): 445–49. Note: The Spingarn Medal had never been awarded to youth.

57. Patterson, *Brown v. Board of Education,* 112. See also biography of Orval Eugene Faubus, *Encyclopedia of Arkansas History and Culture,* available at http://encyclopediaofarkansas.net/encyclopedia/entry-detail.aspx?entryID=102 (accessed July 12, 2007).

58. Press release on the "Negro Girl Becomes First Grad of Integrated School in North Carolina." See also William H. Chafe, *Civilities and Civil Rights: Greensboro, North Carolina and the Black Freedom Struggle* (New York: Oxford Univ. Press, 1980), 72–74 and Kevin Sack, "For Civil Rights Pioneer, a Life of Quiet Struggle," *Los Angeles Times,* May 9, 2004, accessed June 12, 2012, http://articles.latimes.com/2004/may/09/nation/na-josephine9

59. Sack, "For Civil Rights Pioneer, a Life of Quiet Struggle." See also Josephine Boyd Bradley's radio interview by Warren Olney (which took place on the fiftieth anniversary of *Brown v. Board of Education*), available at http://web.mac.

com/paul.tullis/iWeb/Site/Blog/D5AFAF25-9C64-4A43-AB95-9A71506C2BA9.
html (accessed July 1, 2007).

60. Ibid.

61. Ibid.

62. See press release on the "Negro Girl Becomes First Grad of Integrated School in North Carolina."

63. See monthly report of the Youth and College Division, June 1–Aug. 1, 1958, in *NAACP Papers,* pt. 19, ser. D, reel 17. Note: The 1959 Annual Report of the Youth and College Division stated that Boyd had received a $1,500 scholarship from the Jessie Smith Noyes Foundation.

64. See Bradley radio interview by Olney. See also Sack, "For Civil Rights Pioneer." Josephine Boyd Bradley earned a PhD from Emory University in 1995. She formerly chaired the Department of African and African American Studies and Africana Women's Studies at Clark Atlanta University in Atlanta, Georgia.

65. *The Crisis* 65 (Dec. 1958): 622.

66. The march was initially conceived and planned by A. Philip Randolph. He was able to secure support from the NAACP to back the march. See letter from Roy Wilkins to A. Phillip Randolph, Sept. 12, 1958, and letter from Herbert Wright to NAACP Youth and College Units on Eastern Seaboard, Oct. 25, 1958, in *NAACP Papers,* Youth File, Box III E55, Folder 11.

67. See "Youth March for Integrated Schools," *The Crisis* 65 (Dec. 1958): 628. See also *NAACP Papers,* Youth File, Box III E47, Folder 6.

68. See *NAACP Papers,* Youth File, Box III E47, Folder 6.

69. See "Youth March for Integrated Schools," 628. See also *NAACP Papers,* Youth File, Box III E47, Folder 6; and Youth March for Integrated Schools (Oct. 25, 1958 and Apr. 18, 1959), available at http://mlk-kpp01.stanford.edu/index.php/encyclopedia/encyclopedia/enc_youth_march_for_integrated_schools_25_october_1958_and_18_april_1959/ (accessed Apr. 19, 2012).

70. See "Youth March for Integrated Schools," *The Crisis* 65 (Dec. 1958): 628. See also *NAACP Papers,* Youth File, Box III E47, Folder 6.

71. Monthly Report of the Youth and College Division, Oct. 1958, in *NAACP Papers,* pt. 19, ser. D, reel 17. See outline of program for Youth March for Integrated School, in *NAACP Papers,* Youth File, Box III E55, Folder 11. See also Federal Education Policy and the States, 1945–2009, The Eisenhower Years: Desegregation, available at http://www.archives.nysed.gov/edpolicy/research/res_essay_eisenhower_desegregation.shtml and Youth March for Integrated Schools (Oct. 25, 1958 and Apr. 18, 1959), available at http://mlk-kpp01.stanford.edu/index.php/encyclopedia/encyclopedia/enc_youth_march_for_integrated_schools_25_october_1958_and_18_april_1959/ (accessed Apr. 19, 2012).

72. See 1959 Annual Report of the Youth and College Division, in *NAACP Papers,* pt. 19, ser. D, reel 16. See also Youth March for Integrated Schools (Oct. 25, 1958 and Apr. 18, 1959) available at http://mlk-kpp01.stanford.edu/index.php/encyclopedia/encyclopedia/enc_youth_march_for_integrated_schools_25_october_1958_and_18_april_1959/ (accessed Apr. 19, 2012).

73. See Youth March for Integrated Schools (Oct. 25, 1958, and Apr. 18, 1959), available at http://mlk-kpp01.stanford.edu/index.php/encyclopedia/encyclopedia/enc_youth_march_for_integrated_schools_25_october_1958_and_18_april_1959/ (accessed Apr. 19, 2012).

74. See 1959 Annual Report of the Youth and College Division, in *NAACP Papers,* pt. 19, ser. D, reel 16.

75. See also Youth March for Integrated Schools (Oct. 25, 1958, and Apr. 18, 1959) available at http://mlk-kpp01.stanford.edu/index.php/encyclopedia/encyclopedia/enc_youth_march_for_integrated_schools_25_october_1958_and_18_april_1959/ (accessed Apr. 19, 2012).

76. Ibid.

77. Ibid.

78. Youth from the NAACP held membership in and affiliated with both of these organizations since their inception in the 1940s. See 1959 Annual Report of the Youth and College Division, in *NAACP Papers,* pt. 19, ser. D, reel 16.

79. "Not Pushing Integration, says NAACP," *Nashville Banner,* Aug. 7, 1959. See also Pinckney Keel, "Oliver Asks NAACP Keep Hands Off," *Nashville Banner,* Aug. 3, 1959.

80. Lovett, *Civil Rights Movement in Tennessee,* 55.

81. James Talley, "Fill Grades 1–3, NAACP Urges," *Tennessean,* Aug. 3 1959. See also Sonya Ramsey, *Reading, Writing, and Segregation: A Century of Black Women Teachers in Nashville* (Urbana-Champaign: Univ. of Illinois Press, 2008), 77.

82. Talley, "Fill Grades 1–3, NAACP Urges," *Tennessean,* Aug. 3, 1959.

83. Ibid.

84. Lovett, *Civil Rights Movement in Tennessee,* 55.

85. Ramsey, *Reading, Writing, and Segregation,* 84.

86. Lovett, *Civil Rights Movement in Tennessee* 56. See also Ramsey, *Reading, Writing, and Segregation,* 85.

87. Ramsey, *Reading, Writing, and Segregation,* 85.

88. Ibid., 84–87. See also Talley, "Fill Grades 1–3, NAACP Urges," *Tennessean,* Aug. 3, 1959.

89. Ramsey, *Reading, Writing, and Segregation,* 101. In 1963, Nashville and Davidson County merged to form the Metropolitan Nashville-Davidson County government. In 1964, the city and county schools were combined.

90. See John W. Edwards's (president of the Durham Youth Council) letter to Herbert Wright, Sept. 14, 1961, in *NAACP Papers,* pt. 19, ser. D, reel 5.

91. See monthly report for the Youth and College Division for May 1961, in *NAACP Papers,* pt. 19, ser. D, reel 17.

92. See Jessie P. Guzman, *Race Relations in the South—1961: A Tuskegee Institute Report* (Tuskegee: The Department of Records and Research, 1962), in *NAACP Papers,* pt. 19, ser. D, reel 16.

93. Ibid., 12.

94. Ogletree, *All Deliberate Speed,* 128. According to Ogletree, even as late as 1964, only one-fiftieth of all black youth attended desegregated schools in the south.

95. Morris, *Origins of the Civil Rights Movement,* 51.

96. Troy Jackson, *Becoming King: Martin Luther King Jr. and the Making of a National Leader* (Lexington: Univ. Press of Kentucky, 2008), 29–30.

97. Ibid.

98. Ibid., 53.

99. Levine, *Freedom's Children,* 24.

100. Troy Jackson, *Becoming King,* 72.

101. Levine, *Freedom's Children,* 24.

102. Ibid., 54. For a more comprehensive discussion of the Montgomery Bus Boycott, see Taylor Branch, *Parting the Waters: America in the King Years, 1954–1963* (New York: Simon and Schuster, 1988), 146–54. See also Jo Ann Gibson Robinson, *The Montgomery Bus Boycott and the Women Who Started It* (Knoxville: Univ. of Tennessee Press, 1987).

103. Morris, *Origins of the Civil Rights Movement,* 54.

104. See "Progress Report—Nation-Wide Membership Campaign" for the Montgomery Youth Council, in *NAACP Papers,* pt. 19, ser. D, reel 1.

105. *The Crisis* 103 (January 1996): 34–35.

106. This information was obtained from Mrs. Johnnie Carr and Doris Crenshaw, who made a presentation on July 11, 2006, at the NEH Summer Institute on Civil Rights hosted by the W. E. B. Du Bois Institute at Harvard University. Mrs. Carr stated that she was the assistant advisor to the Montgomery Youth Council and that Mrs. Crenshaw was a member. Notably, Montgomery Youth Council activities came to an end in 1956, as the NAACP was banned in Alabama until 1965. For reorganization of the Montgomery Youth Council, see Morris, *Origins of the Civil Rights Movement,* 51.

107. Levine, *Freedom's Children,* 27.

108. See Monthly Report of the Youth and College Division, Apr. 1–May 31, in *NAACP Papers,* pt. 19, ser. D, reel 17. See also the 1956 Annual Report of the Youth and College Division, in *NAACP Papers,* pt. 19, ser. D, reel 16.

109. See the 1956 Annual Report of the Youth and College Division, in *NAACP Papers,* pt. 19, ser. D, reel 16.

110. Jackson, *Becoming King,* 116–17, 143–44.

5. "More Than a Hamburger and a Cup of Coffee"

1. Morris, *Origins of the Civil Rights Movement,* 193.

2. See the 1956 Annual Report of the Youth and College Division, in *NAACP Papers,* pt. 19, ser. D, reel 16.

3. Ronald Walters, "Standing Up in America's Heartlands: Sitting in before Greensboro," *American Vision* 8 (Feb. 1993): 20–23. See also Ronald Walters, "The Great Plains Sit-In Movement, 1958–1960," *Great Plains Quarterly* 16 (Spring 1996): 85–94.

4. Walters, "Standing Up in America's Heartland," 20.

5. Ibid.

6. Ibid.

7. See letter from Chester I. Lewis Jr. to Herbert Wright, Aug. 14, 1958, in *NAACP Papers*, pt. 19, ser. D, reel 3. See also Herbert Wright, memorandum to Mr. Moon, Aug. 20, 1958, in *NAACP Papers*, pt. 19, ser. D, reel 16.

8. See Chester I. Lewis Jr., letter to Herbert Wright, Aug. 14, 1958, in *NAACP Papers*, pt. 19, ser. D, reel 3.

9. Davis W. Houck and David E. Dixon, eds., *Women and the Civil Rights Movement, 1954–1965* (Jackson: Univ. Press of Mississippi, 2009), 118.

10. Morris, *Origins of the Civil Rights Movement*, 193.

11. Ibid. See also Aldon Morris, "Black Southern Sit-In Movement: An Analysis of the Internal Organization," *American Sociological Review* 46 (Dec. 1981): 750–51.

12. Davis D. Joyce, ed., *Alternative Oklahoma: Contrarian Views of the Sooner State* (Norman: Univ. of Oklahoma Press, 2007), 55.

13. See the Monthly Report of the Youth and College Division, June 1–Aug. 31, 1958, in *NAACP Papers*, pt. 19, ser. D, reel 17. See also Quintard Taylor's *In Search of the Racial Frontier: African Americans in the American West, 1528–1990* (New York: W. W. Norton and Co., 1998), 285.

14. Taylor, *In Search of a Racial Frontier*, 285. See also *The Crisis* 65 (Dec. 1958): 612–13.

15. See the 1958 Annual Report for the Youth and College Division, in *NAACP Papers*, pt. 19, ser. D, reel 16.

16. Joyce, *Alternative Oklahoma*, 56.

17. See 1959 National Youth Work Committee Report, in *NAACP Papers*, Youth File, Box III E47, Folder 6.

18. See Margaret B. Kreig, letter to Herbert Wright, Oct. 4, 1960, in *NAACP Papers*, pt. 19, ser. D, reel 6.

19. Houck and Dixon, *Women in the Civil Rights Movement*, 120.

20. See letter titled "To Whom It May Concern" written by Laplois Ashford, national youth secretary, on July 6, 1963, in *NAACP Papers*, pt. 19, ser. D, reel 5.

21. Joyce, *Alternative Oklahoma*, 56.

22. Charles Payne, *I've Got the Light of Freedom: The Organizing Tradition and the Mississippi Freedom Struggle* (Berkeley: Univ. of California Press, 1995), 265–83. See also Charles Payne, "Men Led, but Women Organized: Movement Participation of Women in the Mississippi Delta," in *Women in the Civil Rights Movement: Trailblazers and Torchbearers*, ed. Vicki L. Crawford, Jacqueline Anne Rouse, and Barbara Woods (Bloomington: Indiana Univ. Press, 1990), 1–12.

23. See the monthly report of the Youth and College Division for February, in *NAACP Papers*, pt. 19, ser. D, reel 17.

24. Ibid.

25. See the 1959 Annual Report of the Youth and College Division, in *NAACP Papers*, pt. 19, ser. D, reel 16.

26. See the monthly report of the Youth and College Division for February, in *NAACP Papers*, pt. 19, ser. D, reel 17.

27. Ibid.

28. Morris, "Black Southern Sit-In Movement," 748.

29. Walters, "Standing Up in America's Heartland," 23.

30. Morris, "Black Southern Sit-In Movement," 750.

31. Christina Greene, *Our Separate Ways: Women and the Black Freedom Movement in Durham, North Carolina* (Chapel Hill: Univ. of North Carolina Press, 2005), 26.

32. Morris, "Black Southern Sit-In Movement," 755.

33. "Special Report on Sit Downs: NAACP Staff Activity in the Sit Downs." See also *NAACP Papers*, pt. 19, ser. D, reel 17, and Roy Wilkins and Tom Mathews, *Standing Fast: The Autobiography of Roy Wilkins* (New York: Viking Press, 1982), 268.

34. Carson, *In Struggle*, 9.

35. See "Origins of the Sit-ins: A Sibling Remembers," interview with Gloria Jean (Blair) Howard by Eugene Pfaff, Sept. 15, 1982, Greensboro VOICES, University Libraries, Univ. of North Carolina at Greensboro, at http://www.object ofhistory.org/objects/brieftour/lunchcounter/ (accessed July 5, 2007. See Chafe, *Civilities and Civil Rights*, 82–83.

36. See "Special Report on Sit Downs: NAACP Staff Activity in the Sit Downs." See also , oral interview, "How It Originated Joseph McNeil's Story," interview with Joseph McNeil by Eugene Pfaff, Oct. 14, 1979, Greensboro VOICES, University Libraries, Univ. of North Carolina at Greensboro, available at http://www.objectofhistory.org/objects/brieftour/lunchcounter/?order=2 (accessed July 5, 2007). McNeil asserted that the early sit-in demonstrations, particularly the ones carried out by the Oklahoma City Youth Council, influenced his activism. See also Chafe, *Civilities and Civil Rights*, 79–85.

37. See "Special Report on Sit Downs: NAACP Staff Activity in the Sit Downs."

38. Ibid.

39. Ibid. See also de Schweinitz, *If We Could Change the World*, 189.

40. Chafe, *Civilities and Civil Rights*, 71. See also Deidre B. Flowers, "The Launching of the Student Sit-in Movement: The Role of Black Women at Bennett College," *Journal of African American History* 90 (Winter 2005): 57; and "Special Report on Sit Downs: NAACP Staff Activity in the Sit Downs."

41. "Special Report on Sit Downs: NAACP Staff Activity in the Sit Downs." Note: Secondary sources give different figures for the number of students who actually participated in the second demonstration at Woolworth's. In the "Special Report on Sit Downs," Herbert Wright, the national youth director, asserted that approximately sixty to sixty-five students returned. This work will use the figures given in the "Special Report on Sit Downs."

42. "Special Report on Sit Downs: NAACP Staff Activity in the Sit Downs."

43. Ibid.

44. Ibid.

45. Ibid.

46. Ibid.

47. Ibid.

48. V. P. Franklin, "Patterns of Student Activism at Historically Black Universities in the United States and South Africa, 1960–1977," *Journal of African American History* 88 (Spring, 2003): 206–7.

49. Ibid.

50. See documents on Donald Moss's expulsion from Southern University Law School, in *NAACP Papers,* pt. 19, ser. D, reel 9.

51. Franklin, "Patterns of Student Activism," 206–7.

52. See monthly report of the Youth and College Division, June 1–Aug. 31, 1960, in *NAACP Papers,* pt. 19, ser. D, reel 17.

53. See Roy Wilkins's comments, in *The Crisis* 67 (June–July 1960): 372.

54. Richard L. Plaut, "Prospects for the Entrance and Scholastic Advancement of Negroes in Higher Educational Institutions," *Journal of Negro Education* 36 (Summer 1967): 230.

55. See monthly reports of the Youth and College Division, June 1–Aug. 31, 1960, in *NAACP Papers,* pt. 19, ser. D, reel 17. See also the 1960 Annual Report of the Youth and College Division, in *NAACP Papers,* pt. 19, reel 16.

56. "Fisk Board Backs Sit-ins," *Tennessean,* Apr. 30, 1960.

57. Ibid.

58. Vincent Fort, "The Atlanta Sit-In Movement," in *Atlanta, Georgia, 1960–1961: Sit-ins and Student Activism* (Brooklyn, NY: Carlson Publishing Inc., 1989), 156.

59. Ibid.

60. Robert Churchwell, "Attorney Says NAACP Stands Behind Sit-Ins," *Nashville Banner,* Apr. 7, 1960.

61. Garry Fullerton, "NAACP Backing Them Sitters Told," *Tennessean,* Apr. 7, 1960.

62. See monthly report of the Youth and College Division, Feb. 1–Apr. 30, 1960, in *NAACP Papers,* pt. 19, ser. D, reel 17.

63. Ibid.

64. Ibid. During the early stage of the student sit-in demonstrations, the NAACP cooperated with civil rights groups (such as CORE, SNCC, and SCLC) in advancing the sit-in demonstrations. However, this relationship deteriorated as the protest movement accelerated.

65. See "Special Report on Sit Downs: NAACP Staff Activity in the Sit Downs."

66. Ibid. See also Allan Sindler's "Youth and the American Negro Protest Movement: A Local Case Study of Durham, North Carolina," in *NAACP Paper,* pt. 19, ser. D, reel 9.

67. "Special Report on Sit Downs: NAACP Staff Activity in the Sit Downs."

68. Ibid. See also the 1961 Report of National Youth Work Committee, in *NAACP Papers*, Youth File, Box III E47, Folder 7.

69. 1961 Report of National Youth Work Committee, in *NAACP Papers*, Youth File, Box III E47, Folder 7.

70. Ibid.

71. Ibid.

72. Ibid. See also the 1960 Annual Report of the Youth and College Division, in *NAACP Papers*, pt. 19, ser. D, reel 16.

73. 1961 Report of National Youth Work Committee, in *NAACP Papers*, Youth File, Box III E47, Folder 7.

74. Ibid.

75. Ibid.

76. See Monthly Report of the Youth and College Division, Feb. 1–Apr. 30, 1960, in *NAACP Papers*, pt. 19, ser. D, reel 17. See also petition in support of the sit-down protest from the White House Conference on Children and Youth, in *NAACP Papers*, pt. 19, ser. D, reel 16.

77. See Monthly Report of the Youth and College Division, Feb. 1–Apr. 30, 1960, in *NAACP Papers*, pt. 19, ser. D, reel 17.

78. Ibid.

79. Lau, *Democracy Rising*, 216.

80. Ibid.

81. Ibid., 217.

82. Ibid.

83. Ibid.

84. Ibid. See also Herbert Wright, speech given at the mass meeting for students from South Carolina State and Claflin Colleges, 1960, in *NAACP Papers*, pt. 19, ser. D, reel 6, and the press release on "Protest Leader Employed for Summer Work with NAACP Youth," in *NAACP Papers*, pt. 19, ser. D, reel 20.

85. See Orangeburg County Teachers' Association Resolution, in *NAACP Papers*, pt. 19, ser. D, reel 6. See also Herbert Wright, speech given at the mass meeting for students from South Carolina State and Claflin Colleges; and press release, "Protest Leader employed for Summer Work with NAACP Youth," in *NAACP Papers*, pt. 19, ser. D, reel 20.

86. See Herbert Wright, speech given at the mass meeting for students from South Carolina State and Claflin Colleges.

87. See *The Crisis* 68 (Apr. 1961): 235.

88. Ibid., 237.

89. Ibid.

90. Ibid., 237–38.

91. See Wright's summer report on youth work in South Carolina, in *NAACP Papers*, pt. 19, ser. D, reel 20.

92. Gloster Current, memorandum to Roy Wilkins, Nov. 7, 1960, in *NAACP Papers,* pt. 19, ser. D, reel 20.

93. Baldwin left the association in 1958 (having only held the position less than a year) to return to school to pursue a PhD in political science. See 1965 Report from National Youth Work Committee, in *NAACP Papers,* Youth File, Box III E47, Folder 9. See also *The Crisis* 68 (Mar. 1961): 168.

94. Julie Wright, Special Report, in *NAACP Papers,* Youth File, Box III E55, Folder 2.

95. Wright, Special Report on Summerville, South Carolina, in *NAACP Papers,* pt. 19, ser. D, reel 20. See also Wright, Special Report, in *NAACP Papers,* Youth File, Box III E55, Folder 2.

96. Wright, Special Report, in *NAACP Papers,* Youth File, Box III E55, Folder 2.

97. Ibid.

98. Ibid.

99. Ibid.

100. Ibid.

101. Wright, Special Report on Summerville, South Carolina, in *NAACP Papers,* pt. 19, ser. D, reel 20. See also Wright, Special Report, in *NAACP Papers,* Youth File, Box III E55, Folder 2.

102. Wright, Special Report, in *NAACP Papers,* Youth File, Box III E55, Folder 2.

103. Ibid.

104. Ibid.

105. Aaron Henry and Constance Curry, *Aaron Henry: The Fire Ever Burning* (Jackson: University Press of Mississippi, 2000), 64.

106. Ibid. 64–65.

107. Ibid., 73.

108. Ibid., 68–81. See also Charles Payne, *I've Got the Light of Freedom,* 58–59.

109. Henry and Curry, *Aaron Henry,* 74.

110. Ibid., 74–76.

111. Ibid., 92.

112. See monthly report by Julie Wright, Sept. 6, 1961, in *NAACP Papers,* pt. 19, ser. D, reel 20.

113. Ibid.

114. See 1961 Annual Report on Youth Work, in *NAACP Papers,* pt. 19, ser. D, reel 6. See also Raymond Arsenault, *Freedom Riders: 1961 and the Struggle for Racial Justice* (New York: Oxford Univ. Press, 2006): 30.

115. See 1961 Annual Report on Youth Work, in *NAACP Papers,* pt. 19, ser. D, reel 6. See also monthly report of Julie Wright, Aug. 18–Sept. 1, 1961, in *NAACP Papers,* Youth File, Box III E55, Folder 2.

116. John Dittmer, *Local People: The Struggle for Civil Rights in Mississippi* (Urbana: Univ. of Illinois Press, 1994), 121.

117. Ibid.

118. Henry and Curry, *Aaron Henry,* 112.

119. Dittmer, *Local People,* 122.

120. Ibid., 176.

121. Ibid., 177.

122. Henry and Curry, *Aaron Henry,* 112–14.

6. "And If Not Now, When?"

1. See Report of the National Youth Work Committee, May 1962, in *NAACP Papers,* Youth File, Box III E47, Folder 7.

2. See biographical sketch of Laplois Ashford, in *NAACP Papers,* pt. 19, ser. D, reel 7.

3. Laplois Ashford, memorandum to Roy Wilkins, Nov. 15, 1962 on the youth and college division program, in *NAACP Papers,* pt. 19, ser. D, reel 7.

4. See 1962 National Youth Work Committee Report, in *NAACP Papers,* Youth File, Box III E47, Folder 7.

5. Laplois Ashford, memorandum to Roy Wilkins, Nov. 15, 1962, in *NAACP Papers,* pt. 19, ser. D, reel 7.

6. Ibid.

7. Greyhound Corporation, letter to Laplois Ashford, Dec. 4, 1962, in *NAACP Papers,* pt. 19, ser. D, reel 7.

8. See memorandum to Wilkins and Current concerning Ashford's hospitalization, in *NAACP Papers,* pt. 19, ser. D, reel 7.

9. See document "Do You Want To Be A Task Force Worker," which defines and outlines the role of a task force, in *NAACP Papers,* Youth File, Box III E55, Folder 13. See also *NAACP Papers,* pt. 19, ser. D, reel 20; and the Report for the Youth and College Division for May 25 to July 24, 1960, in *NAACP Papers,* pt. 19, ser. D, reel 17. In Clarksdale, Mississippi, this specialized task force was called the Bravados. In Jackson, Mississippi, this specialized task force was called the Matadors.

10. *NAACP Papers,* pt. 19, ser. D, reel 20, and the Report for the Youth and College Division for May 25 to July 24, 1960, in *NAACP Papers,* pt. 19, ser. D, reel 17. See also Laplois Ashford, memorandum to Roy Wilkins, June 5, 1963, in *NAACP Papers,* Youth File, Box III E47, Folder 2.

11. Timothy Tyson, *Radio Free Dixie: Robert Williams and the Roots of Black Power* (Chapel Hill: Univ. of North Carolina Press, 1999), 153, 192, 211.

12. Ibid., 80. See also Marcellus Barksdale, "Robert F. Williams and the Indigenous Civil Rights Movement in North Carolina, 1961," *Journal of Negro History* 69 (Spring 1982): 73.

13. Tyson, *Radio Free Dixie,* 38.

14. Ibid., 42–43.

15. Ibid., 46–63.

16. Barksdale, "Robert F. Williams," 74.

17. Tyson, *Radio Free Dixie,* 84–86, 98, 217.

18. Ibid., 92–93. See also Walter Rucker, "Crusader in Exile: Robert Williams and the International Struggle for Black Freedom in America," *Black Scholar* 36 (June 2006): 19.

19. Tyson, *Radio Free Dixie,* 101,

20. Ibid., 109.

21. Ibid., 109–10.

22. Ibid., 119, 134.

23. Ibid., 94.

24. Ibid., 145.

25. Ibid., 145–46.

26. Ibid., 147–49.

27. Ibid., 149. See also *The Crisis* 66 (June–July 1959): 325–29.

28. Tyson, *Radio Free Dixie,* 149–50.

29. Ibid., 149–51. See also *The Crisis* 66 (June–July 1959): 325–29.

30. Tyson, *Radio Free Dixie,* 213–14.

31. Ibid., 264.

32. Ibid., 266.

33. Ibid., 266–67. See Marcellus Barksdale, "Robert Williams," 78.

34. Barksdale, "Robert Williams," 78.

35. Tyson, *Radio Free Dixie,* 281.

36. Ibid., 285–86.

37. See Laplois Ashford, memorandum to Roy Wilkins, June 13, 1963, in *NAACP Papers,* pt. 19, ser. D, reel 14. See also Laplois Ashford, memorandum to Roy Wilkins, June 13, 1963, in *NAACP Papers,* Youth File, Box III E47, Folder 2.

38. Ashford, memorandum to Roy Wilkins, June 13, 1963, in *NAACP Papers,* pt. 19, ser. D, reel 14.

39. Ibid.

40. Ibid.

41. Ibid.

42. See Laplois Ashford, memorandum to Roy Wilkins, June 13, 1963, in *NAACP Papers,* Youth File, Box III E47, Folder 2.

43. Brian William Suttell, "Countdown to Downtown: The Civil Rights Protest Movement in Downtown Fayetteville, North Carolina" (MA thesis, North Carolina State University, 2007), 16. See also Catherine Lutz, *Homefront: A Military City and the American Twentieth Century* (Boston: Beacon Press, 2001), 122.

44. Suttell, "Countdown to Downtown," 16.

45. Ibid., 17. See also William H. Chafe, *Civilities and Civil Rights: Greensboro, North Carolina, and the Black Struggle for Freedom* (New York: Oxford Univ. Press, 1980), 110.

46. Glenn T. Eskew, *But for Birmingham: The Local and National Movements in the Civil Rights Struggle* (Chapel Hill: Univ. of North Carolina Press, 1997), 201–97.

47. Ibid., 299–317.

48. Suttell. "Countdown to Downtown," 18.

49. Ibid., 33

50. NAACP Press Release on June 13, 1963, in *NAACP Papers,* pt. 19, ser. D, reel 14.

51. Ibid.

52. Ibid. Suttel maintains that twenty-five demonstrators were arrested, but the NAACP Press Release states that twenty-six were arrested. See also NAACP Press Release, in *NAACP Papers,* Youth File, Box III E47, Folder 2.

53. Suttell, "Countdown to Downtown," 33–34. See also Catherine Lutz, *Homefront,* 122. On this same day, Alabama governor George Wallace refused to allow Vivian Malone and James Hood to integrate the University of Alabama; however, after President John F. Kennedy intervened—federalizing the National Guard to assist with the integration process, Malone and Hood became the first two blacks to attend the school.

54. Suttell, "Countdown to Downtown," 37.

55. NAACP Press Release, June 13, 1963, in *NAACP Papers,* pt. 19, ser. D, reel 14.

56. Suttell, "Countdown to Downtown," 38.

57. Ibid., 38–40.

58. Ibid., 71–74.

59. Ibid., 74.

60. Ibid., 74–77.

61. Ibid., 80. See also Lutz, *Homefront,* 123–24.

62. Suttell, "Countdown to Downtown," 82–87.

63. Special Report of Julie Wright, Field Secretary, for Mar. 27–Apr. 14, in *NAACP Papers,* Youth File, Box III E55, Folder 2.

64. Ibid. See also *The Crisis* 68 (May 1961): 291–92; see the Mississippi Civil Rights Project, the Tougaloo Nine, available at http://mscivilrightsproject.org/index.php?option=com_content&view=article&id=448:the-tougaloo-nine&catid=295:organization&Itemid=33. Accessed May, 16, 2013.

65. Special Report of Julie Wright, Field Secretary, for Mar. 27–Apr. 14, in *NAACP Papers,* Youth File, Box III E55, Folder 2.

66. *The Crisis* 68 (May 1961): 291–92.

67. Special Report of Julie Wright, field secretary, for Mar. 27–Apr. 14, in *NAACP Papers,* Youth File, Box III E55, Folder 2.

68. Ibid.

69. Ibid.

70. Ibid.

71. Ibid.

72. Dittmer, *Local People,* 158.

73. Payne, *I've Got the Light of Freedom,* 58.

74. Dittmer, *Local People,* 160.

75. Ibid.

76. Ibid, 162.

77. Ibid., 163.

78. Theodore Henry Jr. letter to Laplois Ashford, Aug. 12, 1963, in *NAACP Papers,* pt. 19, ser. D, reel 4.

79. Dittmer, *Local People,* 164.

80. Ibid., 165.

81. Ibid., 164–65.

82. Ibid., 165.

83. See monthly report of Julie Wright, Nov. 14, 1961, in *NAACP Papers,* Youth File, Box III E55, Folder 2. See also Morris, *Origins of the Civil Rights Movement,* 240.

84. See monthly report of Julie Wright, Oct. 13, 1961, in *NAACP Papers,* pt. 19, ser. D, reel 20.

85. See monthly report of Julie Wright, Oct. 5–Nov. 8, 1961, in *NAACP Papers,* pt. 19, ser. D, reel 20. See also monthly report of Julie Wright, Nov. 14, 1961, in *NAACP Papers,* Youth File, Box III E55, Folder 2.

86. Ibid.

87. James Forman, *The Making of Black Revolutionaries* (New York: Macmillan, 1972), 250.

88. See monthly reports of Julie Wright, Dec. 8, 1961–Feb. 7, 1962, in *NAACP Papers,* pt. 19, ser. D, reel 20.

89. Morris, *Origins of the Civil Rights Movement,* 242–43.

90. Forman, *Making of Black Revolutionaries,* 362.

91. Ibid.

92. See monthly reports of Julie Wright, Dec. 8–Feb. 7, 1962, in *NAACP Papers,* pt. 19, ser. D, reel 20.

93. Gloster Current, letter to Julie Wright, Oct. 16, 1963, in *NAACP Papers,* pt. 19, ser. D, reel 14.

94. John Bradley and Robert Blow, letter to Laplois Ashford, Nov. 5, 1962, in *NAACP Papers,* pt. 19, ser. D, reel 14.

95. Laplois Ashford, memorandum to Current, Morsell, and Wilkins, May 24, 1963, in *NAACP Papers,* pt. 19, ser. D, reel 5.

96. 1964 Youth Council Constitution, in *NAACP Papers,* pt. 19, ser. D, reel 20. See also the Report of the National Work Committee Meeting, Mar. 1963, in *NAACP Papers,* pt. 19, ser. D, reel 14.

97. See press release on Medgar Evers's death, in *NAACP Papers,* pt. 19, ser. D, reel 4.

98. See the numerous flyers by the Jackson Movement, in *NAACP Papers,* pt. 19, ser. D, reel 4.

99. Forman, *Making of Black Revolutionaries,* 354.

100. See Report of Youth Secretary, July 25–Aug. 2, 1964, in *NAACP Papers,* pt. 19, ser. D, reel 17.

101. Ibid.

102. Ibid.

103. See Laplois Ashford, memorandum to John Morsell, July 14, 1964, in *NAACP Papers,* pt. 19, ser. D, reel 20.

104. Ibid.

105. Dittmer, *Local People,* 178.

106. Ibid., 177–78.

107. According to John Dittmer, Medgar Evers was initially reluctant to work with SNCC and CORE. However, Evers and CORE and SNCC members did develop "mutual respect." They worked together within the COFO, but Charles Evers "ignored COFO leaders and tried to undermine their programs." Ibid., 178.

108. See Donald White, letter to Roy Wilkins, Feb. 4, 1964, in *NAACP Papers,* pt. 19, ser. D, reel 9.

109. Ibid.

110. R. Hunter Morey, letter to Roy Wilkins, Feb. 4, 1964, in *NAACP Papers,* pt. 19, ser. D, reel 9.

111. Report of the Youth and College Division, June 25–July 25, 1964, in *NAACP Papers,* pt. 19, ser. D, reel 17.

112. Ibid.

113. Report of Youth Field Director Sherrill Marcus, Oct. 1965, in *NAACP Papers,* pt. 19, ser. D, reel 17.

114. See press release, "Tennessee College Grad in Engineering Named National Youth Director," in *NAACP Papers,* Youth File, Box III E40, Folder 9. See also letter to "Members of the National Youth Work Advisory Committee," July 22, 1965, in *NAACP Papers,* Youth File, Box III E47, Folder 9.

115. See "Tennessee College Grad in Engineering Named National Youth Director," and also memorandum to "Youth Council, Young Adult Council, and College Chapters Presidents, Secretaries, and Advisors," in *NAACP Papers,* Youth File, Box III E40, Folder 9.

116. See "Tennessee College Grad in Engineering Named National Youth Director," in *NAACP Papers,* Youth File, Box III E40, Folder 9.

117. Eugene Hampton Jr., memorandum to "Youth Council, Young Adult Council, and College Chapters, Presidents, Secretaries, and Advisors," in *NAACP Papers,* pt. 19, ser. D, reel 10, and in *NAACP Papers,* Youth File, Box III E40, Folder 9. (The memorandum is found in both sources.)

118. Ibid.

119. See the Community Action Project, in *NAACP Papers,* pt. 19, ser. D, reel 8.

120. Ibid.

121. See Progress Report on the Community Action Project, in *NAACP Papers,* pt. 19, ser. D, reel 8.

122. Ibid.

123. Ibid.

Epilogue

1. Raines, *My Soul Is Rested,* 135–36.

2. Ibid., 137.

Bibliography

Primary Sources

Archival Sources

Auburn, Alabama
> Ralph Brown Draughon Library, Auburn University
>> Papers of the NAACP (microfilm)

Atlanta, Georgia
> Special Collections, Emory University
>> Papers of the NAACP (microfilm)

Nashville, Tennessee
> Nashville Room, Nashville Public Library
>> Papers of the Congress of Racial Equality (microfilm)
>> Papers of the Student Nonviolent Coordinating Committee (microfilm)
>> Papers of the Southern Council on Human Relations (microfilm)

New York, New York
> Schomburg Center for Research in Black Culture
>> Montgomery Branch NAACP (Youth Council) Minutes, 1954–1955
>> Catherine Clarke Collection (Freedom Summer/COFO)

Newspapers/Periodicals Consulted

Note: These black newspapers and periodicals were chosen mainly because they have information on the activities of the NAACP youth councils and college chapters, particularly *The Crisis,* the official organ of the NAACP. Information found in these newspapers and periodicals on the NAACP youth councils, spanning the years 1936–1965, were examined.

Atlanta Daily World
Baltimore Afro-American
California Eagle
Chicago Defender
The Crisis
Freedom Ways
Harlem Liberator
Journal of Negro History
Los Angeles Sentinel

Norfolk Journal and Guide

Opportunity

Phylon

Pittsburgh Courier

Tennessean

The Movement

Nashville Banner

Washington Afro-American

Oral Histories

Note: I was fortunate to have met Johnnie Carr and Doris Crenshaw on July 11, 2006 and Attorney Vernon Jordan on July 18, 2006, at the W. E. B. Dubois Institute at Harvard University (sponsored by the NEH Institute on Civil Rights) and to have asked questions about their involvement with the NAACP youth councils.

Mrs. Johnnie Carr (former assistant advisor for the Montgomery NAACP Youth Council)

Ms. Doris Crenshaw (former vice president of Montgomery NAACP Youth Council)

Attorney Vernon Jordan (former member of the Atlanta NAACP Youth Council and NAACP southeastern field worker)

Secondary Sources

Books

Anderson, Carol. *Eyes Off the Prize: The United Nations and the African American Struggle for Human Rights, 1944–1955.* Cambridge, UK: Cambridge University Press, 2003.

Anderson, Terry H. *The Movement and the Sixties: Protest in America from Greensboro to Wounded Knee.* New York: Oxford University Press, 1995.

Apel, Dora. *Imagery of Lynching: Black Men, White Women, and the Mob.* New Brunswick, NJ: Rutgers University Press, 2004.

Arsenault, Raymond. *Freedom Riders: 1961 and the Struggle for Racial Justice.* New York: Oxford University Press, 2006.

Ayers, Edward L. *The Promise of the New South: Life after Reconstruction.* New York: Oxford University Press, 1992.

Badger, Anthony J. *The New Deal: The Depression Years, 1933–1940.* New York: Noonday Press, 1989.

Baker, Ella. "Developing Community Leadership." In *Black Woman in America,* edited by Gerda Lerner. New York: Vintage Books, 1973.

Bartley, Numan V. *The New South, 1945–1980.* Baton Rouge: Louisiana State University Press, 1995.

Bates, Daisy. *The Long Shadow of Little Rock: A Memoir.* New York: David McKay, 1962. Bayor, Ronald. *Race and the Shaping of Twentieth-Century Atlanta.* Chapel Hill: University of North Carolina Press, 1996.

Beals, Melba P. *Warriors Don't Cry: A Searing Memoir of the Battle to Integrate Little Rock's Central High.* New York: Pocket Books, 1994.

Bell, Derrick. *Silent Covenants: Brown v. Board of Education and the Unfulfilled Hopes of Racial Reform.* New York: Oxford University Press, 2004.

Berg, Manfred. *The Ticket to Freedom: The NAACP and the Struggle for Black Political Integration.* Gainesville: University Press of Florida, 2005.

Biondi, Martha. *To Stand and Fight: The Struggle for Civil Rights in Postwar New York City.* Cambridge, MA: Harvard University Press, 2003.

Boyle, Kevin. *Arc of Justice: A Saga of Race, Civil Rights, and Murder in the Jazz Age.* New York: Henry Holt and Company, 2004.

Branch, Taylor. *Parting the Waters: America in the King Years, 1954–1963.* New York: Simon and Schuster, 1998.

———. *Pillar of Fire: America in the King Years 1963–65.* New York: Simon and Schuster, 1998.

Bunche, Ralph J. *The Political Status of the Negro in the Age of FDR,* edited by Dewey W. Grantham. 1940. Reprint. Chicago: University of Chicago Press, 1973.

Carney, Jessie. *Notable Black America Women.* Detroit: Gale Research, 1992.

Carson, Clayborne. *In Struggle: SNCC and the Black Awakening of the 1960s.* Cambridge, MA: Harvard University Press, 1981.

Carter, Robert. *A Matter of Law: A Memoir of the Struggle in the Causes of Equal Rights.* New York: The New Press, 2005.

Cashin, Sheryll. *The Failures of Integration: How Race and Class Are Undermining the American Dream.* New York: Public Affairs, 2004.

Chafe, William H. *Civilities and Civil Rights: Greensboro, North Carolina, and the Black Struggle for Freedom.* New York: Oxford University Press, 1981.

Chafe, William, Raymond Gavins, and Robert Korstad, eds. *Remembering Jim Crow: African Americans Tell About Life in the Segregated South.* New York: The New Press, 2001.

Chappell, David. *Inside Agitators: White Southerners in the Civil Rights Movement.* Baltimore: Johns Hopkins University Press, 1994.

Clark, Septima. *Echo in My Soul.* New York: E. P. Dutton, 1962.

———. *Ready from Within: The Story of Septima Clark,* with Cynthia S. Brown. Navarro, CA: Wild Tree Press, 1986.

Carter, Dan T. *Scottsboro: Tragedy of the American South.* Baton Rouge: Louisiana State University Press, 1969.

Cecelski, David. *Along Freedom Road: Hyde County, North Carolina, and the Fate of Black Schools in the South.* Chapel Hill: University of North Carolina Press, 1994.

Cobb, James. *The Most Southern Place on Earth: The Mississippi Delta and the Roots of Regional Identity.* New York: Oxford University Press, 1992.

Cobb, James, and Michael V. Namorato. *The New Deal and the South.* Jackson: University of Mississippi Press, 1984.

Cohen, Robert. *When the Old Left Was Young: Student Radicals and America's First Mass Student Movement, 1929–1941.* New York: Oxford University Press, 1993.

Collier-Thomas, Bettye, and V. P. Franklin, eds. *Sisters in the Struggle: African American Women in the Civil Rights-Black Power Movement.* New York: New York University Press, 2001.

Cone, James H. *Martin and Malcolm and America: A Dream or a Nightmare.* Maryknoll, NY: Orbis Books, 1991.

Crawford, Vicki, Jacqueline Rouse, and Barbara Woods, eds. *Women in the Civil Rights Movement: Trailblazers and Torchbearers, 1941–1965.* Bloomington: Indiana University Press, 1990.

Cryer, Daniel Walter. *Mary White Ovington and the Rise of the NAACP.* Ann Arbor, MI: University Microfilms International, 1980.

Curry, Constance. *Silver Rights.* San Diego: Harcourt Brace, 1995.

Curry, Constance, et al. *Deep in Our Hearts: Nine White Women in the Freedom Movement.* Athens: University of Georgia Press, 2000.

Daniel, Pete. *Lost Revolutions: The South in the 1950s.* Chapel Hill: University of North Carolina Press, 2000.

Davis, Angela. *Angela Davis: An Autobiography.* New York: Random House, 1974.

Davis, Leroy. *A Clashing of the Soul: John Hope and the Dilemma of African American Leadership and Black Higher Education in the Early Twentieth Century.* Athens: University of Georgia Press, 1998.

D'Emilio, John. *Lost Prophet: The Life and Times of Bayard Rustin.* New York: Free Press, 2003.

De Schweinitz, Rebecca. *If We Could Change the World: Young People and America's Long Struggle for Racial Equality.* Chapel Hill: University of North Carolina Press, 2009.

Dittmer, John. *Local People: The Struggle for Civil Rights in Mississippi.* Urbana: University of Illinois Press, 1994.

Dudziak, Mary. *Cold War Civil Rights: Race and the Image of American Democracy.* Princeton, NJ: Princeton University Press, 2000.

Dunbar, Anthony. *Against the Grain: Southern Radicals and Prophets, 1929–1959.* Charlottesville: University Press of Virginia, 1981.

Durr, Virginia. *Outside the Magic Circle: The Autobiography of Virginia Foster Durr,* edited by Hollinger Barnard. Tuscaloosa: University of Alabama Press, 1985.

Egerton, John. *Speak Now Against the Day: The Generation Before the Civil Rights Movement in the South.* New York: Alfred A. Knopf, 1994.

Eskew, Glenn. *But for Birmingham: The Local and National Movements in the Civil Rights Struggle.* Chapel Hill: University of North Carolina Press, 1997.

Estes, Steve. *I Am A Man: Race, Manhood, and the Civil Rights Movement*. Chapel Hill: University of North Carolina Press, 2005.

Evans, Sara. *Personal Politics: The Roots of Women's Liberation in the Civil Rights Movement and the New Left*. New York: Vintage Books, 1980.

Farmer, James. *Lay Bare the Heart: An Autobiography of the Civil Rights Movement*. Fort Worth: Texas Christian University Press, 1985.

Fairclough, Adam. *Martin Luther King, Jr*. Athens: University of Georgia Press, 1990.

———. *Race and Democracy: The Civil Rights Struggle in Louisiana, 1915–1972*. Athens: University of Georgia Press, 1995.

———. *To Redeem the Soul of America: The Southern Christian Leadership Conference and Martin Luther King, Jr*. Athens: University of Georgia Press, 1987.

Fergus, Devin. *Liberalism, Black Power and the Making of American Politics, 1965–1980*. Athens: University of Georgia Press, 2009.

Finch, Minnie. *The NAACP, Its Fight for Justice*. Metuchen, NJ: Scarecrow Press, 1981.

Fleming, Cynthia Griggs. *Soon We Will Not Cry: The Liberation of Ruby Doris Smith Robinson*. Lanham, MD: Rowman and Littlefield, 1998.

Flynt, J. Wayne. *Dixie's Forgotten People: The South's Poor Whites*. Bloomington: Indiana University Press, 1979.

———. *Poor but Proud: Alabama's Poor Whites*. Tuscaloosa: University of Alabama Press, 1989.

Forman, James. *The Making of Black Revolutionaries: A Personal Account*. New York: Macmillan, 1972.

Fort, Vincent. "The Atlanta Sit-in Movement, 1960–1961: An Oral Study." In *Atlanta, Georgia, 1960–1961: Sit-ins and Student Activism,* edited by David J. Garrow, 119–169. Brooklyn, NY: Carlson Publishing, 1989.

Frederickson, George. *Black Liberation: A Comparative History of Black Ideology in the United States and South Africa*. New York: Oxford University Press, 1995.

Frederickson, Kari. *The Dixiecrat Revolt and the End of the Solid South, 1952–1968*. Chapel Hill: University of North Carolina Press, 2001.

Frost, Jennifer. *"An Interracial Movement of the Poor": Community Organizing and the New Left in the 1960s*. New York: New York University Press, 2001.

Gaines, Kevin. *Uplifting the Race: Black Leadership, Politics, and Culture in the Twentieth Century*. Chapel Hill: University of North Carolina Press, 1986.

Gardner, Michael R. *Harry Truman and Civil Rights: Moral Courage and Political Risks*. Carbondale: Southern Illinois University Press, 2002.

Garrow, David. *Bearing the Cross: Martin Luther King Jr., and the Southern Christian Leadership Conference*. New York: Perennial Classics, 1986.

———, ed. *We Shall Overcome: The Civil Rights Movement in the United States in the 1950's and 1960's*. Vol. 3. Brooklyn, NY: Carlson Publishing, 1989.

———, ed. *Birmingham, Alabama, 1956–1963: The Black Struggle for Civil Rights*. Brooklyn, NY: Carlson Publishing, 1989.

————, ed. *The Walking City: The Montgomery Bus Boycott, 1955–1956.* Brooklyn, NY: Carlson Publishing, 1989.

Gavins, Raymond. *"The NAACP in North Carolina in the Age of Segregation."* In *New Directions in Civil Rights Studies,* edited by Armstead L. Robinson and Patricia Sullivan, 105–25. Charlottesville: University of Virginia Press, 1991.

Giddings, Paula. *When and Where I Enter: The Impact of Black Women on Race and Sex in America.* New York: William Morrow, 1984.

Gilliard, Deric. *Living in the Shadows of a Legend: Unsung Heroes and "Sheroes" Who Marched with Martin Luther King, Jr.* Decatur, GA: Gillard Communications Publication, 2002.

Gilmore, Glenda. *Gender and Jim Crow: Women and the Politics of White Supremacy in North Carolina, 1896–1920.* Chapel Hill: University of North Carolina Press, 1996.

Goldfield, David R. *Black, White, and Southern: Race Relations and Southern Culture, 1940 to the Present.* Baton Rouge: Louisiana State University Press, 1990.

Grant, Joanne. *Ella Baker: Freedom Bound.* New York: John Wiley and Sons, 1998.

Greene, Christina. *Our Separate Ways: Women and the Black Freedom Movement in Durham, North Carolina.* Chapel Hill: University of North Carolina Press, 2005.

————. *"'The New Negro Ain't Scared No More!': Black Women Activism in North Carolina and the Meaning of Brown."* In *From Grass-roots to the Supreme Court: Brown v. Board of Education and American Democracy,* edited by Peter Lau. Durham: Duke University Press, 2004.

Greenberg, Cheryl Lynn, ed. *A Circle of Trust: Remembering SNCC.* New Brunswick, NJ: Rutgers University Press, 1998.

Greenberg, Jack. *Crusaders in the Courts: Legal Battles of the Civil Rights Movement.* New York: Twelve Tables Press, 2004.

Haines, Herbert. *Black Radicals and the Civil Rights Movement.* Knoxville: University of Tennessee Press, 1988.

Hale, Grace Elizabeth. *Making of Whiteness: The Culture of Segregation in the South 1890–1940.* New York: Pantheon, 1998.

Hall, Jacquelyn Dowd. *Revolt Against Chivalry: Jesse Daniel Ames and the Women's Campaign Against Lynching.* New York: Columbia University Press, 1979.

Harding, Vincent. *There Is a River: The Black Struggle for Freedom in America.* New York: Harcourt Brace Jovanovich, 1981.

Henry, Aaron and Constance Curry. *Aaron Henry: The Fire Ever Burning.* Jackson: University Press of Mississippi, 2000.

Higginbotham, Evelyn. *Righteous Discontent: The Women's Movement in the Black Baptist Church, 1880–1920.* Cambridge, MA: Harvard University Press, 1993.

Hines, Darlene Clark. *Black Victory: The Rise and Fall of the White Primary in Texas.* Millwood, NY: KTO Press, 1979.

Hines, Darlene et al. *The African American Odyssey.* Upper Saddle River, NJ: Pearson Press, 2006.

Hobson, Fred. *But Now I See: The White Southern Racial Conversion Narrative.* Baton Rouge: Louisiana State University Press, 1999.

Hogan, Wesley C. *Many Minds, One Heart: SNCC's Dream for a New America.* Chapel Hill: University of North Carolina Press, 2007.

Holsaert, Faith S. et al., eds. *Hands on the Freedom Plow: Personal Accounts by Women in SNCC.* Urbana-Champaign: University of Illinois Press, 2010.

Horne, Gerald. *Communist Front? The Civil Rights Congress, 1946–1956.* Rutherford, NJ: Fairleigh Dickinson University Press, 1988.

Houck, Davis W., and David E. Dixon, eds. *Women in the Civil Rights Movement, 1954–1965.* Oxford: University of Mississippi Press, 2009.

Hudson-Weems, Clenora. *Emmett Till: The Sacrificial Lamb in the Modern Civil Rights Movement.* New York: Bedford Publishers, 1996.

Hughes, Langston. *Fight for Freedom: The Story of the NAACP.* New York: Berkeley, 1962.

Inscoe, John C., ed. *Georgia in Black and White: Exploration in the Race Relations of a Southern State, 1865–1950.* Athens: University of Georgia Press, 1994.

Jackson, Troy. *Becoming King: Martin Luther King Jr. and the Making of a National Leader.* Lexington: University Press of Kentucky, 2008.

Jacobson, Matthew Frye. *Whiteness of a Different Color: European Immigrants and the Alchemy of Race.* Cambridge, MA: Harvard University Press, 1998.

Janken, Kenneth Robert. *White: The Biography of Walter White, Mr. NAACP.* New York: The New Press 2003.

Jonas, Gilbert. *Freedom's Sword: The NAACP and the Struggle Against Racism in America, 1909–1969.* New York: Routledge, 2005.

Jones, Jacqueline. *Labor of Love, Labor of Sorrow: Black Women, Work, and the Family from Slavery to the Present.* New York: Vintage Books, 1986.

Jordan, Vernon, with Annette Gordon Reed. *Vernon Can Read!: A Memoir.* New York: Basic Civitas Books, 2001.

Joseph, Peniel. *Waiting 'Til The Midnight Hour: A Narrative History of Black Power in America.* New York: Henry Holt and Company, 2006.

Joyce, Davis, ed. *Alternative Oklahoma: Contrarian Views of the Sooner State.* Norman: University of Oklahoma Press, 2007.

Kelley, Robin. *Freedom Dreams: The Black Radical Imagination.* Boston, MA: Beacon Press, 2002.

———. *Hammer and Hoe: Alabama Communist During the Great Depression.* Chapel Hill: University of North Carolina Press, 1990.

———. *Race Rebels: Culture, Politics, and the Black Working Class.* New York: Free Press, 1994.

King, Martin L. *The Autobiography of Martin Luther King, Jr.* Edited by Clayborne Carson. New York: Warner Books, 1998.

Kuhn, Clifford M., Harlon E. Joye, and E. Bernard West. *Living Atlanta: An Oral History of the City, 1914–1948.* Athens: University of Georgia Press, 1990.

Lau, Peter. *Democracy Rising: South Carolina and the Fight for Black Equality Since 1865*. Lexington: University Press of Kentucky, 2006.

Lawson, Steven. *Black Voting Rights in the South, 1944–1969*. New York: Columbia University Press, 1976.

Lawson, Steven, and Charles Payne. *Debating the Civil Rights Movement, 1945–1968*. Lanham, MD: Rowman and Littlefield, 1998.

Lee, Chana Kai. *For Freedom's Sake: The Life of Fannie Lou Hamer*. Urbana: University of Illinois Press, 1999.

Lefever, Harry G. *Undaunted by the Fight: Spelman College and the Civil Rights Movement 1957–1967*. Macon, GA: Mercer University Press, 2005.

Lewis, Andrew B. *The Shadows of Youth: The Remarkable Journey of the Civil Rights Generation*. New York: Macmillan, 2009

Lewis, David Levering. *W. E. B. Dubois: The Fight for Equality and the American Century, 1919–1963*. New York: Holt, 2000.

Lewis, John. *Walking With the Wind: A Memoir of the Movement*. New York: Harcourt Brace and Company, 1998.

Lindenmyer, Kriste. *The Greatest Generation Grows Up: American Childhood in the 1930s*. Chicago: Ivan R. Dee, 2005.

Lipsitz, George. *The Possessive Investment in Whiteness: How White People Profit From Identity Politics*. Philadelphia: Temple University Press, 1998.

Lovett, Bobby L. *The Civil Rights Movement in Tennessee: A Narrative History*. Knoxville: University of Tennessee Press, 2005.

Lutz, Catherine. *Homefront: A Military City and the American Twentieth Century*. Boston, MA: Beacon Press, 2001.

Malcolm X. *The Autobiography of Malcolm X: As Told to Alex Haley*. New York: Ballantine Books, 1964.

Marable, Manning. *Race, Reform, and Rebellion: The Second Reconstruction in Black America, 1945–1990*. Jackson: University Press of Mississippi, 1991.

———. *W. E. B. Du Bois: Black Radical Democrat*. Boulder, CO: Paradigm Publishers, 2005.

Marsh, Charles. *God's Long Summer: Stories of Faith and Civil Rights*. Princeton, NJ: Princeton University Press, 1997.

Martin, Waldo. *No Coward Soldiers: Black Cultural Politics and Post War America*. Cambridge, MA: Harvard University Press, 2005.

McKuskey, Audrey Thomas, and Elaine Smith. *Mary McLeod Bethune: Building a Better World*. Bloomington: Indiana University Press, 1999.

McNeil, Genna Rae. *Goundwork: Charles Hamilton and the Struggle for Civil Rights*. Philadelphia: University of Pennsylvania Press, 1983.

Meier, August, and Elliott Rudwick. *Along the Color Line: Exploration in the Black Experience*. Urbana: University of Illinois Press, 2002.

———. *CORE: A Study in the Civil Right Movement, 1942–1968*. Urbana: University of Illinois Press, 1975.

Meyer, Stephen Grant. *As Long As They Don't Move Next Door: Segregation and Racial Conflict in American Neighborhoods.* Lanham, MD: Rowman and Littlefield, 2000.

Miller, Eben. *Born along the Color Line: The 1933 Amenia Conference and the Rise of a National Civil Rights Movement.* New York: Oxford University Press, 2012.

Mills, Kay. *This Little Light of Mine: The Life of Fannie Lou Hamer.* New York: Penguin Plume, 1993.

Minchin, Timothy. *What Do We Need a Union For? The Textile Workers Union of America in the South, 1945–1955.* Chapel Hill: University of North Carolina Press, 1997.

Mjagkij, Nina. *Light in the Darkness: African Americans and the YMCA, 1852–1946.* Lexington: University Press of Kentucky, 1994.

———. *Men and Women Adrift: The YMCA and the YWCA in the City.* New York: New York University Press, 1997.

Moody, Anne. *Coming of Age in Mississippi.* New York: Dell, 1968.

Morgan, Ted. *Reds: McCarthyism in Twentieth-Century America.* New York: Random House, 2004.

Morris, Aldon. *The Origins of the Civil Rights Movement: Black Communities Organizing for Change.* New York: Free Press, 1984.

Murphy, Sara Alderman. *Breaking the Silence: Little Rock's Emergency Committee to Open Our Schools, 1958–1963.* Fayetteville: University of Arkansas Press, 1997.

National Association for the Advancement of Colored People. *An Appeal to the World! A Statement on the Denial of Human Rights to Minorities in the Case of Citizens of the Negro Descent in the United States of America and the Appeal to the United Nations for Redress.* New York: NAACP, 1947.

National Negro Congress. *A Petition to the United Nations on behalf of 13 Million Oppressed Negro Citizens in the United States of America.* New York: National Negro Congress, 1946.

Norrell, Robert J. *Reaping the Whirlwind: The Civil Rights Movement in Tuskegee.* New York: Vintage, 1986.

Odum, Howard. *Race and Rumors of Race: The American South in the Early Forties.* Chapel Hill: University of North Carolina Press, 1943.

Ogletree, Charles. *All Deliberate Speed: Reflections on the First Half Century of Brown v. Board of Education.* New York: W. W. Norton and Company, 2004.

Olson, Lynne. *Freedom's Daughters: The Unsung Heroines of the Civil Rights Movement from 1830 to 1970.* New York: Scribner, 2001.

Ovington, Mary White. *Black and White Sat Down Together: The Reminiscences of an NAACP Founder.* New York: Feminist Press at the City University of New York, 1995.

Painter, Nell I. *The Narrative of Hosea Hudson: His Life as a Negro Communist in the South.* Cambridge, MA: Harvard University Press, 1979.

Patterson, James T. *Brown v. Board of Education: A Civil Rights Milestone and Its Troubled Legacy.* New York: Oxford University Press, 1994.

Pauley, Garth E. *The Modern President and Civil Rights: Rhetoric on Race from Roosevelt to Nixon.* College Station: Texas A&M University Press, 2001.

Payne, Charles. *I've Got the Light of Freedom: The Organizing Tradition and the Mississippi Freedom Struggle.* Berkeley CA: University of California Press, 1995.

Phillips, Kimberely L. *Alabama North: African-Americans Migrants, Community, and Working-Class Activism in Cleveland, 1915–1945.* Chicago: University of Illinois Press, 1999.

Pitre, Merline. *In Struggle Against Jim Crow: Lulu B. White and the NAACP, 1900–1957.* College Station: Texas A&M University Press, 1999.

Plummer, Brenda Gayle. *Rising Wind: Black Americans and US Foreign Affairs, 1935–1960.* Chapel Hill: University of North Carolina Press, 1996.

———. *Window on Freedom: Race, Civil Rights, and Foreign Affairs, 1945–1988.* Chapel Hill: University of North Carolina Press, 2003.

Raines, Howell, ed. *My Soul Is Rested: Movement Days in the Deep South Remembered.* New York: Penguin Books, 1977.

Ramsey, Sonya. *Reading, Writing, and Segregation: A Century of Black Women Teachers in Nashville.* Chicago: University of Illinois Press, 2008.

Ransby, Barbara. *Ella Baker and the Black Freedom Movement: A Radical Democratic Vision.* Chapel Hill: University of North Carolina Press, 2003.

Record, Wilson. *Race and Radicalism: The NAACP and the Communist Party in Conflict.* Communism in America Life Series, edited by Clinton Rossiter. Ithaca, NY: Cornell University Press, 1964.

Reed, Christopher Robert. *The Chicago NAACP and the Rise of Black Professional Leadership, 1910–1966.* Bloomington: Indiana University Press, 1997.

Reed, Linda. *Simple Decency and Common Sense: The Southern Conference Movement, 1938–1963.* Bloomington: Indiana University Press, 1991.

Reed, Merl E. *Seedtime for the Modern Civil Rights Movement: The President's Committee on the Fair Employment Practices, 1941–1946.* Baton Rouge: Louisiana State University Press, 1991.

Reiman, Richard. *The New Deal and American Youth: Ideas and Ideals in the Depression Decade.* Athens: University of Georgia Press, 1992.

Robinson, Cedric J. *Black Marxism: The Making of the Black Radical Tradition.* Chapel Hill: University of North Carolina Press, 2000.

Robinson, James. *Road Without Turning: The Story of the Reverend James H. Robinson.* New York: Farrar, Straus and Company, 1950.

Robinson, Jo Ann Gibson. *The Montgomery Bus Boycott Movement and the Women Who Started It.* Edited by David Garrow. Knoxville: The University of Tennessee Press, 1987.

Robnett, Belinda. *How Long? How Long? African American Women in the Struggle for Civil Rights.* New York: Oxford University Press, 1997.

———. "Women in the Student Non-Violent Coordinating Committee: Ideology, Organizational Structure, and Leadership." In *Gender in the Civil Rights Move-*

ment, edited by Peter Ling and Sharon Monteith, 131–68. New York: Garland, 1999.

Roediger, David R. *Colored White: Transcending the Racial Past.* Berkeley, CA: University of California Press, 2002.

———. *The Wages of Whiteness: Race and the Making of the American Working Class.* London: Verso, 1991.

Romero, Francine Sanders. *Civil Rights Policy Making in the United States: An Institution Perspective.* Westport, CT: Praeger, 2002.

Rosenberg, Gerald. *The Hollow Hope: Can Courts Bring About Social Change?* Chicago: The University of Chicago Press, 1991.

Ross, Barbara Joyce. *J. E. Spingarn and the Rise of the NAACP, 1911–1939.* New York: Atheneum, 1972.

Ross, Rosetta E. *Witnessing and Testifying: Black Women, Religion and Civil Rights.* Minneapolis, MN: Fortress Press, 2003.

Sacks, Karen. *Caring by the Hour: Women, Work, and Organizing at Duke Medical Center.* Urbana: University of Illinois Press, 1988.

Savage, Barbara. *Broadcasting Freedom: Radio, War, and the Politics of Race, 1938–1948.* Chapel Hill: University of North Carolina Press, 1999.

Schneider, Mark R. *"We Return Fighting": The Civil Rights Movement in the Jazz Age.* Boston, MA: Northeastern University Press, 2002.

Shabazz, Amilcar. *Advancing Democracy: African Americans and the Struggle for Access and Equity in Higher Education in Texas.* Chapel Hill: University of North Carolina Press, 2004.

Shapiro, Herbert. *White Violence and Black Response: From Reconstruction to Montgomery.* Amherst: University of Massachusetts Press, 1988.

Shaw, Stephanie J. *What a Woman Ought to Be and to Do: Black Professional Women During the Jim Crow Era.* Chicago, IL: University of Chicago Press, 1996.

Sikora, Frank. *Until Justice Rolls Down: The Birmingham Church Bombing Case.* Tuscaloosa: University of Alabama Press, 1991.

Sitkoff, Harvard. *A New Deal for Blacks: The Emergence of Civil Rights as a National Issue.* New York: Oxford University Press, 1978.

Smith, Jessie Carney. *Notable Black American Women.* Detroit, MI: Gale Research, 1992.

Sorensen, Lita. *The Scottsboro Boys Trial: A Primary Source Account.* New York: Rosen Publishing Group, 2004.

St. James, Warren D. *NAACP, Triumphs of a Pressure Group, 1909–1980.* Smithtown, NY: Exposition Press, 1980.

Sugrue, Thomas. *The Origins of the Urban Crisis: Race and Inequality in Postwar Detroit.* Princeton, NJ: Princeton University Press, 1996.

Sullivan, Patricia. *Days of Hope: Race Democracy in the New Deal Era.* Chapel Hill: University of North Carolina Press, 1996.

———. *Lift Every Voice: The NAACP and the Making of the Civil Rights Movement.* New York: The New Press, 2009.

Taylor, Quintard. *In Search of the Racial Frontier: African Americans in the American West, 1528–1990*. New York: W. W. Norton & Company, 1998.

Theoharis, Jeanne F, and Komozi Woodard, eds. *Freedom North: Black Freedom Struggles outside the South, 1940–1980*. New York: Palgrave Macmillan, 2003.

Tindall, George. *The Emergence of the New South, 1913–1945*. Baton Rouge: Louisiana State University Press, 1967.

Tushnet, Mark V. *The NAACP's Legal Strategy Against Segregated Education, 1925–1950*. Chapel Hill: University of North Carolina Press, 1987.

Tyson, Timothy B. *Radio Free Dixie: Robert F. Williams and the Roots of Black Power*. Chapel Hill: University of North Carolina Press, 1999.

Verney, Kevern, and Lee Sartain, eds. *Long Is the Way and Hard: One Hundred Years of the NAACP*. Fayetteville: University of Arkansas Press, 2009.

Von Eschen, Penny M. *Race Against the Empire: Black Americans and Colonialism, 1937–1957*. Ithaca, NY: Cornell University Press, 1997.

Washburn, Patrick. *A Question of Sedition: The Federal Government's Investigation of the Black Press During World War II*. New York: Oxford University Press, 1986.

Weisbrot, Robert. *Freedom Bound: A History of America's Civil Rights Movement*. New York: W. W. Norton and Company, 1990.

West, Thomas, and James W. Mooney eds. *To Redeem A Nation: A History and Anthology of the Civil Rights Movement*. St. James, NY: Brandywine Press, 1993.

Whalen, Charles, and Barbara Whalen. *The Longest Debate: A Legislative History of the 1964 Civil Rights Act*. New York: Mentor Books, 1985.

White, Deborah Gray. *Too Heavy of a Load: Black Women in Defense of Themselves, 1894–1994*. New York: W. W. Norton and Company, 1999.

White, E. Frances. *Dark Continent of Our Bodies: Black Feminism and the Politics of Respectability*. Philadelphia: Temple University Press, 2001.

White, Walter. *A Man Called White: The Autobiography of Walter White*. New York: Viking Press, 1948.

Wilkerson, Yolanda B. *Interracial Programs of Student YWCA's*. New York: Woman's Press, 1948.

Wilkins, Roy, and Tom Mathews. *Standing Fast: The Autobiography of Roy Wilkins*. Introduction by Julian Bond. New York: Viking Press, 1982.

Williams, Juan. *Eyes on the Prize: America's Civil Rights Years 1954–1965*. New York: Penguin Books, 2002.

Wilson, Sondra K. *In Search of Democracy: The NAACP Writings of James Weldon Johnson, Walter White, and Roy Wilkins (1920–1977)*. New York: Oxford University Press, 1999.

Woodard, Komozi. *A Nation Within a Nation: Amiri Baraka (LeRoi Jones) and Black Power Politics*. Chapel Hill: University of North Carolina Press, 1999.

Wormley, Stanley L., and Lewis H. Fenderson. *Many Shades of Black*. New York: William Morrow and Company, 1969.

Wright, Gavin. "Economic Consequences of the Southern Protest Movement." In *New Direction in the Civil Rights Studies.* Edited by Armstead L. Robinson and Patricia Sullivan. Charlottesville: University Press of Virginia, 1991.

Zangrando, Robert. *The NAACP Crusade against Lynching, 1909–1950.* Philadelphia: Temple University Press, 1980.

Scholarly Articles

Bates, Beth Tompkins. "A New Crowd Challenges the Agenda of the Old Guard in the NAACP, 1939–1941." *American Historical Review* 102 (April 1997): 340–77.

Bernd, Joseph L. "White Supremacy and the Disenfranchisement of Blacks in Georgia, 1946." *Georgia Historical Quarterly* 66 (1982): 492–513.

Bracey, John H., Jr., and August Meier. "Allies or Adversaries?: The NAACP, A. Phillip Randolph, and the 1941 March on Washington." *Georgia Historical Quarterly* 75, no. 1 (Spring 1991): 1–17.

Brown, Flora Bryant. "NAACP Sponsored Sit-ins by Howard University Students in Washington, D.C., 1943–1944." *Journal of Negro History* (September 2000): 275–83.

Bynum, Thomas L. "We Must March Forward: Juanita Jackson and the Origins of the NAACP Youth Movement." *Journal of African American History* 94 (Fall 2009): 487–508.

Chalfen, Michael. "Rev. Samuel B. Wells and Black Protest in Albany, 1945–1965." *Journal of Southwest Georgia History* 9 (Fall 1994): 37–64.

Collins, James. "Taking the Lead: Dorothy Williams, NAACP Youth Councils, and Civil Rights Protest in Pittsburgh 1961–1964." *Journal of African American History* (Spring 2003): 105–10.

Cox, Oliver. "Provisions for Graduate Education Among Negroes, and the Prospects of a New System." *Journal of Negro Education* 9 (January 1940): 22–31.

Dalfiume, Richard. "The Forgotten Years of the Negro Revolution." *Journal of American History* 55 (1968): 90–106.

Daniel, Pete. "Going Among Strangers: Southern Reactions to World War II." *Journal of American History* 77, no. 3 (December 1990): 886–911.

Dudziak, Mary L. "Desegregation as a Cold War Imperative." *Stanford Law Review* 41, no. 61 (November 1988): 61–120.

Fairclough, Adam. "Being in the Field of Education and Also Being Negro...Seems... Tragic': Black Teachers in the Jim Crow South." *Journal of American History* 87, no. 1 (June 2000): 65–91.

Franklin, V. P. "Patterns of Student Activism at Historically Black Universities in the United States and South Africa, 1960–1977." *Journal of African American History* 88 (Spring, 2003): 206–7.

Gaines, Kevin, Clayborne Carson, Mary L. Dudziak, Adam Fairclough, Scott Kurashige, Darryl Michael Scott, Charles Payne, and Lani Guinier. "Round Table: *Brown v. Board of Education,* Fifty Years After." *Journal of American History* 90, no. 1 (June 2004): 19–118.

Hall, Jacqueline Dowd. "The Long Civil Rights Movement and the Political Uses of the Past." *Journal of American History* 91(March 2005): 1233–63.

Kelleher, Daniel. "The Case of Lloyd Gaines: The Demise of the Separate but Equal Doctrine." *Journal of Negro History* 56 (October 1971): 262–71.

King, Desmond. "The Racial Bureaucracy: African Americans and the Federal Government in the Era of Segregated Race Relations." *Governance* 12 (October 1999): 345–77.

Lawson, Steven. "Freedom Then, Freedom Now: The Historiography of the Civil Rights Movement." *American Historical Review* 96 (April 1991): 456–71.

Martin, Charles H. "The Civil Rights Congress and Southern Black Defendants." *Georgia Historical Quarterly* 71, no. 1 (Spring 1987): 25–52.

Mayer, Michael S. "With Deliberation and Some Speed: Eisenhower and the Brown Decision." *Journal of Southern History* 52, no. 1 (February 1986): 43–76.

Meier, August, and John Bracey, Jr. "The NAACP as a Reform Movement, 1909–1965: 'To Reach the Conscience of America.'" *Journal of Southern History* 59, no. 1 (February 1993): 3–30.

McWhorter, Diane. "The Day Autherine Lucy Dared to Integrate the University of Alabama," *Journal of Blacks in Higher Education* 32 (Summer 2001): 100–101.

Nasstrom, Kathryn L. "Down to Now: Memory, Narrative, and Women's Leadership in the Civil Rights Movement in Atlanta, Georgia." *Gender and History* 11, no. 1 (April 1999): 113–44.

Payne, Charles. "Ella Baker and Models of Social Change." *Signs* 14, no. 4 (Summer 1989): 885–99.

Plaut, Richard. "Prospects for the Entrance and Scholastic Advancement of Negroes in Higher Educational Institutions." *Journal of Negro Education* 36 (Summer 1967): 230–37.

Roark, James L. "American Black Leaders: The Response to Colonialism and the Cold War, 1943–1953." *African Historical Studies* 4 no. 2 (1971): 253–70.

Rucker, Walter. "Crusader In Exile: Robert Williams and the International Struggle for Black Freedom in America." *Black Scholar* 36 (June 2006): 19.

Sugrue, Thomas. "Crabgrass-Roots Politics: Race, Rights, and the Reaction against Liberalism in the Urban North, 1940–1954." *Journal of American History* 82 (September 1995): 551–78.

Walters, Ronald. "Standing Up in America's Heartlands: Sitting in Before Greensboro." *American Vision* 8 (February–March 1993): 20–23.

———. "The Great Plains Sit-In Movement, 1958–1960." *Great Plains Quarterly* 16 (Spring 1996): 85–94.

Wynn, Neil. "The Impact of the Second World War on the American Negro." *Journal of Contemporary History* 6 (1971): 42–53.

Online Resources

"A Guide to Juanita Jewel Shank Craft Collection, 1939–1983." http://www.Lib. utexas.edu/taro/utcah/00086/cah-00086.html Accessed May 21, 2007.

"Barbers Refuse to Comment on Pickets' Effect." *Daily Collegian.* December 15, 1948. http://digitalnewspapers.libraries.psu.edu/Default/Scripting/ArticleWin.asp? From=Archive&Source=Page&Skin=collegian&BaseHref=DCG/1948/12/15& PageLabel=1&EntityId=Ar00100&ViewMode=HTML Accessed May 20, 2007.

Beauchamp, Clinton, and Amanda Turner. "The Desegregation of Clinton Senior High School: Trial and Triumph." http://www.jimcrowhistory.org/resources/ pdf/hs_es_clintonhs_deseg.pdf (accessed July 1, 2007).

"Born of Controversy: The G.I. Bill of Rights." http://www.gibill.va.gov/GI_Bill_info/ history.htm Accessed May 21, 2007.

Chalkley, Tom. "Mother Figure." *Baltimore City Paper.* May 17, 2000. http://www. citypaper.com/printStory.asp?id=2483 Accessed November 17, 2006.

"Dr. Lillie M. Carroll Jackson: Mother of Freedom (1889–1975)." http://www.naacp baltimore.org/bio-jackson.html Accessed November 17, 2006.

"Federal Education Policy and the States, 1945–2009, The Eisenhower Years: Desegregation." http://www.archives.nysed.gov/edpolicy/research/res_essay_ eisenhower_desegregation.shtml Accessed April 19, 2012.

Howard, Gloria Jean Blair "Origins of the Sit-ins: A Sibling Remembers." http:// www.objectofhistory.org/objects/brieftour/lunchcounter/ Accessed July 5, 2007.

"Maryland Women's Hall of Fame: Juanita Jackson Mitchell." http://www.mdarchives. state.md.us/msa/educ/exhibits/womenshall/html/mitchell.html Accessed November 17, 2006.

McMillan, George. "'The Ordeal of Bobby Cain': Racial Confrontation at a Newly Integrated Southern High School." http://historymatters.gmu.edu/d/6254/. Accessed July 2, 2007.

"Mrs. Juanita Jackson Mitchell, Esq.: Avowed Freedom Fighter." http://www.naacp baltimore.org/bio-mitchell.html. Accessed November 17, 2006.

McNeil, Joseph. "How It Originated Joseph McNeil's Story." http://www.objectof history.org/objects/brieftour/lunchcounter/?order=2. Accessed July 5, 2007.

"NAACP to Hold Rally against Discrimination." *The Collegian.* December 11, 1948. http://digitalnewspapers.libraries.psu.edu/Default/Scripting/ArticleWin.asp? From=Archive&Source=Page&Skin=collegian&BaseHref=DCG/1948/12/11 &PageLabel=1&EntityId=Ar00103&ViewMode=HTML. Accessed May 20, 2007.

Olney, Warren. "*Brown v. Board of Education* Fiftieth Anniversary Interview with Josephine Boyd Bradley." http://web.mac.com/paul.tullis/iWeb/Site/Blog/ D5AFAF25–9C64–4A43-AB95–9A71506C2BA9.html. Accessed July 1, 2007.

"Orval Eugene Faubus." *Encyclopedia of Arkansas History and Culture.* http:// encyclopediaofarkansas.net/encyclopedia/entry-detail.aspx?entryID=102 Accessed July 12, 2007.

"Picket Line to Continue in Barber-NAACP Fight." *Daily Collegian*. December 14, 1948, http://digitalnewspapers.libraries.psu.edu/Default/Skins/collegian/Client. asp?Skin=collegian&AppName=2. Accessed May 20, 2007.

"Robert 'Bobby' Cain Jr." *Tennessee Encyclopedia of History and Culture*. http:// tennesseeencyclopedia.net/imagegallery.php?EntryID=C002. Accessed July 2, 2007.

Smolovik, Cindy C. "Biographical/Historical Note: Juanita Jewel Shank Craft." http://www.dallaslibrary.org/ctx/archives/craft.html. Accessed 21 May 2007.

"The NAACP to Boycott Local Barbershops." *Daily Collegian*. December 10, 1948. http://digitalnewspapers.libraries.psu.edu/Default/Scripting/ArticleWin.asp? From=Archive&Source=Page&Skin=collegian&BaseHref=DCG/1948/12/10& PageLabel=1&EntityId=Ar00101&ViewMode=HTML Accessed May 20, 2007.

Weber, Jake. "'There's a Lot to Fight For': 'Little Rock Nine' Member Ernest Green Highlights Civil Rights Movement." *Albion View*. http://www.albion.edu/ ac_news/AlbionViews2005–06/ernestgreen.asp. Accessed 2 July 2007.

Youth March for Integrated Schools. October 25, 1958, and April 18, 1959. http:// mlk-kpp01.stanford.edu/index.php/encyclopedia/encyclopedia/enc_youth_ march_for_integrated_schools_25_october_1958_and_18_april_1959/. Accessed April 19, 2012.

Unpublished Works

Bragg, Susan. "Marketing the 'Modern' Negro: Race, Gender, and the Culture of Activism in the NAACP, 1909–1941." PhD diss., University of Washington, 2007.

Hoecker, Robin. "The Black and White Behind the Blue and White: A History of Black Protest at Penn State." BA thesis, Pennsylvania State University, 2001.

Suttell, Brian William. "Countdown to Downtown: The Civil Rights Movement in Downtown Fayetteville, North Carolina." MA thesis, North Carolina State University, 2007.

Thompson, Bruce. "The Civil Rights Vanguard: The NAACP and the Black Community in Baltimore, 1931–1942." PhD diss., University of Maryland, 1996.

Index

college clubs, segregation in, xvi, 39, 58, 166n70

colleges and universities, white: black students attending, xvi, 57–59, 103, 171n55, 172n57; interracial groups in, 166nn69–70; segregation in, 39, 58–61, 171n55. *See also* scholarships

Colligan, Eugene, *Nation's Progress,* 11, 158n2

colonialism, fight against, 26, 40

Columbia, South Carolina: direct action demonstrations in, 108–9; NAACP Youth Council, wade-in by, 105

Columbia University NAACP Chapter, 47, 58, 166n70

Colvin, Claudettte, 93

Commander, Gerald, 115

Commandos (NAACP youth task force), 120–21, 127–28, 139

Commission on Higher Education (Truman Administration), 59

Committee on Cooperative Enterprise in Europe (U.S. government), 17–18

Committee on Direct-Action (Howard University), 39

Communists: allegations of infiltration of NAACP, xvi–xvii, 52, 64, 65–67, 89, 114, 121, 139, 173n86; at Second World Youth Congress, 24, 25, 161n3; in youth organizations, 161–62n8, 169n20

Community Action Program (CAP), xix, 145–46, 150

Congress of Industrial Organizations (CIO), 9, 16, 55

Congress of Racial Equality (CORE), 30, 190n107; NAACP youth joining, 139, 141, 142, 150; sit-in demonstration involvement, 95, 102, 105, 135; support for NAACP activities, xv, 116, 183n64; tensions with NAACP, 143, 150; wealthy white donors, 53, 170n37; youth activism in, xiii, 149

Connor, Eugene "Bull," 129–30

consumer cooperative movement, 17–18

Cooper, Esther, 43

CORE. *See* Congress of Racial Equality (CORE)

Cornell University NAACP College Chapter (Ithaca, NY), 47, 60, 166n70;

allegations of Communist infiltration, 65–67, 173n86

Costigan-Warner Anti-Lynching Bill, 7. *See also* antilynching legislation

Council of Federated Organizations (COFO), xix, 142, 150, 190n107

Council on the United Civil Rights Leadership, 170n37

Craft, Juanita Jewel, xvii, 61–62, 69–70

Crawley, William, 132

Crenshaw, Doris, 180n105

crime, campaigns against, 36, 42

Crisis, The (NAACP official organ), xiv

Crowder, Richard, 126

Crump, Marjorie, 90

Cunningham, Eleanor, 62

Current, Gloster B., 43, 63, 109–10, 141; and Jackson, Mississippi, demonstrations, 136, 138

Curry, Izola, 88

Dallas, Texas, NAACP Youth Council, desegregation of Texas State Fair, xvii, 61–62, 69–70, 149

d'Avila, Sarah H., 50

Davis, Benjamin O., 62

Davis, Josephine Jett, 163n26

Davis, Roosevelt J., 131

Davis, Sidney, 83

Deep South: direct action demonstrations in, 51–52, 53–56, 70; Hurley's work in, 35–36. *See also* Jim Crow laws and practices; South, the

defense industry, hiring of blacks in, 32, 33, 34

De La Beckwith, Byron, 138–39

Delany, Hubert, 45, 167n1

democracy, 121, 130; Second World War as fight for, 23, 30–31, 33, 41, 42, 45; youth fight for, xiv, 30, 43–44, 163–64n33

De Schweinitz, Rebecca, xiii, xiv, 19, 20, 64, 82

Detroit, Michigan: NAACP Branch, 51; NAACP Youth Council, **74**

Dies Committee (House Committee on Un-American Activities), 161n3

Diggs Civil Rights Law (Michigan), 51, 64

Hart, Frederick, 109
Hastie, William, 50, **74**
Hattie Cotton Elementary School (Nashville), bombing of, 91
Henderson, Albert, 35, 67
Henderson, Elmer, 50
Henderson, Vivian W., 90
Henry, Aaron, 113–14, 115, 116–17
Henry, Theodore, 138
Hicks, Chester E., 82
High, Lucius, 111
high school students: combatting drop-out rates, 145; participation in protests, 105, 106, 131, 136, 137–38; in youth councils, 38, 165n67. *See also* youth councils, NAACP
hiring practices, discriminatory: for black professors, 60–61; in department stores, 153n14; outlawing, 32, 42; protests against, 33, 99, 111, 113–17, 129, 145. *See also* "Don't Buy Where You Can't Work" campaigns; employment, equal
history, black: promotion of, xv, 12, 33, 41; textbooks distorting, 11–12, 158n52
History of the American People (Muzzey), 11, 158n52
Hitler, Adolf, 32, 41. *See also* Nazism
Hodges, Luther H., 102
Hollings, Ernest F., 109
Holmes, Martha, 92
Hood, James, 188n53
Hopkins, John, 135
House Un-American Activities Committee. *See* Dies Committee (House Committee on Un-American Activities)
housing: fighting discrimination in, 40, 145; segregated campus, xvi, 39, 58–59, 166n70
Houston, Charles Hamilton, 12–13, **71**
Houston, Texas: equal education campaign in, 11; NAACP Youth Council, 11, 20–21, **74**
Howard University NAACP Chapter (Washington, D.C.), desegregation of Little Palace Cafeteria, xvi, 39–40, 166n71, 166n76
Hughes, Langston, 36; *Scottsboro Limited*, 8
Hughes, Rosie, xvii

human rights: global struggle for, 23, 41; NAACP's fight for, 40, 49, 174n96; youth agenda for, 41, 44, 68. *See also* civil rights activism
hunger, campaigns to alleviate, 18. *See also* antipoverty programs
Hurley, Ruby, **76**; and Albany, Georgia, campaign, 140–41; and allegations of Communist infiltration of youth division, 65–67, 173n86; appointed NAACP youth director, 34–35; and challenging segregation in states with civil rights laws, 51; and direct action demonstrations, 41–42; and Emmet Till's murder, 80; legacy of, 147, 149, 164n54; revitalization of youth division by, 37, 42, 68, 69, 165n62; and tensions between youth councils and senior branches, 63–56, 67; work in Deep South, 35–36; and youth legislative conferences, 48–49, 50

ICC. *See* Interstate Commerce Commission (ICC) ruling of 1961, testing
Ike Smalls Award, 37, 165n63
Illinois Central Railroad Company, demonstration against, 116
imperialism, fight against, 25, 26
Indiana Theater (East Chicago, Indiana), desegregation of, 54
inequalities. *See* education, equal, denied to blacks; employment, equal, denied to blacks; hiring practices, discriminatory; justice system, southern, inequities in
injustices, protesting, 19, 25, 80, 147, 148
inner-city communities, fighting segregation, xix, 145–46, 149, 150
integration. *See* schools, public, desegregation of
Interdenominational Ministerial Alliance (Jackson, MS), 134
Interstate Commerce Commission (ICC) ruling of 1961, testing, xviii–xix, 115, 119–20, 140–41
Irwin, Frank E., 82
isolationism, 25, 161–62n8
Italy, invasion of Ethiopia, 25

J. C. Penney Co. (Fayetteville, NC), sit-in demonstration at, 131

Jackson, Esther, 9, 10

Jackson, George, 9

Jackson, Joseph, 133

Jackson, Juanita, 1–22, **72**; on antilynching bill, 7–9; appointed NAACP youth director, xv, 2, 4–5, 6, 161n3; and citizenship training schools, 18–19; and direct action demonstrations, 17–18, 41–42, 154n4; and economic conditions, 15–16; and equal education campaigns, 12, 13–14, 154n4; legacy of, 21–22, 35, 147; marriage to Clarence Mitchell, 21, 26, 162n12; and Scottsboro Boys case, 20, 21

Jackson, Lillie (mother of Juanita), 3–4, 21, 88, 154n5

Jackson, Marion, 4

Jackson, Mississippi: direct action campaign in, 133–39; NAACP Youth Council, 135–37, 136

Jackson, Troy, 93

Jackson Central High School (Jackson, MS) students, protests by, 137

Jackson NAACP Intercollegiate Chapter, 134, 135

Jackson State College, student protests, 133, 135

Jackson State University NAACP Chapter, demonstrations by, 143

James, Mary E., **74**

Jessen, H. H., 110

Jessie Gerring VFW Post (East Chicago, Indiana), and theater desegregation campaign, 55

Jessie Smith Noyes Foundation, scholarships from, 81, 87, 178n63

Jim Crow laws and practices: Hurley's experience with, 35–36; injustices of, 119–20, 129; in the military, 12, 47–48, 168–69n15; protests against, xiv, 3, 21, 29, 113–17, 120–21, 148, 157n45; sit-in demonstrations challenging, xvi, 94, 95, 97, 104, 106–7; violence by whites to preserve, 103

John A. Brown Department Store (Oklahoma City), sit-ins at, 97–98

Johns, Ralph, 100, 101

Johnson, Lyndon B., antipoverty programs of, xix, 145–46, 150

Johnson, Mordecai, 40, 166n76

Johnson C. Smith University NAACP Chapter (Charlotte, NC), supporting sit-ins, 101

Johnston, W. Jay, 20

Jones, Madison S., as NAACP youth director, 31, 34, 37, 66, 164n50

Jones, Russell, 43

Jordan, Vernon, 140

justice system, southern, inequities in, 19–21, 80, 113, 123, 125

Kansas City, Missouri: NAACP Youth Council, 105; National Youth Administration office, 31

Kasper, Frederick John, 81–83, 84, 90, 91, 176n37

Katz Drug Store (Oklahoma City), sit-in at, 97

Keating, Kenneth B., 50

Kellum, Laura, 20, **72**

Kennedy, John F., 50; and school segregation, 139, 188n53

Kentucky (KY), youth councils in, 69

Kester, Howard, 17

King, Coretta Scott, 88

King, Martin Luther, Jr., 88, 89–90; and Birmingham protests, 129–30; and Montgomery Bus Boycott, 93; nonviolence preferred by, 126, 132

kissing case (Monroe County, NC), 123–24

Korean Conflict, antisegregation campaigns during, 47, 48, 169n16

Kress department stores, sit-in demonstrations at, xviiii; Baton Rouge, Louisiana, 102; Greensboro, North Carolina, 101, 105; Louisville, Kentucky, 95; Oklahoma City, xviii, 97; Orangeburg, South Carolina, 108

Ku Klux Klan, 27–30, 41, 121, 122

labor movement, NAACP youth involvement in, 16, 18, 32. *See also* Congress of Industrial Organizations (CIO)

Lacey, Joseph, 94

Servicemen's Readjustment Act of 1944. *See* G.I. Bill of Rights, discriminatory implementation of

sharecroppers, 9, 16–17, 18, 32

Sharpe Street Memorial M.E. Church Community House (Baltimore), **71**

Shaw, Brodus F., 124–25

Shaw University NAACP Chapter (Raleigh, NC), supporting sit-ins, 101

Sherrod, Charles, 140

Shields-Collins, Betty, 24

Shores, Arthur, **76**

Shull, Lynwood, 46, 168n4

Shuttleworth, Fred, 129

Simkins, George, 101

Simmons Pharmacy (Summerville, SC), sit-in at, 111–12

Simpson, David Ezell, 123

Sipuel, Ada, 59–60

sit-in demonstrations, **78,** 95–108; challenging Jim Crow laws, xvi, 94, 95, 97, 104, 106–7; desegregation through, xvi, xvii–xix; expulsion of students for participation in, 102–3, 106; NAACP support of, 103, 104, 105–6, 109; as precedent for 1960s civil rights movement, xiv, 99, 149; SNCC's use of, xix, 166n71, 183n64. *See also under individual NAACP chapters and councils and individual cities*

Sitman's Drugstore (Baton Rouge, LA), sit-in demonstration in, 102

Skidmore College NAACP Chapter (Saratoga Springs, NY), 166n70

slums, urban, xix, 145–46, 149, 150

Smalls, Ike, 37, 165n63

Smith, Ferdinand, 66

Smith, Joy, 91

Smith, Kelly, 91

Smith, Lamar, murder of, 36

Smith, R. L. T., 137

Smith, Wilma, 116

Smith v. Allwright (1944), xv–xvi, 40, 113. *See also* elections

SNCC. *See* Student Nonviolent Coordinating Committee (SNCC)

SNYC. *See* Southern Negro Youth Congress (SNYC)

Socialists, 1, 24, 65. *See also* Communists

social justice, 7, 18–20, 21–22, 25, 30

soldiers: black, 48, 133, 168–69n15; white, 132. *See also* military, segregation in; veterans, black

sororities. *See* Greek letter organizations, segregation in

South, the: civil rights movement in, 51–52, 53, 108, 135; crimes against blacks in, 36; direct action demonstrations in, 61–62, 69–70, 92, 94, 95–117, 149, 153n4; educational inequalities in, 157–58n50; justice system in, 19–21, 80, 113, 123, 125; resistance to desegregation in, 79, 80–82, 117, 144. *See also* Deep South; *and individual southern states and cities*

South Carolina (SC), direct action demonstrations in, 107–13

South Carolina State NAACP Chapter, sit-ins by, 107–8

Southern Christian Leadership Conference (SCLC): direct action demonstrations by, 102, 104–5, 116, 129, 136, 183n4; NAACP's tensions with, 135, 136; wealthy white donors to, 53

Southern Negro Youth Congress (SNYC), xv, 1, 157n45; collective security policy endorsed by, 24; support for antilynching bill, 8, 9

Southern Tenant Farmers' Union (STFU), 16–17, 32

Southern University (Baton Rouge, LA), student demonstrations at, 102–3

Soviet Union, nonaggression pact with Germany, 161–62n8

Spann, C. O., 109

Spingarn, Arthur, 7

Spingarn, Joel E., 13

St. Augustine College NAACP Chapter (Raleigh, NC), supporting sit-ins, 101

St. Clair Drake, J. G., 7–8

St. Louis NAACP Branch (MO), support for sit-ins, 98–99

Stark Theological Seminary (Columbia, SC), sit-ins by, 108

Sterlings, Aurelio, 67

STFU. *See* Southern Tenant Farmers' Union (STFU)

Stokes, Olivia Pearl, 43

27–30; resistance to desegregation, 144; violence perpetrated by, xvi, 29, 45–46, 79–80, 96, 103, 106–7, 122, 127. *See also* discrimination, racial; racism; segregation

Whitney, S. Leon, 134

Wichita, Kansas, NAACP Youth Council, sit-ins by, xvii–xviii, 95–97, 99, 149

Wilkins, Roy, 88, 89; on armed resistance to violence, 125, 126; on direct action demonstrations, 103, 109, 138; on Eugene Hampton appointment, 144; and kissing case, 123

William Penn High School (High Point, NC), supporting sit-ins, 101

Williams, Aubrey, 14

Williams, Avon, 81, 90–91

Williams, Cardelia, 61

Williams, J. C., 27

Williams, Mabel, 122

Williams, Margaret, 10

Williams, Mitchell, 56

Williams, Walter, 135

Williams Robert, 121–22; advocating armed resistance to violence, 124–25, 127; and kissing case, 123–24

Williams v. Zimmerman (1936), 10–11. *See also* schools, public, desegregation of

Willis, O. W., 82

Wilmington, Delaware: Community Action Program, 145–46; NAACP Youth Council, 145–46

Wilmington, North Carolina, NAACP Youth Council, 131

Wilson, Woodrow (Monroe, NC, veteran), 122

Winfield, B. J., 122

Winston-Salem Teachers College NAACP Chapter (NC), supporting sit-ins, 101

withholding patronage campaigns, xviii, 112, 149

Wofsy, Leon, 169n20

women, black: role in civil rights activism, 34–35, 98, 100, 122; as victims of white racist practices, 85–86, 124–25, 131

women, white, white men's patriarchal view of, 124–25

Women's Political Council (WPC), 92

Woodard, Isaac, tragedy of, 45–46, 48, 168n4

Woodson, Carter G., *The Negro in Our History*, 11

Woolfolk, Mary Anna, **74**

Woolworth's department stores. *See* F. W. Woolworth department stores, sit-ins at

Works Progress Administration (WPA), 14

World War I. *See* First World War

World War II. *See* Second World War

World Youth Assembly, 81

World Youth Congresses, 41; First, 161n1; Fourth, 43; Second, 23–26, 161n3

Wortham, Offie, 89

WPA. *See* Works Progress Administration (WPA)

WPC. *See* Women's Political Council (WPC)

Wright, Herbert, 52, 88, 119; appointed NAACP youth director, 68, 69; and scholarships for black students, 58, 172n57; and sit-in demonstrations, 102, 106, 108

Wright, Julie: and Albany, Georgia, campaign, 140–41; as field secretary, 109–13, 115–16; and Jackson, Mississippi, protests, 133–35; and sit-in demonstrations, 108

Wright, Roy, 19

Wright, Stephen J., 103–4

YAC. *See* Young Adult Council (YAC, NAACP)

Yard, Molly, 9

YCAW. *See* Youth Committee Against War (YCAW)

YMCA. *See* Young Men's Christian Association (YMCA)

Young Adult Council (YAC, NAACP), xv, 90, 142, 179n78

Young Communist League, 1

Young Men's Christian Association (YMCA), xv, 1, 8

Young People's Socialist League (YPSL), 1, 24

Young Women's Christian Association (YWCA), xv, 1, 8

youth, black: building racial pride in, 12, 33; economic conditions among, 16, 17–18; lack of employment opportunities, 14–16, 31–32; in military, 33–34; at Second World Youth Congress, 25–26

Youth Committee Against War (YCAW), 24, 25, 30, 161–62n8

youth cooperatives, 17–18

youth councils, NAACP, xviii, 67, **77,** 155n22, 156n27; accusations of Communist infiltration, xvi–xvii, 64, 65, 169n20; age range, 155n21, 169n19; college chapters' collaboration with, 23, 37–39, 165n65; constitution of, 6, 141–42; direct action demonstrations by, xiii–xvi, 41–42, 117, 150–51; expansion of, 35, 109; fighting discrimination in the military, 47–48; fundraising by, 52, 156n37; high school students in, 38, 165n67; and implementation of *Brown v. Board of Education,* 80–92; junior, 5, **75;** objectives of, 5–6, 41, 44, 119, 147–48; origins in the 1930s, 1–22, 147; during Second World War, 33–34; supervision of, xix, 5, **38;** tensions with senior NAACP officials, xvii, 44, 53, 62–69, 139, 141–42, 143, 149–50; Textbook Survey, 11, 158n53. *See also* junior college chapters, NAACP

Youth March for Integrated Schools (NAACP, 1958), xvii, 88, 89, 178n66

YPSL. *See* Young People's Socialist League (YPSL)

YWCA. *See* Young Women's Christian Association (YWCA)

Zimmerman, Williams v. (1936), 10–11. *See also* schools, public, desegregation of